day trips® series

day trips® from
austin

eighth edition

getaway ideas for the local traveler

revised by jackie sheckler finch

Globe
Pequot

Essex, Connecticut

All the information in this guidebook is subject to change. We recommend that you call ahead to obtain current information before traveling.

Globe Pequot

An imprint of Globe Pequot, the trade division of The Rowman & Littlefield Publishing Group, Inc.
4501 Forbes Blvd., Ste. 200
Lanham, MD 20706
www.rowman.com

Distributed by NATIONAL BOOK NETWORK

Copyright © 2022 by the Rowman & Littlefield Publishing Group, Inc.
Previous editions by Paris Permenter and John Bigley
Maps: © 2022 by the Rowman & Littlefield Publishing Group, Inc.

British Library Cataloguing in Publication Information available

Library of Congress Control Number: 2022936862

[ISBN] 978-1-4930-6581-3 (paper)
[ISBN] 978-1-4930-6582-0 (electronic)

∞™ The paper used in this publication meets the minimum requirements of American National Standard for Information Sciences—Permanence of Paper for Printed Library Materials, ANSI/NISO Z39.48-1992.

contents

southeast

south

southwest

west

day trip 01

day trip 02

day trip 03

day trip 04

northwest

day trip 01

day trip 02

day trip 03

day trip 04

day trip 05

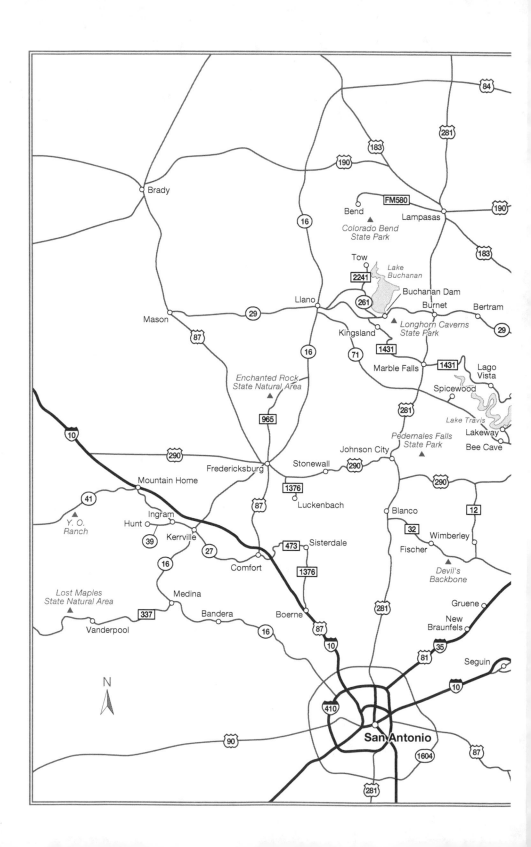

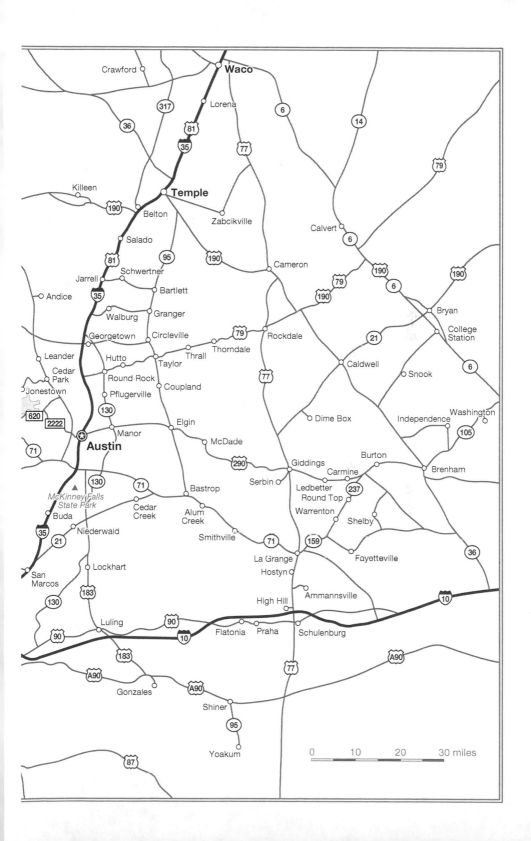

about the author

Jackie Sheckler Finch has written about a wide array of topics—from birth to death with all the joy and sorrow in between. An award-winning journalist and photographer, Jackie has done more than two dozen travel guidebooks for Globe Pequot and is a member of The Society of American Travel Writers and The Midwest Travel Journalists Association. She has been named the Mark Twain Travel Writer of the Year a record five times, in 1998, 2001, 2003, 2007, and 2012. One of her greatest joys is taking to the road to find the fascinating people and places that wait over the hill and around the next bend.

acknowledgments

Many thanks to the hospitable folks of Texas for answering my endless questions. My appreciation to public relations officials and to the Texas residents and business owners who took the time to share what makes day trips from Austin so varied and special.

Gratitude to my Globe Pequot editor, Greta Schmitz, for inviting me to take this treasure-filled trip. It has been a delight and a pure pleasure.

This book is dedicated to my family—Kelly Rose; Mike Peters; Sean Rose; Stefanie, Will, Trey, and Arianna Scott; and Logan Peters.

A special remembrance to my husband, Bill Finch, whose spirit goes with me every step of the way through this journey.

introduction

Most people have a mental image of Texas as miles of rugged, uncivilized land where the outlines of cattle and lonely windmills stretch above the horizon. But that's just one side of the Lone Star State, known as the "land of contrast." Texas also boasts high-tech cities, piney woods, sandy beaches, rolling hills, and fertile farmland—much of it within a two-hour drive of Austin.

The region covered in this book is as diverse as the more than 30 cultures who helped found the state. German, Czech, Mexican, Polish, and even Alsatian settlers brought their traditions to Texas in the 1800s. The influences of these pioneers are still apparent today in the varied festivals and ethnic foods that vacationers come here to enjoy.

The day trips within this book span terrain ranging from farmland to rocky hills. This difference in topography is the result of an ancient earthquake that created the Balcones Fault, which runs north to south. The fault line, slightly west of I-35, forms the dividing line between the eastern agricultural region and what is known as the Hill Country to the west.

Many of the attractions lie along the route taken by numerous Winter Texans who flock here during the cooler months. So, whether you're heading for the Rio Grande Valley, the coast, or the Mexican border, you'll find a wealth of useful tips and information in this guide as you pass through Central Texas. Be sure to check the sections marked "Especially for Winter Texans," which will help you identify special services, festivals, and parks aimed at making you feel right at home.

You'll find that Texans are friendly folk who wave on country roads and nod as they pass you on the sidewalk. Talk to local citizens as you wind through the back roads for even more travel tips and a firsthand look at the varied cultures that make up the pieces of your journey.

 # using this travel guide

hours of operation

In some cases, hours are omitted in the listings because they are subject to frequent changes. Instead, phone numbers and websites are provided as a resource for up-to-date information.

credit cards

In the interest of accuracy and because they are subject to change, attraction prices are given in general terms. Always remember to call ahead. You can assume all establishments listed accept major credit cards unless otherwise noted. If you have questions, contact the establishments for specifics.

pricing key

For Accommodations: Room prices are designated as $$$ (Expensive: more than $200 for a standard room); $$ (Moderate:$100-$200); and $ (Inexpensive: less than $100).

For Restaurants: Per-person restaurant prices are designated as $$$ (Expensive: more than $50 per person); $$ (Moderate: $25-$50); and $ (Inexpensive: less than $25).

travel tips

carry a road map

Although we've included directions, it's best to carry a Texas road map as you travel. It's also advisable to carry a county map for a better look at farm-to-market (FM) roads and ranch-to-market (RM) roads. To get brochures on Texas attractions and a free copy of the Texas Travel Guide, call (800) 452-9292 or visit traveltexas.com/plan-ahead/travel-guide. The guide is coded to a free Texas state map also provided by the highway department. These maps are also available from any of the tourist information centers located on routes into Texas and at the Texas State Capitol in Austin. The tourist information centers are open daily, except Thanksgiving, Christmas, and New Year's Day.

The expansiveness of Texas sets it apart from other states. Note the scale of the map. With 266,807 square miles of land, Texas is the second-largest state in the country. One inch on the state road map spans 23 miles.

Driving varies with terrain: In the western Hill Country, towns are far apart and roads can be slow and winding. To the east, population is more dense, and day trips involve quiet, slow drives along farm-to-market and ranch-to-market roads.

For Texas travel questions, call (800) 452-9292 from anywhere in the US or Canada.

be wary of weather conditions

As a general rule, the Austin region enjoys a very temperate climate. Winters are mild, with just about 25 freezing days annually. Snow is råre and, when it does occur, causes businesses and schools to close and roads to congest quickly.

The most pleasant seasons in the region are spring and fall. You'll find many Austin-area festivals are scheduled during these pleasant weekends, times when temperatures are in the 70–80°F range.

Austin receives less than 30 inches of rain annually, most of it arriving during the spring. Thunderstorms are common from April through September, especially during the late afternoon as temperatures rise. Tornadoes are most likely during May and June.

The biggest weather threat comes in the form of flash floods, especially in the Hill Country. The steep slopes, rocky terrain, and shallow topsoil of the region mean that even a few inches of rain can turn dry creek beds into roaring rivers capable of sweeping cars off the road. Drownings occur annually when drivers attempt to cross roadways covered with water.

avoid midday heat

In summer, Texas is hotter than a sizzling fajita. In this weather, it's best to drive in the early-morning hours or after sunset. If you are traveling with children or pets, never leave them in a closed car; temperatures soar to oven-like heights in just minutes.

watch out for stray livestock

When driving through open-ranch cattle country on farm-to-market or ranch-to-market roads, be on the lookout for livestock and deer wandering across roads, especially near dusk. Deer can be a driving hazard even in populated regions.

highway designations

Federal highways are designated US. State routes use TX. Farm-to-market roads are defined as FM, and ranch-to-market roads are designated RM. County roads (which are not on the Texas state map) are identified as CR. The only official ranch road (RR) is RR 1, the highway on the LBJ Ranch.

where to get more information

Day Trips from Austin attempts to cover a variety of bases and interests, but those look-ing for additional material can contact the following agencies by phone, mail, or the web. Regarding the latter, when checking out the various destinations, be aware that online reviews may be contradictory and conflicting. Everyone's experience can be different, and the web allows for a forum for these diverse opinions. So call the place directly and be con-scious of ratings such as AAA and the Better Business Bureau. Many of the areas have chain hotels and restaurants, which are generally not included in the listings in each chapter. Within each chapter, we provide contact information for chambers of commerce and/or convention and visitor bureaus. Here are some additional general resources:

- **Office of the Governor, Economic Development and Tourism.** Traveltexas.com. This official Texas tourism website offers a free state map, narrated walking tours that you can download to your iPod, and the annual Texas Travel Guide.

- **Statewide Road Conditions.** (800) 452-9292; drivetexas.org. Call or visit the website for up-to-date information on road conditions including construction, closures, flooding, or accidents that may affect your plans.

- **Texas Department of Transportation.** txdot.gov/inside-txdot/division/travel.html. The website is a great resource for weather information, maps, travel safety tips, and more.

- **Texas Travel Information Centers.** 112 E. 11th St., Austin, TX 78701; (512) 463-8586 or (800) 452-9292; txdot.gov. This travel center, located at the Texas Capitol Visitors Center in Austin, is one of 12 official travel centers in Texas (and the only one within the scope of this book). Each offers maps, the Texas Travel Guide, brochures, and professional assistance on trip planning.

austin area overview

Welcome to Austin, the state capital and gateway to attractions in Central Texas. With Austin as your base, you'll have a chance to visit both rugged hills to the west and miles of scenic roads and interesting small towns to the east.

Austin is a high-tech city, with an economy based on computer-related industries and state government. The city of Austin takes in more than 950,807 residents, including a University of Texas population of more than 50,950 students and faculty from around the world. This gives Austin an international feel, with many ethnic restaurants and specialty grocery stores. Many people have relocated here, attracted by the clean industry and beautiful weather. Over the past decade, Austin has burst its boundaries and now encompasses a sprawl of about 2.2 million residents in the metropolitan area.

New residents aren't the first to discover the beauty of Austin. When Mirabeau B. Lamar, the president-elect of the Texas Republic, set out to hunt buffalo in the fall of 1838, he returned home with a much greater catch than a prize buffalo: a home for the new capital city. Lamar fell in love with a tiny settlement surrounded by rolling hills and fed by cool springs. Within the coming year, the government arrived and construction on the capitol building was begun. Austin was on its way to becoming a city.

Since those early days there's been no looking back. Today Austin is a city on the move. Hollywood has discovered this big city with a small-town atmosphere, and it's not uncommon these days to see film crews blocking off an oak-lined street. High-tech industries have also migrated to Austin, making this area Texas's answer to Silicon Valley.

But for all the changes that have occurred in this capital city, Austin is still very much a town with a past that the city is proud to preserve and show off to its visitors.

A visit to Austin should begin downtown, where the Colorado River slices through the heart of the city. Once an unpredictable waterway, the Colorado has now been tamed into a series of lakes, including two within the Austin city limits. The 22-mile-long Lake Austin begins at the foot of the Hill Country and flows through the western part of the city.

Lake Austin flows into Lady Bird Lake (named for former First Lady, the late Lady Bird Johnson). This narrow stretch of water, formerly known as Town Lake, meanders for 5 miles through the center of downtown Austin. Several hotels overlook the beautifully planted greenbelts that line the lakeshore. In the late afternoon hours, locals grab their sneakers and head to Zilker Park or the lake shores for a jog or leisurely walk. When the sun sets on summer days, attention turns to the lake's Congress Avenue bridge, the location of the country's largest urban colony of Mexican free-tailed bats. The bats make their exodus after sunset to feed on insects in the Hill Country.

Many of Austin's historical buildings are found downtown, and the granddaddy of them all is the State Capitol. Tours introduce you to this pink-granite building that holds the distinction of being the tallest state capitol in the US.

The Governor's Mansion (gov.texas.gov) lies just south of the Capitol. After an extensive renovation, the mansion is open for free guided tours Wednesday, Thursday, and Friday from 2 to 4 p.m. Call (512) 305-8524 for reservations.

Continuing south of the Capitol is the Driskill Hotel, Austin's most historic hotel. Since 1886 this property has been a stopover for dignitaries, heads of state, legislators, and vacationers from around the globe.

The Capitol, the Governor's Mansion, and the Driskill are all historical Austin landmarks, but they're just babes when compared to the French Legation, Austin's oldest existing home. Located in east Austin at 802 San Marcos, this is the only foreign legation in the country ever built outside of Washington, DC. (Wondering why it was built in Austin? Don't forget: Texas was once a separate country—complete with its own foreign ambassadors!)

Austin's most famous museum is the Lyndon Baines Johnson Presidential Library, located on the University of Texas campus. Special exhibits illustrate the Vietnam conflict, the civil rights movement, and the advances in education that took place during these years. Visitors can also view extravagant gifts received from other countries, a limousine used by the president, and family memorabilia.

On the southern end of the University of Texas campus, you'll find the Blanton Museum of Art. One of the largest university art museums in the country, the Blanton's collection includes more than 17,000 works and is recognized for its old master paintings as well as modern and contemporary American and Latin American art. And off-campus but within easy walking distance lies the Bob Bullock Texas State History Museum, which showcases the history of the Lone Star State from European exploration to recent times.

After a day of touring, Austin presents plenty of other entertainment options. The heart of Austin's nightlife is Sixth Street, a historic 7-block area with many nightclubs and restaurants, as well as eclectic shops that are open during the day. And if you get hungry in the

live music capital of the world

Austin has earned its nickname thanks to the large number of live music venues scattered throughout the city. On any given night, about 100 venues ranging from concert halls to alternative bars to honky-tonks move to the sound of live music. The city has drawn many well-known names who select Austin not just for performances but for their home. Today Austin is home to Robert Plant, Willie Nelson, Asleep at the Wheel, Natalie Maines of The Chicks, Eric Johnson, and others.

capital city, have no fear—Austin is home to more restaurants and bars per capita than any other city in the nation.

And if all that dining creates a need for a little activity, fun comes in many forms. In the warm months, Austin really lives up to its nickname, "The River City," since everyone takes to Lake Austin and nearby Lake Travis to enjoy swimming, scuba diving, waterskiing, and boating. Golfers find plenty of challenges in this area as well.

Austin spreads out into the suburban communities of Round Rock, Cedar Park, Oak Hill, and others. But beyond the reach of Austin's bedroom communities, you'll find a Texas that's largely unchanged. Bowling alleys still set pins by hand, businesses close on Friday nights during high school football season, and pickup trucks seem to outnumber every other form of transportation. Some of the best barbecue in the world comes from the small towns nestled in the Hill Country, a region so called because of its rugged terrain. The topographical change represents the 1,800-mile Balcones Fault, which has separated the western Hill Country from the flat eastern farmland ever since a 3.5-minute earthquake 30 million years ago.

This part of Texas gives you a chance to slow down, meet some local folks, and enjoy a good old-fashioned chicken-fried steak at the local diner.

For brochures, maps, and general questions on Austin area attractions, call (800) 926-ACVB or (512) 474-5171; write Austin Convention and Visitors Bureau, 111 Congress Ave., Ste. 700, Austin, TX 78701; or check out austintexas.org.

While you're downtown, stop by the Austin visitor center (866-462-8784 or 512-478-0098) for information, tour tickets, and a chance to shop Austin's official gift shop. The center is located at 602 E. Fourth St. and is open daily.

north

day trip 01

north

interstate gems:
pflugerville, round rock, georgetown, salado

Heading north of Austin on congested I-35, this day trip steps from one of the state's most populated cities to the quickly growing bedroom communities and suburbs, then travels beyond commuter range to towns that still maintain the flavor of small-town Texas. Since the 1800s, this area has been primarily agricultural, settled by immigrant farmers from Sweden, Germany, and Czechoslovakia.

pflugerville

Heading north on I-35 you won't notice that you've left Austin and reached Pflugerville (pronounced "FLOO-gur-vil") unless you look for the signs. Technically about 15 miles north of the capital city, Pflugerville proper is located 4 miles east of I-35 on FM 1825 (look for I-35 exit 247).

Austin's urban sprawl has caught up to this place named for German immigrant Henry Pfluger. What began as a small town just after the Civil War became the fastest-growing community in Texas in the 1980s. Growth continues today but the community still holds onto its distinctive spirit in its historic downtown.

Continue east on FM 1825 past the subdivisions and strip centers to where FM 1825 becomes Pecan Street. Soon you'll see small-town Texas, especially if you turn north on Railroad Street and continue for 1 block to Main Street. Here you'll find the true "downtown" Pflugerville, with dining, shopping, and nightlife in historic buildings.

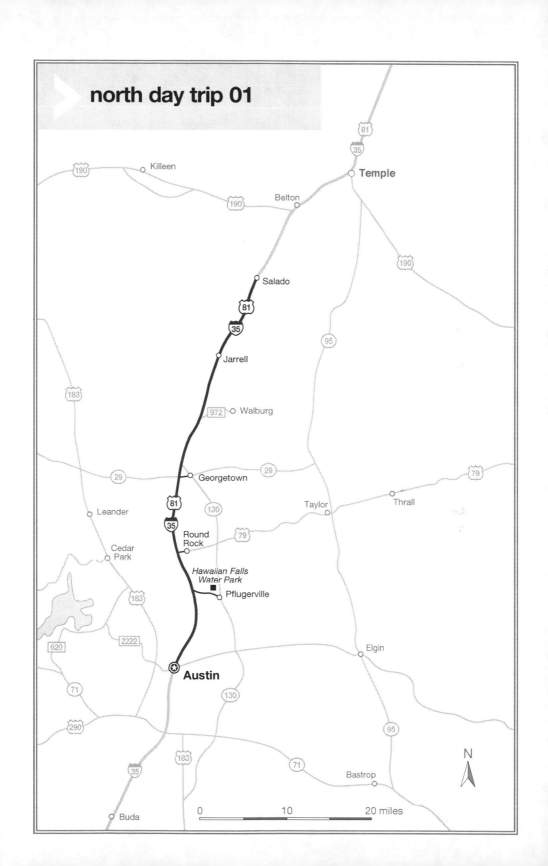

Those historic buildings and the general Pflugerville setting have been the backdrop for many movies. Pflugerville's Chamber of Commerce (101 S. Third St.; 512-251-7799; pfchamber.com) is proud to point out its "PflugerWood" connection thanks to its role in movies, including *A Perfect World, Best Little Whorehouse in Texas, Courage Under Fire, The Newton Boys, Secondhand Lions,* and *What's Eating Gilbert Grape?*

During the third weekend in October, crowds flock to this bedroom community from the capital city for Pflugerville's annual Deutchen Pfest (deutchenpfest.com) complete with a parade, music, rides, food, and more.

where to go

Gilleland Creek Park and Pool. 700 N. Railroad Ave.; (512)-990-6350; pflugervilletx.gov. Wonderful 11.9-acre facility with a Junior Olympic–size swimming pool, playscape, hike-and-bike trail, outdoor exercise area, and lighted pavilion with picnic tables, BBQ pit, and grill. Fee.

Heritage House Museum. 901 Old Austin Hutto Rd.; (512) 990-0635; library.pflugervilletx .gov. This local history museum traces the lives of early Pflugerville residents through exhibits of artifacts and other memorabilia in a home dating from 1913. Open first Sun of each month from 1 to 4 p.m., also open Tues during Pfarmers Market (Mar through Dec) from 3 to 7 p.m. Free admission.

Lake Pflugerville. 18216 Weiss Ln.; (512) 990-6400; pflugervilletx.gov. We love this 180-acre lake located on the east side of the city, an easy getaway for dog walking, fishing, or a relaxing stroll. The lake and surrounding parkland make up a very popular recreation area for residents who come to swim, fish, windsurf, and hike or bike the 3-mile trail. Free to use; kayaks can be rented at the public facility on the north shore of the lake.

where to shop

Pfarmers Market. 901 Old Austin Hutto Rd.; (512) 990-6355. Held on Tues from May through Oct in Heritage Park, this extensive market features all manner of locally grown fruits and vegetables, bakery goods, canned food, and free-range meats. The market also offers craft items for sale, and musicians entertain shoppers on certain dates.

Ruffles & Rust. 101 W. Pecan St.; (512) 252-9300; rufflesandrusttexas.com. Texas products, gourmet food, fashions, jewelry, home decor, gift items, and much more in locally owned boutique.

where to eat

Hanovers Draught Haus. 108 E. Main St.; (512) 670-9617; hanoversaustin.com. Known for its live music (every Wed, Thurs, Fri, and Sat night), its draft beer selection, and its large beer garden, you'll also find barbecue at this historic building. The structure dates to 1903, when it began as a saloon; later it was converted to a lumberyard and hardware store. Today the lively place is well known in the world of Austin live music. Families are welcome until 8 p.m., at which time only patrons age 21 and over are permitted. $.

Pecan Street Station Deli & Grill. 1005 Pecan St. West; (512) 251-0296; pecanstreet station.com. This eatery just west of the downtown area specializes in comfort food favorites like hamburgers, hot dogs, subs, and other deli sandwiches served in a large dining room or on the adjoining patio. An all-you-can-eat salad bar is another popular option. Check the website for hours of operation. $.

Rio Grande Tex Mex Restaurant. 15821 Central Commerce Dr.; (512) 252-1800; rio grandemex.com. Although the name of this restaurant says "Tex Mex," it also features some Mexican specialties like charbroiled platters of beef, chicken, or shrimp and their *puerco cascabel*, pork tips cooked in homemade Cascabel sauce. Open daily. $–$$.

round rock

With a population nearing 125,000, this booming suburban community located north on I-35 is named for the circular rock formation that lies in the middle of Brushy Creek.

Round Rock was the scene of a Wild West shoot-out a century ago. Sam Bass was a well-known outlaw in these parts back then, a stagecoach and train robber who boasted that he'd never killed a man. Bass planned to make his first bank robbery in Round Rock, but things went awry when the Texas Rangers learned of his scheme. They were waiting as Bass and his gang rode into town on July 19, 1878, and they gravely wounded him during a gun battle in the 100 block of E. Main Street. Bass fled from town and died two days later.

This colorful figure was buried in the old Round Rock cemetery, situated on what's now known as Sam Bass Road. The grave is near an interesting slave cemetery, a reminder of the cotton industry and plantation system that once dominated this area.

Round Rock was also once a part of the stagecoach route that stretched from Browns-ville, Texas, to Helena, Arkansas. Frontiersmen used the round rock to judge the depth of Brushy Creek before crossing. Today visitors still can see coach tracks in the Brushy Creek riverbed, just west of I-35.

Today Round Rock is home to the Round Rock Express (512-255-BALL; milb.com), a AAA minor-league baseball franchise. The city boasts an expansive sports facility off I-35 at US 79 near Old Settlers Park. The team comes to the community thanks to Texas baseball great Nolan Ryan.

where to go

Blue Starlite Mini Urban Drive-In Cinema. 800 Harrell Pkwy; (512) 850-6127; bluestar litedrivein.com. For a blast from the past, visit this mini drive-in cinema that takes only 15

> ## on the sam bass trail
>
> *Texas has more buried treasure than any other state, much of it tied to outlaw Sam Bass. The robber hid from the law in the town of Round Rock. Bass was in Round Rock, making plans for a bank robbery, until a final shoot-out with the Texas Rangers on July 19, 1878. Before he died, however, many say that he hid much of the loot from his train, stagecoach, and bank robberies somewhere in the area.*
>
> *The outlaw allegedly buried $30,000 in the community of McNeil. No treasure was ever recovered, and today there is little remaining of McNeil, located in the northern part of Travis County near Round Rock.*

to 40 cars a night. Blue Starlite features childhood favorite movies, classics, indie films, pop culture faves, and much more.

Dell Diamond. 3400 E. Palm Valley Blvd.; (512) 255-2255; milb.com. The home field of the Round Rock Express, the AAA affiliate of the Texas Rangers, Dell Diamond is a modern ball-park seating over 8,000 fans with an additional 3,000 vantage points on the grassy outfield berm. The park, which opened in 2000, has numerous food concessions, a state-of-the-art scoreboard, and even a swimming pool and hot tub located beyond the right-field wall. Guided tours of the park are offered year-round. Fee.

where to shop

Round Rock Premium Outlets. 4401 I-35 North; (512) 863-6688; premiumoutlets.com. Located between Round Rock and Georgetown on the east side of the interstate, this outlet mall boasts 125 shops, mostly upscale brands such as Ann Taylor, Michael Kors, and Polo Ralph Lauren. Open daily.

where to eat

Governor's Kitchen at Bluebonnet Beer Company. 1700 Bryant Dr. #107; (512) 774-4258; bluebonnetbeerco.com. The Governor's Kitchen offers snacks, salads, sandwiches, and charcuterie plates. A favorite is the Oktoberfest Beer Brat, a cream ale braised German sausage, sauerkraut, spicy mustard served on a pretzel roll with house chips. Established in 2013, Bluebonnet Beer Co. offers a variety of ales, IPAs, and seasonal beers. $.

georgetown

Georgetown is an elegant community of over 71,000 residents that rests on the border of farmland to the east and ranch land to the west. Located 10 miles north of Round Rock on I-35, this was once an active agricultural center. Today Georgetown is home to many Austin commuters and 1,500 students at Southwestern University, the oldest college in Texas.

Georgetown's first residents were the Tonkawa tribe, a resourceful group of Native Americans that drove buffalo off the bluffs of the San Gabriel River. Years later, the town of Georgetown was founded by a group of men that included George Washington Glasscock. After he donated the land for the town, it was named in his honor. Glasscock had come to Texas from the East after running a river barge business for a time in Illinois with Abraham Lincoln.

Georgetown became a cattle center after the Civil War and the starting point of many northern cattle drives. The community grew but remained a small town into the late 1900s. Austin's runaway growth during the 1980s eventually turned Georgetown into a bedroom community divided by I-35. To the west is "new" Georgetown, with many subdivisions, including nationally known Sun City, along Williams Drive on the way to Lake Georgetown. "Old" Georgetown sits east of the highway, and among its main attractions are the winding North and South San Gabriel Rivers, which join together in shady San Gabriel Park.

Georgetown has refined its recipe for community charisma as the city has grown and prospered. Serving as seat of the seventh-fastest-growing county in the nation, Georgetown continues to hang onto its cozy charm. Even with a growing population, it is proud to say that it's still the kind of place where folks can walk around the square and be welcomed by a smile and a friendly nod. Georgetown may have just found the secret ingredient: historic preservation.

North of the courthouse square, San Gabriel Park has served for centuries as a gathering site. Native Americans camped on the verdant grounds, pioneers met here, and early Georgetown residents congregated on the riverbanks for parades and meetings, including one event that featured speaker Sam Houston.

Today, park lovers enjoy shady picnics under the oak and pecan trees. Children romp on the playscape while anglers try their luck from the grassy riverbanks. Crystal-clear springs bubble up at three sites on the park grounds, and often you can watch these little "salt and pepper" springs spew up chilly water.

Upstream, the North San Gabriel River has been controlled to create Lake Georgetown, a 1,310-acre lake popular with anglers, boaters, water-skiers, and swimmers.

where to go

Georgetown Visitors Center. 103 W. Seventh St., on the square; (800) 436-8696 or (512) 930-3545; visitgeorgetown.org. Stop by for a copy of a Georgetown map, brochures on area attractions, and walking tour booklets. The center also sells many Georgetown items, from posters to T-shirts. Open Mon through Sat 9 a.m. to 5 p.m. and Sun 1 to 5 p.m.

Blue Hole. W. Second Street and Rock Street. In the heart of Georgetown, where the waters of the San Gabriel River reflect limestone cliffs, a revitalization project has made this beautiful spot a place to be appreciated by residents and visitors once more. At Blue Hole, walkers and joggers journey along the wide paths that wind beside waters as green as fresh spring leaves. On quiet mornings anglers try their luck with just the sound of an occasional cardinal singing its friendly song in the distance. Free admission.

Inner Space Cavern. West off I-35 exit 259 at 4200 S. I-35 Frontage Rd.; (512) 931-2283; innerspacecavern.com. Discovered during the construction of the interstate, this cave is a cool getaway for summer travelers and was once a hideaway for animals as well. A skull of a peccary (a piglike hoofed mammal) estimated to be a million years old has been found here, along with bones of a giant sloth and a mammoth.

Enter the cavern on a cog railroad car, traveling down from the visitor center to the well-lit, easy-to-follow trail. Along the way, guides point out features of Inner Space, including large stalactite and stalagmite formations. Some of the larger formations of the cavern are "The Warriors," two stalagmites that have grown together, the "Flowing Stone of Time" in the Outer Cathedral, and "Ivory Falls," a beautiful flow of white stalactites. The cavern uses sound and light displays to create special effects, including the grand finale of the tour: a show at the "Lake of the Moon."

After reaching cave level aboard a small trolley, follow your guide for a tour of cave formations, a small lake, and evidence of those prehistoric visitors. Kids also enjoy the Inner Space Mining Company, where they can pan for gems and minerals. For a thrilling ride, try the Saber Tooth tandem zip ride where one or two riders are strapped in for a 130-foot lift into the air, then zoom backwards for 630 feet. The lift stops at the top for a quick view, then heads back at up to 33 mph. Open daily. Fee.

Lake Georgetown. FM 2338, 3.5 miles west of town; (512) 930-5253. Built on the north fork of the San Gabriel River, this lake spans 1,310 surface acres. Three public parks offer swimming, fishing, boating, camping, and hiking as well as the chance to spot a protected golden-cheeked warbler and black-capped vireo. Public facilities include **Jim Hogg Park** with overnight camping, electric and water hookups, and boat ramp; **Cedar Breaks Park** with picnic facilities and campsites with electric hookups; **Russell Park** for picnicking and camping; and **Tejas Camp** for picnics and hikes among oak-shaded trails. Free admission; fee for camping.

The 17-mile **Good Water Loop** follows the upper end of the lake. The trail was named in honor of the Tonkawa, a people who made the region near the San Gabriel River their home. Known for their flint arrowheads and tools, these Native Americans called this region *takatchue pouetsu*, or "land of good water." This loop is part of the 26-mile San Gabriel River Trail, which completely encircles Lake Georgetown.

The trail is marked by mileposts as it snakes its way along the lake, passing through several historical points of interest. One such spot is Russell Crossing, later known as the **Second Bootys Crossing,** located near milepost 1. In the late 1860s, Frank Russell resided at this crossing, and his rock house served as a postal substation. Mail was carried in saddlebags to the local residents.

Between mileposts 2 and 3, hikers can see **Crockett Gardens,** a natural spring. A flour mill operated here in 1855, and a few decades later the first strawberries in Williamson County were grown in truck gardens at this site. Today the remains of the springhouse and corrals can still be seen.

Besides man-made attractions, hikers are also surrounded by natural beauties. White-tailed deer, coyote, skunk, raccoon, ringtail, armadillo, and opossum thrive in this area. From Feb to Aug, the region is home to the endangered golden-cheeked warbler, a small bird that nests in older juniper trees.

San Gabriel Park. Off Austin Avenue at 445 E. Morrow St.; (512) 930-3595; parks.george town.org. This park, just south of the junction of the North and South San Gabriel Rivers, includes a children's playscape, picnic sites, sunken gardens, a swimming pool, and a walking trail. We love the park for quiet picnics in the shade of the tall pecan trees. Open daily. Free admission.

Southwestern University. 1001 E. University Ave.; (512) 863-6511; southwestern.edu. Southwestern holds the title of Texas's first institution of higher learning. Call for a guided tour. Open daily. Free admission.

The Williamson Museum. 716 S. Austin Ave.; (512) 943-1670; williamsonmuseum.org. This local history museum is itself housed in a historic structure, the 1911 Farmers State Bank building. Today the Beaux Arts–style building contains exhibits that range from cattle

poppy fields

In late March, the fields and yards around Georgetown bloom with the vibrant color of red poppies. Georgetown holds the title of the "Red Poppy Capital of Texas," with both native and cultivated varieties growing throughout the town.

The poppies originate from seeds imported to the town by Henry Purl "Okra" Compton. During his service in World War I in Europe, he collected seeds and planted them around his mother's home upon his return.

Today the poppies brighten yards and highway right-of-ways from late March through May. Look for white signs indicating a "Poppy Zone" as you travel through town.

drives to Williamson County during wartime. You can't miss the museum: Just look for the statue of "Three-Legged Willie" out front. The statue memorializes Robert McAlpin Williamson, a Texas Ranger and Republic of Texas Supreme Court justice. Williamson's leg was bent by arthritis, necessitating the need for a wooden leg fastened to his knee, giving him the nickname for which he is still known today. Open Wed through Fri noon to 5 p.m. and Sat 10 a.m. to 5 p.m. Free admission.

where to shop

Georgetown has more than a dozen antiques shops. For a free map of the shops listing hours and specialties, call (800) 436-8696, click on visitgeorgetown.org, or stop by the visitor center on the square, where other brochures are also available.

Diva Chicks Boutique. 823 S. Austin Ave.; (512) 630-2022; facebook.com/divachicksinc .com. This trendy boutique features comfortable but stylish fashions from clothing to accessories. Open daily.

Georgetown Antique Mall. 110 W. Eighth St.; (866) 594-7542; georgetownantiquemall .com. This expansive shop features antiques from many dealers, ranging from collectibles to glassware to furniture. Open Mon through Sat 10 a.m. to 6 p.m.

Rough and Ready Antiques. 602 S. Main St.; (512) 819-0463; facebook.com/roughand ready. This shop specializes in early Texas furniture as well as architectural details. Open daily 10 a.m. to 5 p.m.

The Windberg Art Gallery. 7100 I-35 North; (512) 869-5588; windbergartcenter.com. Georgetown is home to the renowned artist Dalhart Windberg. Known for his emotional portrayals of American landscapes and settings, the gallery offers both original art and handsome prints. Open Mon through Sat.

where to eat

Black Sugar Caffe. 109 W. Seventh St.; (512) 688-3035; blacksugarcaffe.com. This friendly coffee bar on the courthouse square has become a favorite hangout for locals and visitors alike. The Caffe serves specialty coffees, fresh smoothies, tapas, desserts, pastries, beer, and wine. Open daily. $.

The Monument Cafe. 500 S. Austin Ave.; (512) 930-9586; themonumentcafe.com. Styled like an old-fashioned diner, this family restaurant serves up favorites ranging from chicken-fried steak to burgers. It is also a popular breakfast stop, serving excellent breakfast tacos as well as traditional fare. And, if you need to check email during your day trip, the restaurant also has free Wi-Fi connectivity. Open daily. $–$$.

Wildfire. 812 S. Austin Ave.; (512) 869-FIRE; wildfiretexas.com. *Time* magazine said that this restaurant's blue cornmeal–encrusted catfish was reason enough to move to

Georgetown. Southwestern-inspired cuisine, much of it prepared on an oak-burning grill, rules, although you'll also find dishes such as pancetta-wrapped Atlantic salmon and oak-fired elk tenderloin. Open for lunch and dinner daily. $$$.

where to stay

Campgrounds at Lake Georgetown. (877) 444-6777 or (512) 930-5253; tpwd.texas.gov. All of the Lake Georgetown parks offer camping, a great option especially during the spring and fall months. Cedar Breaks Park has 64 campsites offering water and electric hookups as well as a covered picnic table, fire ring, and grill. The park also has a dump station for RVers; restrooms offer hot showers and flush toilets. More facilities are found at Jim Hogg Park, with 142 sites offering water and electric hookups, each with a covered table, fire ring, and grill. This park also includes a dump station and five large group camping shelters. The sparsest facilities are found at Russell Park, with 27 primitive sites without water or electric hookups. This park does offer 10 screened shelters, each with 2 sets of bunk beds (no mattresses). Tent camping without electricity is available at Russell Park as well as in the largely unimproved Tejas Camp. $.

San Gabriel House. 1008 E. University Ave.; (512) 930-0070; sangabrielhouse.com. This elegant bed-and-breakfast is an Arts and Crafts mansion located directly across University Avenue from Southwestern University. The home has 6 guest rooms with bathrooms, well-tended gardens in the back, and large porches with swings. $$.

salado

Continuing north on I-35 to exit 283, you'll encounter Salado, a shopping stop for interstate travelers. Antiques stores, artists' galleries, and specialty shops fill the historic downtown buildings. Salado (pronounced "sa-LAY-dough") is a Spanish word meaning either "salty" or "amusing," although residents prefer the latter.

This community is located where Salado Creek flows beneath I-35. The site once was a stagecoach stop on the old Chisholm Trail and served the line that stretched from San Antonio to Little Rock, Arkansas.

Today the old rest stop has been converted to the modern Stagecoach Inn, located on the east side of I-35. Visitors' accommodations are found in a modern addition, and the original building, where Sam Houston once delivered an anti-secession speech, has become an elegant restaurant.

The former stagecoach route, now called Main Street, is lined with historic structures housing antiques shops and specialty stores. In all, 18 of these buildings are listed on the National Register of Historic Places, and 23 boast Texas historical markers.

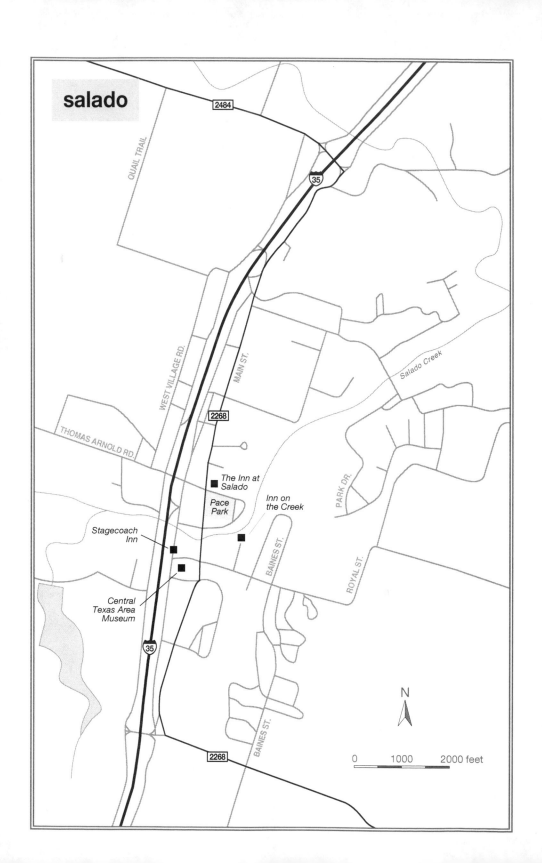

where to go

Pace Park. Pace Park Drive, downtown, off Main Street; (254) 947-5060. This beautiful area, restored following a massive flood in 2009, is filled with tall oaks and is an excellent spot to bring a picnic lunch and wade in the creek. Don't miss the statue of Sirena, located on the banks of the creek. (Previously Sirena was in the creek itself, but after damage from a flood, she was repaired and relocated.) Local artist Troy Kelley created the statue cast in bronze of the legendary Native American maiden who was transformed into a mermaid by a magical fish. In the morning, you can see fog rising from the chilly waters of the pure springs near the statue. Free admission.

Salado Museum & College Park. 423 S. Main St., across from Stagecoach Inn; (254) 947-5232; saladomuseum.org. This museum traces the history of the Salado area and all of the Brazos Trail—the rich farming area near the Brazos River. Its collection includes historic Scottish genealogical records, and it founded Salado's annual Gathering of the Clans of Texas celebration of Scottish heritage. Open weekdays 10 a.m. to 4 p.m. Free admission, but donations are welcome.

where to shop

Shopping is the main drawing card of Salado, and many stores are open daily. Most sell one-of-a-kind, handmade items.

Accents of Salado. 3366 FM 2484; (877) 947-5938; accentsofsalado.com. This shop specializes in European-inspired furniture and accessories for the home. The large showroom is full of unique old-world items with an emphasis on Tuscan-style decor. Open by appointment only.

Mud Pies Pottery. 18 N. Main St.; (254) 947-0281; visitsaladotexas.com/places/mud-pies-pottery/. If it can be made from clay, you'll probably find it here. Each item is crafted by hand, and most kitchen items are dishwasher and oven safe. Open daily.

Salado Glassworks. 2 Peddlers Alley; (254) 947-0339; saladoglassworks.com. The delicate art of glassblowing is on display at this shop featuring the work of Gail Allard. The shop's gallery sells bowls and vases and other unique creations and offers classes in glassblowing. Open Tues through Sun.

The Shoppes on Main in Salado. 22 N. Main St.; (254) 947-0888; facebook.com/Shoppes OnMain. With more than 25 different shops to choose from, you can find everything from furniture to jewelry to original artworks in one central location. Open daily.

Sirril Art Gallery. 1 Royal View Rd.; (469) 877-0374; sirrilartgallery.com. Gallery features works by artist Michael Pritchett as well as collections of artwork from central Texas area artists. Open Tues through Sun.

where to eat

The Barton House. 101 N. Main St.; (254) 947-0441; thebartonhousesalado.com. This elegant restaurant specializes in farm-to-table dishes as well as steaks, pork, and seafood. Our favorite here is the grilled Tuscan marinated quail served with a sherry-maple reduction. An adjacent lounge serves cocktails and features live entertainment. Open for brunch, lunch, and dinner. Check the website or call for days open. $$$.

Robertson's Hams and Choppin' Block. I-35, exit 285 at 1420 N. Robertson Rd.; (800) 458-HAMS or (254) 947-5562; robertsonshams.com. Enjoy a deli sandwich of sugar-cured ham, then shop for kitchen collectibles in the extensive gift shop. $.

Stagecoach Inn. 416 S. Main St.; (254) 947-5111; stagecoachsalado.com. Located right beside I-35, this historic restaurant and inn is a Central Texas favorite, holding a special place in the hearts of many local residents who have celebrated special occasions for generations here. By long-standing tradition, servers recite the day's menu by heart. The restaurant has won awards for its roast prime rib, but offerings also include seafood, chicken-fried steak, baked ham, and grilled steaks. Baskets of hush puppies are a tradition. Open Sun through Thurs 8 a.m. to 8 p.m.; Fri and Sat 8 a.m. to 9 p.m.; adjacent coffee shop open daily for lunch and dinner. Reservations recommended. $$–$$$.

where to stay

For a list of Salado inns and bed-and-breakfasts, visit salado.com/lodging.cfm.

The Inn at Salado. 7 N. Main Street at Pace Park Drive; (800) 724-0027 or (254) 947-0027; inn-at-salado.com. This lovely bed-and-breakfast with 10 rooms and a cottage, all with private baths, is located within walking distance of the main shopping district. Room rates include a full breakfast and free Wi-Fi. $$–$$$.

Inn on the Creek. 602 Center Circle; (877) 947-5554 or (254) 947-5554; inncreek.com. This inn offers 19 private guest rooms in 6 different locations, including the beautiful manor house with its 1882 Victorian elegance. The Manor is not suitable for guests with children under 14. Some rooms boast brass beds; all have private baths. All guests receive an upscale continental breakfast and free Wi-Fi. $$–$$$.

Stagecoach Inn. 416 S. Main St.; (254) 947-5111; stagecoachsalado.com. This throwback to Salado's early days started out as the Shady Villa Inn, an important rest stop on the Chisholm Trail. Today guests stay in a modern addition, and the original building, where Sam Houston once delivered an anti-secession speech, is now an elegant restaurant. The Inn features 48 rooms and suites along with a heated pool and free Wi-Fi. The property features 7 acres of landscaping with lush greenery and native Texas plants. Notable guests have included George Armstrong Custer, Robert E. Lee, and Jesse James. $$.

day trip 02

north

>>>>> **military history:**
belton, killeen, temple

Beyond Georgetown and Salado (see North Day Trip 01 for attractions in those towns), I-35 continues its northward journey to two larger central Texas communities. If you're a military buff, take a short detour to Killeen, home of Fort Hood, one of the largest military bases in the world.

belton

Built on the Leon River and Nolan Creek, this community once named Nolanville was a place where merchants sold goods from wagons and tin cups of whiskey from barrels. Today Belton is a small town of 21,685 residents, best known as home of the University of Mary Hardin–Baylor. The Baptist college began here over a century ago and was once the women's school for Waco's Baylor University. Visit beltonchamber.com for more information.

Two lakes, Stillhouse Hollow Lake and the larger Belton Lake, lie outside the city limits. Both provide fishing, boating, camping, and a quiet retreat only a few minutes from busy I-35.

where to go

Bell County Museum. 201 N. Main St.; (254) 933-5243; bellcountymuseum.org. This National Register property was first a Carnegie library. Today the Beaux Arts–style building and its newer addition house exhibits on Bell County's first century, 1850–1950. Special

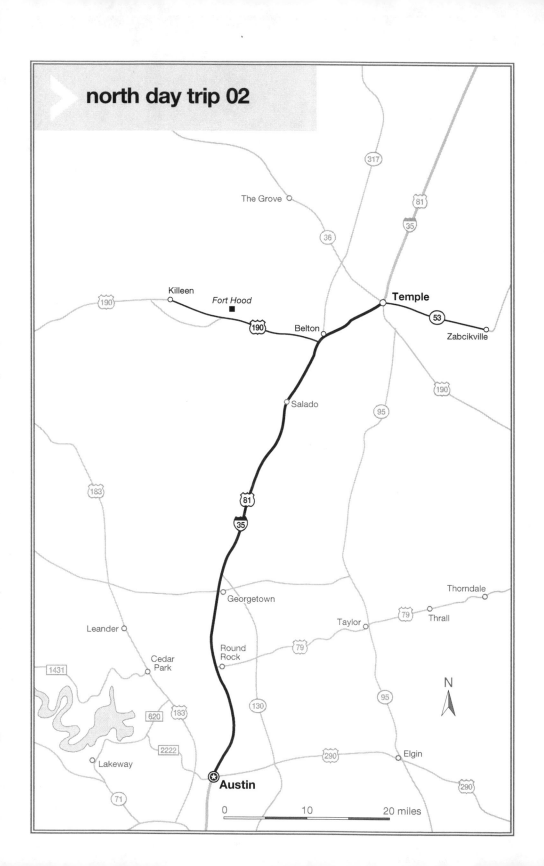

north day trip 02

displays remember Miriam "Ma" Ferguson, Texas's first woman governor, as well as the history of Camp Hood, later to become Fort Hood. Open Tues through Fri noon to 5 p.m.; Sat 10 a.m. to 5 p.m. Free admission.

Belton Lake. TX 317, 5 miles northwest of Belton; (877) 444-6777 for camping reservations, (254) 939-2461; swf-wc.usace.army.mil/belton. Built on the Leon River, this winding 7,400-acre lake features 13 public parks within its 110 miles of shoreline. Trailer sites, camping, nature trails, and boat ramps are available. Fee.

Cochran, Blair and Potts. 221 E. Central Ave.; (254) 939-3333; cbandpotts.com. Something of a living museum, this store's claim as the oldest department store in Texas might well be true. Founded in 1869, it has remained owned by the same family for its entire history. It occupies an entire city block and sells a wide variety of wares. A museum section illustrates the store's history. Open Mon through Sat. Free admission.

Mother Neff State Park. 1921 Park Rd. 14, Moody; (254) 853-2389; tpwd.texas.gov/state-parks/mother-neff. From I-35 take exit 315 to FM 107 west to Moody, continue 6 miles west on FM 107, then take TX 236 for 2 miles to the park. Named for Isabella Neff, the mother of Governor Pat Neff, this park is nestled along the shady bottomland along the Leon River. A nice place for a quiet day of picnicking and walking, the park also offers periodic trailer rides to point out historical areas. In 2015, the park underwent a $6.5 million renovation, with new facilities including a limestone headquarters, maintenance facilities, and a 20-site camping loop. Designed to complement the existing Civilian Conservation Corps structures, the new headquarters building includes exhibits on the CCC's work at the park from 1934 to 1938. $2 daily fee for age 12 and over. Open daily.

Stillhouse Hollow. US 190, 4 miles southwest of Belton; (254) 939-2461; swf-wc.usace.army.mil/stillhouse. Six public parks surround this lake. You'll find the most facilities at Stillhouse Park, the first you'll come to on US 190. Fee.

Summer Fun Water Park. 1410 Waco Rd.; (254) 939-0366; summerfunwaterpark.com. This 7-acre water theme park offers more than 900 feet of water slides to help you cool off in the Texas heat. Hop in an inner tube and enjoy the 750-foot Lazy River ride, or slide into the water from a 40-foot tower. There are picnic and concession areas as well. Open seasonally. Fee.

killeen

Military buffs should take a detour at this point in the journey and head west on US 190 to the city of Killeen. Twenty-five miles west of Belton, this small town is dwarfed by Fort Hood, one of the world's largest military posts.

where to go

Belton Lake Outdoor Recreation Area. Sparta Road, northeast of Fort Hood; (254) 287-4907; hood.armymwr.com. This 890-acre park offers woodland hiking, equestrian trails, fishing, boating, paddleboating, and swimming. Open daily. Fee.

Fort Hood. US 190; (254) 286-5139; hood.army.mil. Established in 1942, Fort Hood spans 339 square miles, encompassing more people and machines than any other post in the free world. The post is home to more than 40,000 soldiers. Access to the base is restricted, but the public is welcome at two museums: the 1st Cavalry Division and the 3rd Cavalry Regiment Museums. Before traveling to the museums, you'll need to make your first stop at the **Marvin Leath Visitors Center** (254-287-9909; hood.army.mil/visitors.center.aspx) located at US 190 at the Main Gate at 69004 T.J. Mills Blvd. To obtain a driving permit for the base, you'll need to show identification and proof of driver's insurance. The visitor center is open daily 5 a.m. to 9 p.m.

1st Cavalry Division Museum. Building 2218, Headquarters Avenue; (254) 287-3626; history.army.mil/museums/fieldmuseums/forthoot_1stCav/index.html. Fort Hood is home to the 1st Cavalry Division Horse Detachment. Wearing authentic 19th-century uniforms, this group performs at exhibitions throughout Texas. The museum traces the history of this division from its days on the western frontier through its berm-busting attacks during Desert Storm. An outdoor area displays more than three dozen pieces of military equipment, including aircraft and tanks. Open daily. Free admission.

3rd Cavalry Regiment Museum. Building 409, 761st Tank Battalion Avenue, near the intersection with 27th Street; history.army.mil/museums/fieldMuseums/forthood_3dCAV/index.html. The history of the US Army's largest armored cavalry regiment from the Civil War through missions in Iraq is illustrated here with exhibits of uniforms, weapons, battle flags, and photos. Outside, a display of military vehicles continues the story of this storied regiment nicknamed "The Brave Rifles." Open daily. Free admission.

Mayborn Science Theater. Central Texas College campus, Bldg. 152, Bell Tower Dr.; (254) 526-1768 (weekdays) or (254) 526-1799 (weekends); starsatnight.org. The centerpiece of this facility, located on the campus of Central Texas College, is a cutting-edge planetarium with its 60-foot dome. Explore the galaxy with sky shows, IMAX films, and laser shows. Open for public shows most days; check website for scheduled times. Fee.

temple

From Killeen and Fort Hood, return to I-35 and continue north to Temple. With more than 74,000 people, this city is the medical center for Central Texas and an important industrial

zabcikville

It's a little too lively to be a true Texas ghost town, but the Czech community of Zabcikville, located 10 miles east of Temple on TX 53, is the next best thing. During its boomtown days in the 1940s, the population reached about 80; today you'll find just a few dozen residents. There's still one good reason to make a detour to this town, though: **Green's Sausage House,** *16483 I-53; (254) 985-2331; greenssausagehouse.com. The only business in town packs in area diners eager to lunch on sausage burgers, hamburgers, and homemade kolaches. An adjacent meat market sells sausage, ham, turkey, bacon, and more.*

producer. Temple was established by the Gulf, Colorado, and Santa Fe Railroad and named for its chief construction engineer, B. B. M. Temple. Temple is also nicknamed "The Wildflower Capital of Texas." Visitors lucky enough to arrive in late March and April are greeted by a variety of native blooms.

where to go

Miller Springs Nature Center. Off FM 2271 north of Lake Belton Spillway at 1473 Farm-To-Market Rd. 2271; (254) 939-2461; millerspringsnaturecenter.org. Set on 260 scenic acres between the Leon River and soaring river bluffs and adjacent to Lake Belton, this natural area gives visitors the opportunity for fishing, hiking, picnicking, and rock climbing. It frequently hosts school groups as part of the Bell County Network for Educational Technology's "classrooms without walls" program. Open daily 8 a.m. to dusk. Free admission.

Temple Railroad and Heritage Museum. 315 W. Avenue B; (254) 298-5172; templeparks .com/facilities_rentals/temple_railroad_heritage_museum/index.php. First housed in the former Moody depot, today this museum is located in a renovated Temple Santa Fe depot. Upstairs you'll find exhibits on the history of trains; outdoors check out the rolling stock like Santa Fe #3423, a 1921 steam locomotive. Open Tues through Sat 10 a.m. to 4 p.m. Fee.

where to eat

Clem Mikeska's Bar-B-Q and Grill. 1217 S. 57th St.; (800) 344-4699 or (254) 778-5481; clembbq.com. A member of the legendary Mikeska family, often referred to as the "first family of Texas barbecue," Clem Mikeska has been serving up 'que since 1965. Clem and his family specialize in sirloin rather than brisket barbecue. You'll also find popular favorites like chicken-fried steak, homemade sausage, coleslaw, potato salad, and banana pudding. Open daily. $.

Pignetti's.14 S. Second St.; (254) 778-1269; pignettis.com. Fine Italian dining and more than 1,300 selections of wine. Pignetti's has been given the Award of Excellence from *Wine Spectator* for over 10 years. Serving brunch on Sat and Sun from 11 a.m. to 3 p.m. with such favorites as crab cake benedict, chicken and waffles, and steak and eggs. A hefty lunch menu is offered Mon through Fri from 11 a.m. to 4 p.m. Dinner menu offers pasta, pizza, salads, steak, pork chops, veal, and fresh catch-of-the-day seafood. $$.

day trip 03

north

>>> **heart of texas:**
lorena, waco

Waco is sometimes called the "Heart of Texas" for its central location in the Lone Star State. This day trip continues North Day Trips 01 and 02, continuing north on I-35 through several small communities before reaching Waco, a city that has a large number of visitor attractions.

lorena

Located 80 miles north of Austin on I-35 at exit 322 (see North Day Trips 01 and 02 for attractions along this drive), the community of Lorena (254-857-4641; ci.lorena.tx.us) was formerly a railroad town. Named for the daughter of a local businessman, Lorena was a thriving town before the Depression. From the 1920s until the late 1960s, Lorena was especially quiet. In 1968 renovation began on several historic structures, and the town returned to life. Today the old part of the city (known as "Olde Town") is home to several antiques and specialty shops.

where to go

Library and Museum of the Lorena Women's Club. 101 Walter St. Since 2000 this small museum has celebrated the 100th Anniversary of the Lorena Women's Club. The museum contains household and agricultural items from Lorena's heyday. A collection of interest to

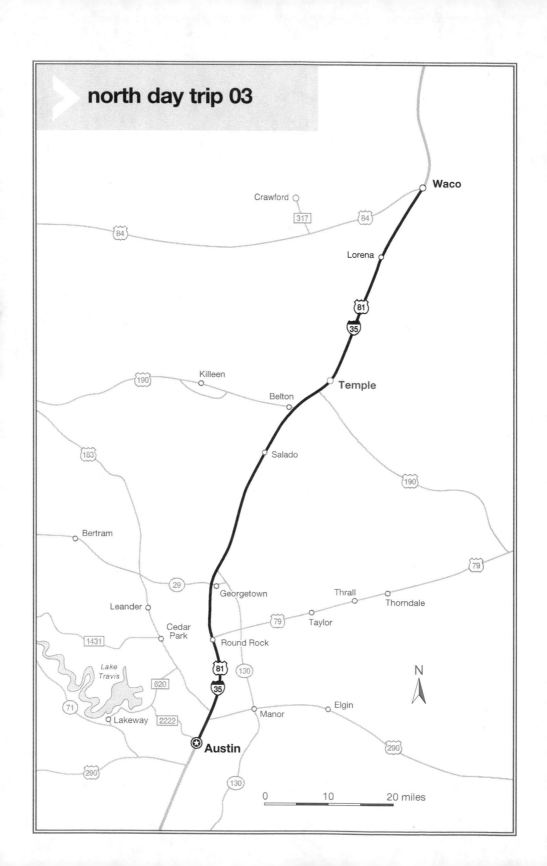

Crawford

Waco

84

317

84

Lorena

81

35

Killeen

190

Temple

Belton

183

Salado

190

Bertram

29

Georgetown

Thrall

Thorndale

79

Leander

Cedar
Park

79

Taylor

1431

Round Rock

Lake
Travis

81

35

130

620

Elgin

71

2222

Manor

Lakeway

Austin

290

290

130

N

0   10   20 miles

historians and former residents, the museum is home to 6,000 donated books and local artifacts. Open the first and last Wed of each month. Free admission.

where to shop

The Village Lamp Lighter. 103 E. Center St.; (254) 857-4435; villagelamplighter.com. This shop, in business for over four decades, showcases lamps and lighting of all types. Open Mon through Sat.

where to eat

Altos De Jalisco Lorena. 216 N. Interstate 35 Frontage Rd.; (254) 857-4787; altosde jalisco.us. Serving breakfast, lunch, and dinner, this Mexican restaurant offers authentic Mexican food with attentive fast service. $–$$.

waco

Continue north on I-35 to Waco, a city of more than 135,000, named for the Hueco people who resided here before the days of recorded history. The Huecos were attracted to this rich, fertile land at the confluence of the Brazos and Bosque Rivers.

Although Spanish explorers named this site "Waco Village" in 1542, over 300 years elapsed before permanent settlement began. At that time, Waco was part of the Wild West, with cattle drives, cowboys, and so many gunslingers that stagecoach drivers called the town "Six-Shooter Junction." (Drivers routinely asked passengers to strap on their guns before the stagecoach reached the rowdy community!)

In the 1870s Waco became a center of trade with the completion of a 470-foot suspension bridge across the Brazos, the longest inland river in Texas. The bridge, which still stands, was designed by the same engineers who constructed New York City's Brooklyn Bridge years later.

Today Waco's Wild West heritage is tempered by a strong religious influence. The city is home to Baylor University, a Baptist liberal arts college of 16,000 students. The university has several excellent museums open to the public.

Some of the most scenic areas in Waco fall along the Brazos River. This waterway slices the city in half and provides miles of shoreline parks, shady walks, and a winding river walk, which begins at Fort Fisher Park and extends to Cameron Park.

where to go

City of Waco Tourist Information Center. Fort Fisher at exit 335B off I-35; (800) WACO-FUN; wacoheartoftexas.com. The visitor center provides helpful maps and brochures, and staff members give advice on Waco attractions, accommodations, and restaurants. The

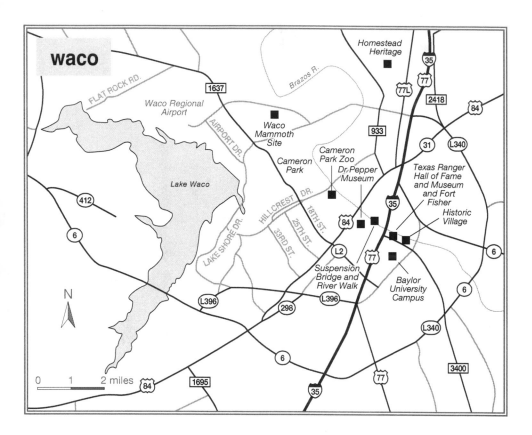

center also offers a great selection of Waco and Texas souvenirs. Open 9 a.m. to 5 p.m. Mon through Sat. Free admission.

The Art Center of Waco. 701 S. Eighth St.; (254) 752-4371; artcenterwaco.org. This exhibit hall and teaching center is located in a one-story brick building that was a former social services center. Built in 1960 and with 9,240 square feet of space, the building allowed the community art center to move downtown from its past home at McLennan Community College. Open weekdays 9 a.m. to 5 p.m. Free admission.

Baylor University. I-35, exit 335B at 1311 S. Fifth St.; (800) 229-5678; baylor.edu. Chartered by the fledgling Republic of Texas in 1845, this Baptist-affiliated university is the oldest continually operating university in the state. Now a nationally ranked liberal arts institution, the Baylor campus fills nearly 1,000 acres in downtown Waco. The university curriculum offers degrees in 141 undergraduate areas, 75'master's programs, and 37 doctoral programs. Major components of the university include the College of Arts & Sciences, the Hankamer School of Business, the School of Education, the School of Engineering & Computer Science, Graduate School, Honors College, Law School, School of Music, the Louise

Herrington School of Nursing, George W. Truett Theological Seminary, and the School of Social Work.

Armstrong Browning Library. 710 Speight Ave., Baylor University campus; (254) 710-3566; baylor.edu/library/index.php?id=973825. The works of Elizabeth Barrett Browning and husband Robert Browning fill this two-story library. The building also boasts the world's largest collection of secular stained-glass windows, which illustrate the works of both writers (including Robert Browning's *The Pied Piper of Hamlin*). Take a guided tour to see the upstairs rooms furnished with the couple's belongings. Open weekdays 9 a.m. to 5 p.m. Free admission.

Mayborn Museum Complex. 1300 S. University Parks Dr.; (254) 710-1110; baylor.edu/mayborn. This expansive museum complex includes exhibits on the region's natural and social history. Learn more about Waco with a visit to the *Waco at the Crossroads of Texas* natural history exhibits, which includes walk-in dioramas of a limestone cave, Texas forest, and Waco mammoth experience. Popular with children are the Discovery Rooms, where 16 themed rooms offer hands-on learning in areas that range from vertebrates to TV weather to Native Americans. Beyond the museum walls the learning continues in 9 wood-frame buildings found on the 13-acre Governor Bill and Vara Daniel Historic Village, a re-creation of a 19th-century cotton town. It includes a schoolhouse, a mercantile store, and, of course, a Wild West saloon. The buildings, once the property of the governor, were moved to this site from a plantation community in Liberty County and restored by Baylor University. Open daily. Free admission.

Cameron Park. 2601 N. University Parks Dr.; (254) 750-5980; waco-texas.com/cms-parksandrecreation. This 416-acre municipal park is one of the largest in the state and holds Miss Nellie's Pretty Place, a beautiful wildflower garden filled with Texas bluebonnets. Free admission.

Cameron Park Zoo. 1701 N. Fourth St. in Cameron Park; (254) 750-8400; cameronparkzoo.com. This zoo features natural habitats and displays including the African Savanna, Gibbon Island, Treetop Village, Asian Forest, and Lemur Island. The newest exhibit area at the zoo is called "Brazos River Country," and explores the Gulf to the Caprock regions through plant and animal life. Open daily. Fee.

Dr Pepper Museum & Free Enterprise Institute. 300 S. Fifth St.; (254) 757-1025; drpeppermuseum.com. The famous Dr Pepper soft drink was invented by pharmacist Dr. Charles Alderton at the Old Corner Drug Store in Waco, which once stood at Fourth Street and Austin Avenue. Today the drugstore is gone, but the original bottling plant remains open as a museum. Interesting exhibits and films offer a look at some early promotional materials, as well as the manufacturing process of the unusual soft drink. (Also of note is the popular advertising slogan promoting Dr Pepper as an energy booster to be consumed at "10, 2, and 4.") After a look through the museum, visit the re-creation of the Old Corner Drug Store fountain for an ice-cream soda or (what else?) a Dr Pepper. Open daily. Fee.

Fort Fisher Park. I-35, exit 335B; (254) 750-8696. This park was once the site of Fort Fisher, an outpost of the Texas Rangers built in 1837. The lawmen established a post here to protect the Brazos River crossing. Today the park contains the City of Waco Tourist Information Center and the Texas Ranger Hall of Fame and Museum. Open daily. Free admission.

Historic Home Visits. Historic Waco Foundation, 810 S. Fourth St.; (254) 753-5166; historicwaco.org. Although a devastating tornado in 1953 destroyed many of Waco's historic structures, some still remain. The public can visit any of four historic homes, all in the downtown area. One of the most interesting stops is East Terrace House, an Italian villa on the east bank of the Brazos. Here guests once slept in unheated dormitories to discourage them from overstaying their welcome! Tours are held Tues through Sun. Fee.

Homestead Heritage. Elm Mott; 608 Dry Creek Rd.; (254) 754-9600; homesteadheritage .com. From I-35 take exit 343, then turn west on FM 308 and continue 3 miles to FM 933. Turn north on FM 933 and continue 1.5 miles to Halbert Lane. Turn left (west) onto Halbert Lane and continue for 0.5 mile to 608 Dry Creek Rd. This 510-acre Christian homesteading community is the site of a 200-year-old Dutch-style barn that showcases the crafts of the village's woodworkers as well as unique quilts, wrought iron, oil lamps, and more. You can take a walking tour of the village to see the potter's house, herb gardens, blacksmith's shop, and the restored 1760 gristmill. Café Homestead, cafehomestead.com, serves locally sourced American cuisine. The on-site Brazos Valley Cheese company produces most of the cheeses that are served at the cafe. Café Homestead serves breakfast, lunch, and dinner. Check the website for days and times. Open 9 a.m. to 5 p.m. Mon through Sat. Free admission.

Lake Waco. FM 1637, 2 miles northwest of the city at 3801 Zoo Park Dr.; (254) 756-5359; swf-wc.usace.army.mil/waco/index.asp. This lake, part of the Bosque River, is a favorite with anglers and boaters. Several marinas and boat ramps offer access. Open daily. Fee.

Suspension Bridge and River Walk. University Parks Drive between Franklin and Washington Streets; (254) 750-8080. Spanning the 800-mile-long Brazos River, this restored suspension bridge was once the longest in the world at 470 feet. Built in 1870, it eliminated the time-consuming process of having to cart cattle across the water by ferry. Today the structure is used as a pedestrian bridge bearing the motto "First Across–Still Across," linking Indian Spring Park on the west bank and Martin Luther King Jr. Park on the east. On the west side, you'll find a walkway to Fort Fisher Park in one direction and Herring Avenue Bridge in the other, 1.5 miles away. The new East Riverwalk section in downtown Waco provides the final 2/3-mile trail of paved, lighted pathway for a continuous 5.5-mile downtown Riverwalk loop from Baylor to Cameron Park. Open daily. Free admission.

Texas Ranger Hall of Fame and Museum. Fort Fisher, 100 Texas Ranger Trail (at exit 335B off I-35); (254) 750-8631; texasranger.org. If you're interested in the taming of Texas, budget a couple of hours for this large museum. Visitors here can see guns of every description used by the Rangers, who had the reputation of lone lawmen who always got their man. Dioramas in the Hall of Fame recount the early days of the Rangers, including their founding by Stephen F. Austin. A 55-minute film shows several times daily. Open daily. Fee.

Texas Sports Hall of Fame. 1108 S. University Parks Dr. (at exit 335B off I-35); (254) 756-1633; tshof.org. This popular attraction is a tribute to the athletes of the Lone Star State. Sports memorabilia highlight more than 350 sports heroes, including an autographed baseball by former Texas Ranger Nolan Ryan, Earl Campbell's letter jacket, and one of Martina Navratilova's Wimbledon rackets, as well as displays featuring prominent Texas high school athletes. Open 9 a.m. to 5 p.m. Mon through Sat. Fee.

Waco Mammoth National Monument. 6220 Steinbeck Bend Rd. (exit 335C off I-35); (254) 750-7946; nps.gov/waco/index.htm. Located northwest of Waco, this attraction features prehistoric Columbian Mammoth bones that were discovered in 1978 and excavated by Baylor University archeologists. Now a public park, the 100-acre site includes a dig shelter reached via a suspended walkway for an overhead view and a scenic trailway with benches and rest areas. The park Welcome Center includes a gift shop and a ticket counter. Open daily 9 a.m. to 5 p.m. Fee.

where to shop

Along with stand-alone shops, several major attractions in Waco also have notable gift shops, including the Art Center Waco, Cameron Park Zoo, Dr Pepper Museum, Homestead Heritage, Texas Sports Hall of Fame, and Texas Ranger Museum.

The Craft Gallery. 7524 Bosque Blvd. in Bosque Square; (254) 751-0693; craftgallery giftstore.com. A host of different vendors present their wares in this collection of shops. In addition to crafted items, you'll find women's and children's apparel, souvenirs, accessories, home decor items, and pre-owned furniture. Open Mon through Sat.

Honey's Home+Style. 1700 Austin Ave.; (254) 754-3311; honeys-home-style.com. This downtown shop is just across the street from the Waco McLennan County Library and specializes in unique home furnishings, antiques, and artworks. Open Tues through Sat.

Spice Village. S. Second Street and Franklin Avenue; (254) 757-0921; spicewaco.com. This shopping emporium with over 80 different shops offering clothing and accessories, antiques, home decor, and souvenirs is housed in the historic Waco Hardware Building near downtown. Open daily.

Waco Downtown Farmers Market. 500 Washington Ave.; wacodowntownfarmersmarket .com. This large farmers' market is held Saturday year-round and features fresh, locally produced fruits and vegetables, jams and jellies, cheeses, and honey as well as arts and crafts. On some Saturdays, live music entertains shoppers, too. Free admission.

where to eat

Health Camp. 2601 Circle Rd.; (254) 752-2186; health-camp-waco.com. In spite of the name, don't look for açaí or quinoa on the menu at this classic burger joint. Perched right on the Waco traffic circle, this casual restaurant has been selling burgers, fries, malts, and shakes since 1949. A stop here is like a step back in time, so forget your diet for one meal and enjoy a famous "Health Burger." Open daily for lunch and dinner. $.

Sergio's Restaurant. 608 Austin Ave.; (254) 714-1297; facebook.com/sergiosrestaurant/. The fare at this low-key restaurant is classic Veracruz-style seafood served in a large dining room decorated with photos of former US president George W. Bush and former Mexican president Vicente Fox. The restaurant was a favorite with the Washington, DC, press corps during the Bush presidency. Large menu, but BYOB. Open Mon through Sat. $$–$$$.

Tru Jamaica. 937 Taylor St.; (254) 304-9288; trujamaica.com. The names says it all—true Jamaican food in Texas. Among the favorites are jerk spiced chicken on a bed of coconut with peas, steamed cabbage, carrots, green pepper with onions and fried plantains; curry goat marinated and stewed in Jamaican curry; and oxtails slowly stewed with herbs and butter beans. Save room for the rum raisin bread pudding or rum cake, a vanilla cake that has Jamaican Overproof Rum in the batter. $.

the western white house

The tiny community of Crawford, with a population of 760 residents, drew inter-national attention with the 1999 arrival of two new residents: George W. and Laura Bush. The then-governor purchased the 1,600-acre ranch, located 8 miles northeast of town on Prairie Chapel Road, and constructed a home that soon became host to world leaders.

*Today Crawford remains a quiet town except when the former president is at the **Prairie Chapel Ranch,** which visitors can drive by. You'll know you're get-ting close when you see signs warning "no stopping, no standing, no parking." The ranch is located on the right side of the road heading north. To reach Craw-ford from Waco, take US 84 west, then turn right onto TX 317.*

where to stay

1700 South 2nd. 1700 S. Second St.; (254) 709-3288 or (512) 507-6712; 1700south2nd .com. Named for its location right across the street from the Baylor campus, this all-suite property has a minimalist vibe with its Japanese-inspired decor. All suites include full kitchens, 2 bedrooms, and 2 baths. $$$.

Colcord House Bed & Breakfast. 2211 Colcord Ave.; (254) 753-5537; wacoheartoftexas .com/places/colcord-house-bed-and-breakfast/. Charming B&B in a 1920 Georgian mansion offers two rooms with private baths in the main house plus a suite with bedroom, sitting room, kitchenette, bath, and private patio in the Carriage House. Full breakfast and airport shuttle.

northeast

day trip 01

northeast

>>> **farming heartland:**
hutto, taylor, thrall

A magnet for immigrant farmers from Sweden and other Scandinavian countries in the 1800s, these fertile blackland prairies and small towns are rapidly evolving into bedroom communities for Austin commuters. Some of the agrarian spirit remains, however, and family farms coexist alongside housing developments and shopping malls.

hutto

Hutto, east of Austin, was once just another blackland farming community. For years the town was, well, pretty much just a wide spot in the road on US 79 between Round Rock and Taylor. Things changed, though, with both the booming of Austin's population and the construction of TX 130. Today Hutto's population boom makes it one of the country's fastest growing communities at 25,320 residents.

Just a block off US 79, though, you'll find "old" Hutto, with historic buildings and small-town atmosphere. You also might spot something a little unusual for a small Texas town: hippo statues. More than 150 of them grace Hutto, ranging from a giant hippo at the Hutto High School to smaller "yard hippos" in front of many businesses and private homes.

Why the hippos? According to local legend, a hippo escaped from a circus train near Hutto around 1915 and was recovered in a local creek. The residents seemed to fall in love with the idea of hippos and soon named their football team the Hutto Hippos (complete with the only hippo football mascot in Texas).

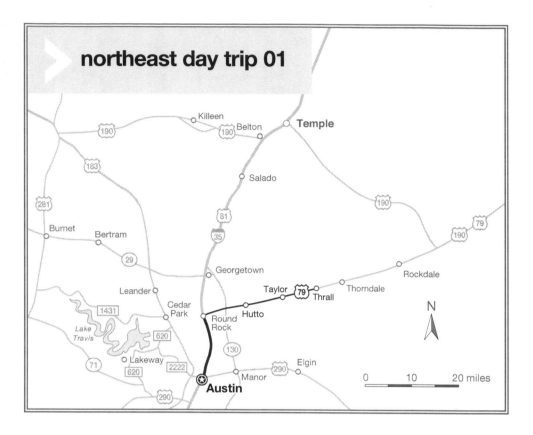

northeast day trip 01

where to go

Henrietta the Hippo Statue. East Street. It's not just anyplace you can pose with a 14,000-pound hippo statue, but here's your chance. This concrete hippopotamus in downtown Hutto was placed here by the chamber of commerce and serves as the town's most popular photo op.

Self-paced Hippo Tour. No, we did not make this up. If Henrietta the Hippo isn't enough for you, enjoy a self-guided tour of the 300-plus hippo statues in Hutto, including Farmer Hippo, Dalmatian Hippo, and even Army Hippo. You'll find a link with a map on the Hutto Convention and Visitors Bureau website, visithutto.com, or stop by the Chamber of Commerce office at 122 East St., (512) 759-4400, huttochamber.com for more information.

taylor

Taylor's biggest claim to fame is its International BBQ Cook-Off in June. (See Festivals and Celebrations at the back of this book.) It also was the hometown of former Texas governor Dan Moody as well as Bill Pickett, an African-American cowboy born in 1860. Pickett originated the practice of "bulldogging"—throwing a bull by twisting its head until it falls. The well-known cowboy also had a habit of biting a steer's upper lip, a trick called "biting the bull" that he practiced on the rodeo circuit.

where to go

Moody Museum. 114 W. Ninth St.; (512) 352-8654; moodymuseum.com. Governor Dan Moody was born in this 1887 home, which today is filled with his furniture and personal belongings. He went to law school at the University of Texas, served in World War I, then returned to become governor at the age of 33. The hometown hero was best known for prosecuting members of the Ku Klux Klan in Williamson County. Open Sat and Sun 2 to 5 p.m. and by appointment. Free admission.

smokin' in taylor

*Don't be alarmed during a June visit if you see smoke rising from the Central Texas town of Taylor, located northeast of Austin. That just means it's time again for the annual **International BBQ Cook-Off,** and contestants from around the Lone Star State are firing up their pits. With military-like precision, using recipes so carefully guarded it would make the Pentagon jealous, these cooks try their hand at preparing the best smoky delectables.*

In a state where you can hardly throw a sausage link without hitting a cook-off, Taylor's is one of the largest and also one of the most prestigious. It draws some of the state's best pitmasters. Although there are no cash prizes, up to 100 teams show up every year to compete for cooking trophies plus prizes for showmanship. Besides the prestige of being able to claim the best brisket, poultry, lamb, goat, pork ribs, seafood, or wild game, the teams come for the pure enjoyment of the competition.

Using secret spices, the pitmasters season the meats and start the slow process of smoking over their chosen wood. Many cooks stay up through the night basting, or "mopping," the meat with marinade to keep it from drying.

Judging takes place on Saturday afternoon, and once the judging is completed, the real fun begins. Cooks are encouraged, although they are not required, to provide the public with a sample of their craft. In the relaxed atmosphere after the judging, cooks also enjoy talking about the art of barbecuing, sometimes even sharing tips and secrets.

Murphy Park. 1600 Veterans Dr.; (512) 352-3675; ci.taylor.tx.us/243/Murphy-Park. This 120-acre park is right in town but a quiet retreat for a picnic or a little birding on the shores of City Lake. Free admission.

where to eat

Louie Mueller Barbecue. 206 W. Second St.; (512) 352-6206; louiemuellerbarbecue.com. One of the most authentic barbecue joints in Texas, where diners eat off white butcher paper in a room decorated with free calendars and a corkboard filled with business cards (all imbued with enough smoke to give them the color of a grocery sack). But none of that matters. What matters is the barbecue: brisket, sausage, pork ribs, and steak. Open Wed through Sat 11 a.m. to 4 p.m. or until sold out. $.

Masfajitas. 1905 N. Main St.; (512) 352-9292; masfajitas.com. If you're looking for an alternative to Taylor's barbecue joints, you can opt for some mainstream Tex-Mex here. Start with a frozen margarita and tortilla soup or chile con queso appetizer, then select a plate of enchiladas, tamales, or burritos. Open daily for lunch and dinner. $–$$.

Smokin' Oak BBQ. 410 W. Seventh St.; (512) 650-8099; facebook.com/smokinoakbbqtx/. Real downhome Texas BBQ. Sandwiches or meat plates with BBQ chicken, brisket, sausage, turkey, beef ribs, plus popular cornbread casserole and potato salad. Scratch-made sweets include chocolate pecan pie. $.

thrall

When oil was discovered in 1915, more than 200 wells were drilled and Thrall's population skyrocketed. As the saying goes, what goes up must come down, and Thrall was back on its way down as soon as oil production diminished. Today it's once again a quiet spot on US 79, composed of a few blocks of homes that run parallel to the railroad.

where to go

Stiles Farm Foundation. US 79, east of Thrall at 5700 FM 1063; (512) 898-2214; stiles farm.tamu.edu. This 2,600-acre farm is administered by the Texas A&M University AgriLife Extension Service. Here new techniques are demonstrated to area farmers and ranchers. Visitors can take guided tours to see everything from hog raising to cotton growing. This is a great chance to have a look at an operating Texas farm and ranch. Call for an appointment. Free admission.

day trip 02

northeast

>>> **texas two-steppin':**
coupland, taylor, circleville, granger,
bartlett, new corn hill, walburg

This day trip encompasses many small farming communities that lie east of I-35. Much of this farmland, largely covered by cotton fields, was first settled by German, Czech, and Austrian immigrants in the mid to late 1800s. Today it remains a quiet slice of Central Texas, with the exception of the local dance halls that draw visitors from Austin and surrounding communities for evenings of live country music and dancing.

coupland

Located 8 miles north of Elgin on TX 95, this small farming community is home to about 180.

where to go

Huntington Sculpture Foundation. 212 N. Broad St. at the corner of Hoxie Street; (512) 856-2334; huntingtonsculpture.org. With its miles of surrounding agricultural land, the last thing you might expect to see in tiny Coupland is a sculpture garden featuring an internationally known artist, but here it is. This garden and studio feature the work of Jim Huntington, whose installations are seen from Japan to Australia. Call for hours at the studio, although the large granite sculptures can be seen outdoors anytime. Free admission; donations accepted.

The Old Coupland Inn and Dancehall. 101 Hoxie St.; (512) 856-2777 (weekends) or (512) 431-9584 (weekdays); couplanddancehall.com. On weekends, tiny Coupland becomes a

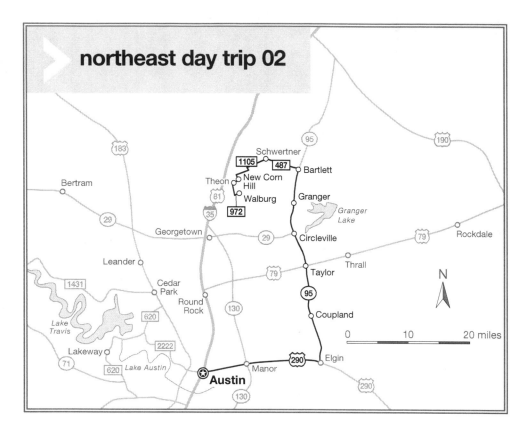

northeast day trip 02

hot spot for major boot-scooting fun at this historic dance hall. Headliners from all over Texas and Nashville have performed here since 1910. If you're planning a late night of dancing, consider staying at the adjacent B&B located just above the dance hall; it's styled like a 1900s bordello. While it may not have ever served as a bordello, the property does have a rich history as a mercantile and even a newsletter publishing company. Open Fri 7 p.m. to midnight, Sat 7 p.m. to 1 a.m., sometimes on Sun. Admission varies with performer.

where to eat

The Old Coupland Inn and Dancehall. 101 Hoxie St.; (512) 856-2777 (weekends) or (512) 431-9584 (weekdays); couplanddancehall.com. Barbecue and steaks take center stage when it comes to dining at this historic dance hall. Start with a half rack of ribs or some stuffed jalapeños, then move on to the serious entrees: mesquite-trimmed sirloin steaks, catfish and shrimp, a mixed barbecue plate, or chicken-fried steak. Work off that big dinner with a twirl around the dance floor on Fri and Sat nights, when country bands keep the evenings lively. Open for dinner Fri and Sat. $$.

taylor

Continue north on TX 95 to Taylor, the largest community on this tour. You'll find Taylor's attractions (and world-renowned barbecue) covered in Northeast Day Trip 01.

circleville

Continue north on TX 95 for approximately 5 miles to the community of Circleville. With a population that hovers around 40 residents, Circleville is not exactly a ghost town, but most of its former businesses, including its railroad stop, gristmill, cotton gin, blacksmith shop, and churches are now just a memory. Only the Circleville Store and Restaurant remain.

where to eat

Circleville Store. 600 S. TX 95; (512) 352-6848.With its tin exterior, the Circleville Store doesn't look like much from the outside, but inside you'll find a classic Texas general store and small restaurant. The menu is pretty basic, offering hamburgers, chicken-fried steak, and grilled steaks and pork chops, but most diners come away satisfied and proud to have discovered this hidden slice of Texas culture. An outdoor stage offers live entertainment on select weekends. Open Tues through Sat. $.

granger

Continue north on TX 95 to the agricultural community of Granger. The home of a cotton gin, Granger is also notable for its brick Davilla Street, the community's main avenue. This street was paved with bricks in 1912, a feat that the *Granger News* said made Granger "the only city in the state of less than 5,000 inhabitants that has paved streets, or is paving them."

Today Granger still has 1,119 residents, and Davilla Street is still paved with red bricks. You'll find the town divided by railroad tracks, with a few businesses both east and west of TX 95.

where to go

Granger Lake. (512) 859-2668; swf-wc.usace.army.mil/granger. Located east of Granger, this 4,064-acre lake was created in 1980 on the San Gabriel River. Today the lake is a favorite with local anglers and boaters; you'll find four parks operated by the US Army Corps of Engineers. Catfish and crappie are top catches in the lake, and lucky anglers also have the chance at white bass and largemouth bass. Birders also frequent the park, especially during the winter migration when birds ranging from American white pelicans to Franklin's gulls may be spotted. Parks are found on the north, west, and south sides of the lake. Fee.

Friendship Park. North shore of the lake off FM 971. Includes a boat ramp and picnicking.

Taylor Park. South shore of the lake off FM 1331. Offers picnicking, camping, and a boat ramp.

Willis Creek Park. Western shore of the lake off CR 348. Offers picnicking, camping, and a boat ramp.

Wilson H. Fox Park. South shore of the lake off FM 1331. Offers picnicking, camping, fish-cleaning stations, and two boat ramps.

where to eat

Cotton Country Club. 212 E. Davilla St.; (512) 859-0700; cottoncountryclub.com. This Texas-size dance hall is open Fri, Sat, and Sun nights only, a time when couples from surrounding farmland—and surrounding cities—pack the dance floor for an evening of boot-scootin' with some top-notch country singers. There is a cover charge for the dance hall (unless it is rented out for a private function), but diners are welcome at the courtyard without cover. Diners find a traditional Texas menu: appetizers of jalapeño poppers, onion rings, and queso and chips followed by favorites like chicken-fried steak, fried shrimp and catfish, steaks, and more. Open Fri 5 p.m. to midnight, Sat 5 p.m. to 1 a.m., Sun 4 to 10 p.m. $$.

bartlett

From Granger follow TX 95 north for 5 miles to reach Bartlett. Once an agricultural boomtown with two weekly newspapers, today Bartlett's a quiet farm town, one so classic that it has appeared in several Hollywood movies, including *Stars Fell on Henrietta* and *The Newton Boys.*

new corn hill

From Bartlett turn west on FM 476 and continue for 5 miles to the intersection with FM 1105. At these crossroads, you'll find the hamlet of Schwertner. From there head south on FM 1105, a pretty drive lined with rolling ranches and farms. Several miles before you reach New Corn Hill, you'll see the twin steeples of the historic Holy Trinity Catholic Church, built in 1913, one of few remaining structures in this town.

And where, you might ask, is Old Corn Hill? That community was consolidated with Jarrell (now on I-35). Some of its residents packed up and headed a few miles east to settle what's now called New Corn Hill.

where to go

Holy Trinity Catholic Church. 8626 FM 1105; (512) 863-3020; holytrinityofcornhill.org. The twin neo-Gothic towers of Holy Trinity Church soar above the tiny town and surrounding farmland and can be seen from miles away. The church was established in 1889 to serve the nearby communities of Theon and Corn Hill, and the present structure was built in 1913. The church still serves area residents and celebrates Mass on Sat and Sun. Free admission.

walburg

Continue south on FM 1105 to the German community of Walburg. First named Concordia, the town was later renamed by the local storekeeper after his hometown in Germany. It has always been small, although it represents many immigrant groups including Germans, Wends, Czechs, Austrians, and Swiss.

where to eat

Dale's Essenhaus. 3900 FM 972; (512) 819-9175; dales-essenhaus.com. Less atmospheric than the larger Walburg Restaurant, Dale's is also known both for its menu and its live country and blues music. The restaurant is especially noted for its Dale's Walburger, a hamburger served with grilled onions, but fried catfish and chicken-fried steak are tops as well. Outside, the biergarten is open Fri and Sat night from Apr through Oct; food and drink are also served outside. Open Mon through Thurs 11 a.m. to 9 p.m., Fri and Sat 11 a.m. to 10 p.m. $–$$.

the walburg boys

The Walburg Restaurant is owned by Ron Tippelt, who originally hails from Munich, Germany. Nearly three decades ago, Tippelt packed up his accordion and headed for Walburg, creating this restaurant with recipes from his homeland. Tippelt's contribution didn't end there, however; he also puts his musical talents to work in the biergarten. The accordionist and yodeler assembled The Walburg Boys, a band that plays Bavarian tunes that encourage patrons to take to the dance floor.

Tippelt is walking in the footsteps of another Munich immigrant: Hy Doering. In 1882 Doering settled in Walburg and built the Walburg Mercantile that today serves as the home of the popular restaurant.

Walburg German Restaurant. 3777 FM 972 at the intersection of FM 1105; (512) 863-8440; walburgrestaurant.net. This restaurant is housed in the 1882 Walburg Mercantile building and features authentic German food and music. Behind the restaurant, a converted cotton gin serves as a biergarten. The restaurant menu includes wiener schnitzel, bratwurst, sauerbraten, and some Texas favorites like chicken-fried steak and catfish. The buffets are particularly popular and include a wide selection of the restaurant's top items. A more limited menu is served in the biergarten. The restaurant hosts several annual celebrations, including Oktoberfest. Open Wed through Sun. $–$$.

day trip 03

northeast

>>> **presidential corridor:**
dime box, caldwell, snook, bryan–college station

Between Austin and College Station lies the "Presidential Corridor," which links Austin's LBJ Library with Bryan–College Station's Bush Library. Head east of Austin on US 290 through the towns of Elgin and McDade (see East Day Trip 01 for attractions along this route) before turning northeast on TX 21 through Caldwell and Bryan–College Station.

dime box

OK, there's not much in the town of Dime Box, but with a name like that, isn't it worth a quick detour? The burg is located just east of TX 21 on FM 141.

The town was originally named for its sawmill, but confusion with towns that had similar names led to its name change. The reason for the unusual moniker? Early residents could drop their mail—and a dime—in a box at the post office for delivery.

Actually, Dime Box began up on TX 21, but when a rail line was built a few miles southeast of town, everyone up and moved. The original settlement became Old Dime Box and today's community is, well, New Dime Box. The story of that namesake is recalled not only in the community's museum but in a transparent box perched alongside FM 141 that contains an oversize Liberty Head dime, a fun photo stop on your day trip.

Dime Box also got national attention in 1945, when it became the country's first community to have 100 percent participation in the new March of Dimes campaign. Dime Box's citizens filled a mailbox with their collected donations and sent the package—mailbox and

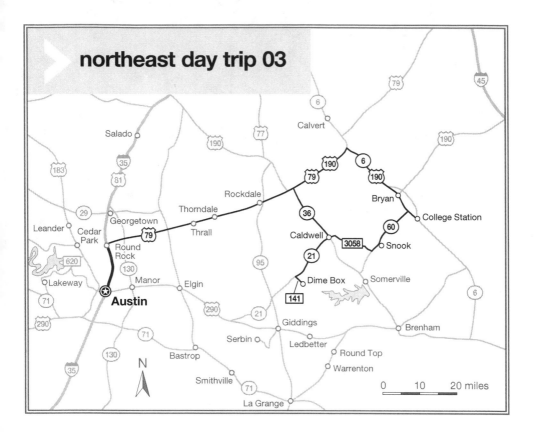

northeast day trip 03

all—to then-president Franklin D. Roosevelt, who responded with a phone call to the city's postmaster and banker.

where to go

Dime Box Museum. Downtown on FM 141; (979) 884-0182. This small museum traces the history of this community that was settled by Czech, British, German, and Polish immigrants. Exhibits include a pocket Communion Bible in Czech, a barber's chair, and other farm and home memorabilia. Open Fri through Sun 1 to 5 p.m. Free admission; donations accepted.

caldwell

Nicknamed the "Kolache Capital of Texas" by the 71st Legislature, Caldwell is located just south of TX 21 on TX 36. This community is the capital of Burleson County (and it's confusing because there's a nearby county named Caldwell County—whose county seat is Lockhart). You'll find a traditional Texas courthouse square downtown.

The biggest event in town takes place the second Saturday of September when Caldwell celebrates its annual Kolache Festival. The event was begun as a way to revive Czech traditions in the region. The kolache, the Czech wedding pastry that can be sweet or savory, is the focal point of the day, with everything from kolache baking contests to eating contests. Along with plenty of kolaches, the event includes Czech traditions such as stenciling, dancing, egg decorating, cane weaving, and dulcimer playing.

where to go

Burleson County Czech Heritage Museum. 200 E. Fawn St.; (979) 567-0000. The longtime links between Caldwell and Prague are traced in this local history collection that includes Czech costumes and household items used by Czech settlers in Texas. The museum works with local schools to preserve Czech traditions through special tours and exhibits. Notable items include a 1737 Bible smuggled into the country inside a loaf of bread. Open Sat 10 a.m. to 2 p.m., June through Sept.; other times by appointment. Free admission.

Burleson County Historical Museum. 100 W. Buck St. (1st floor of the Burleson County Courthouse); (979) 567-7196. The focus of this museum is on early county settlement and history. The museum has a variety of resources and archives for research that may be used on-site. The historical commission assists in research and can try to answer most questions. Open Fri 1 to 5 p.m., or by appointment. Free admission.

snook

From Caldwell you can travel directly to Bryan on TX 21 or take a detour to the small community of Snook.

Like nearby Caldwell and many other neighboring communities, Snook was founded by Czech immigrants. First named Sebesta after a family of early settlers, the town's name was later changed to Snook to honor the postmaster, who arranged for the town to get its own post office.

The liveliest time to visit Snook is in mid-April, when it celebrates Chilifest, a two-day blowout with a chili cook-off and live music drawing up to 35,000 visitors. The festival has featured well-known musicians such as Willie Nelson, Dwight Yoakam, and Pat Green. The proceeds from the annual event benefit local charities.

From Caldwell head east on FM 166 just over a mile to the intersection with FM 3058; turn right (southeast) on FM 3058 and continue until it dead-ends into FM 60. Then turn left and head north about 4 miles to Snook.

kolache country

A sweet reminder of the Old Country—anyone who tastes a freshly baked kolache can recognize that more than apricots, apples, or cottage cheese is wrapped inside the sugar-topped bread roll—the main ingredient of this pastry is a love for tradition. This wedding pastry was traditionally baked weeks before a local ceremony, then given as an invitation to the upcoming event.

Many Czechs immigrated to Texas in the mid-1800s in search of a more prosperous life, and today their descendants proudly pay homage to them each time they reach for a recipe for this tasty concoction.

where to shop

Slovacek Sausage Company. 9687 FM 60; (979) 272-6002; slovacek.com. Slovacek has been cranking out tasty pork and beef sausage since 1957 in tiny Snook. The company has grown to become one of the premier sausage makers in the state. In addition to traditional beef and pork sausage, Slovacek now offers turkey sausage, hams, and hot jalapeño sausage. Most of their products can be purchased by phone and online. Open daily.

where to eat

Sodolak's Original Country Inn. 234 CR 265; (979) 272-6002. Texas-size steaks, burgers, and chicken-frieds fill the menu, but this restaurant's real claim to fame is its chicken-fried bacon. Featured on *Texas Country Reporter*, a television series, this dish features strips of raw bacon dipped in an egg batter, rolled in flour, then deep-fried to a golden crispiness that no doubt makes cardiologists cringe but keeps diners coming back for more. Open daily. $–$$.

bryan–college station

From Snook head northeast on FM 60 into College Station. Home of Texas A&M University, these adjoining communities are populated by over 178,000 residents, and several attractions are of interest to travelers.

Bryan was chartered in 1855 in the area where early colonists led by Stephen F. Austin first settled. The agriculturally rich city still has an emphasis on farming thanks to Texas A&M University, the first public institution of higher learning in Texas. The college is well known for its agriculture, veterinary, and engineering programs, as well as its military Corps of Cadets.

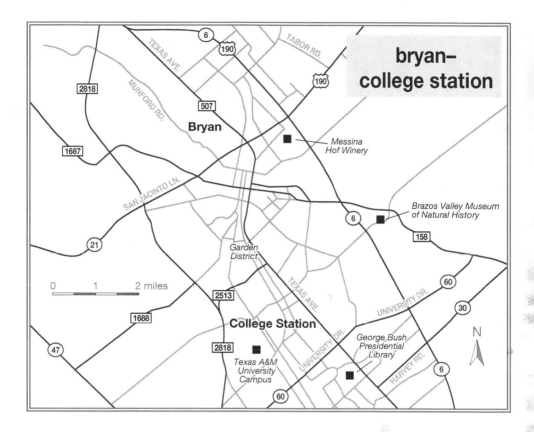

bryan–college station

where to go

Benjamin Knox Gallery. 405 University Dr. East, College Station; (979) 691-2787 or (979) 696-5669; benjaminknox.com. This gallery features the work of Benjamin Knox, known locally as the "University Artist." Along with fine art, the gallery sells gift items, and the Knox Wine Bar has wine, beer, soft drinks, coffee, and signature desserts. Open Mon through Sat 10 a.m. to 6 p.m. Knox Wine Bar is open Thurs through Sat noon to 10 p.m. Free admission.

Brazos Valley Museum of Natural History. 3232 Briarcrest Dr., Bryan; (979) 776-2195; brazosvalleymuseum.org. Bring the whole family to this collection of natural history, with exhibits on life in the Brazos Valley more than 12,000 years ago. Open Tues through Sat 10 a.m. to 5 p.m. Fee. Admission to the museum on the first Tues of each month is only $1.

The Children's Museum of the Brazos Valley. 4114 Lake Atlas Dr., Ste 110; (979) 779-KIDS; cmbv.org. Teaching through hands-on exhibits, this museum gives kids the opportunity to do everything from shopping for groceries to creating a puppet show. Open Tues through Sun. Fee.

George Bush Presidential Library and Museum. 1000 W. George Bush Dr., College Station; (979) 691-4000; bush41.org. The state's second presidential library contains exhibits on the first Bush presidency as well as research materials in the library center. Open daily. Fee.

Messina Hof Winery and Resort. 4545 Old Reliance Rd., Bryan; (800) 736-9463 or (979) 778-9463; messinahof.com. One of Texas's most celebrated wineries offers tours and tastings. Started in 1983, the winery includes 45 acres of vineyards and demonstrates the wine-making skills of the Messina, Italy, and Hof, Germany, regions. Public tours daily. Call for tour hours. Fee for tours and tastings.

Texas A&M University. 400 Bizzell St.; (979) 845-3211; tamu.edu. Several of the school's facilities here in College Station are of special interest to visitors, including the Floral Test Garden (Houston and Jersey Streets). Stroll among hundreds of varieties of flowers planted and studied by university students.

> **Appelt Aggieland Visitor Center.** Rudder Tower in the Memorial Student Center Complex; (979) 845-5851; visit.tamu.edu/visitor-center. A good introduction to the A&M campus, the center offers tours, videos, and exhibits. Open Mon through Fri 8 a.m. to 5 p.m. Free admission.

> **Century Tree.** In the central campus area near the Academic Building. One of the most beloved shrines on campus, this century-old live oak was among the first trees planted on campus. Over the years, generations of Aggies have gathered beneath its low-hanging branches to celebrate engagements and weddings and pose for photos. Free admission.

> **J. Wayne Stark University Center Galleries.** Memorial Student Center, 275 Joe Routt Blvd.; (979) 845-6081; uart.tamu.edu/visit-stark. This large university gallery features American drawings, paintings, and photography with a particular focus on Texas art and artists. Open Tues through Fri. Free admission.

> **M. Benz Gallery of Floral Art.** Horticultural and Forest Sciences Building on the west side of campus; (979) 845-1699; aggie-horticulture.tamu.edu/benz-school/welcome-to-the-benz-school. This museum features everything related to floral art. Open weekdays. Free admission.

> **MSC Forsyth Center Galleries.** 275 Joe Routt Blvd.; (979) 845-9251; uart.tamu.edu/forsyth-permanent-collection. This gallery features both touring exhibits and an extensive glass display. Open Tues through Fri. Free admission.

> **Sam Houston Sanders Corps of Cadets Center.** 12 Short St.; (979) 862-2862; corpscenter.tamu.edu/index.php/sanders-corps-center. Learn more about the Corps of Cadets through College Station's displays that trace the graduates'

service in World Wars I and II, Korea, Vietnam, the Gulf War, and more recent conflicts. Open Mon through Fri 8 a.m. to 5 p.m. Free admission.

Texas A&M Sports Museum. Bernard C. Richardson Zone at Kyle Field; (979) 846-3024; museumsusa.org/museums/info/16128. The long tradition of Aggie sports is featured in this museum with exhibits that include not only all types of A&M sports but also the Aggie band, and interactive computers that display historical footage. Open Mon through Fri 9 a.m. to 5 p.m. and Sat home game days from 9 a.m. to kickoff. Free admission.

where to shop

Catalena Hatters. 203 N. Main St., Bryan; (800) 976-7818 or (979) 822-4423; catalenahats .com. Even if you are an "all hat and no cattle" kind of cowboy or cowgirl, you'll enjoy this shop that has been producing custom hats for over 30 years. Sammy and Carolyn Catalena and their family can build a hat to your specifications or restore a favorite hat to look like new. Open Mon through Sat.

Charli. 505 University Dr. East, College Station; (979) 268 9626; charlionline.com. High fashions from trendy designers are offered at this boutique located just north of the Texas A&M campus. You'll find formal and casual apparel, jewelry, and accessories here. Open daily.

Old Bryan Marketplace. 202 S. Bryan St., Bryan; (979) 779-3245; oldbryan.com. Set inside a historic 1908 building in downtown Bryan, this expansive store offers treasures of all sizes, from furniture and home decor to gifts and women's clothing. Open Mon through Sat.

where to eat

C&J Barbecue. 4304 Harvey Rd., College Station; (979) 776-8969; cjbbq.com. This prize-winning restaurant has hundreds of loyal diners in the College Station area. Their specialties include beef, ribs, sausage, and chicken barbecue plates and sandwiches. C&J also has two other locations: 1010 S. Texas Ave., Bryan (979-822-6033), and 105 Southwest Pkwy., College Station (979-696-7900). All locations are open daily. $$.

Christopher's World Grille. 5001 Boonville Rd., Bryan; (979) 776-2181; christophers worldgrille.com. Chef Christopher Lampo spent 10 years wandering the globe before returning to his home region to restore a 100-year-old ranch house and transform it into a fine-dining destination. Mediterranean, South Pacific, and Louisiana touches grace the menu, which includes pastramied steelhead salmon, Zihuatanejo snapper, Hawaiian pork tenderloin, and the Bleu Filet, a bacon-wrapped seared beef tenderloin topped with blue cheese. Open Tues through Sat 4 to 9 p.m.; reservations encouraged. $$$.

bonfire memorial

*Throughout the state, the Texas Aggies had long been known for their pregame bonfires, a tradition since 1909. On November 18, 1999, the tradition came to a halt when 12 students were killed by the collapse of the massive stack of logs they were constructing. To commemorate the fallen students and the longtime tradition, the university constructed the **Bonfire Memorial,** a circular ring with doorways representing each of the lost students. The History Walk leading up to the memorial traces the tradition's timeline, leading up to the 170-foot-diameter circle representing the size of an actual Aggie bonfire. The memorial is located on the Polo Fields at the TAMU campus.*

where to stay

Hilton Hotel and Conference Center College Station. 801 University Dr. East, College Station; (979) 693-7500; hilton.com. This hotel offers guests a pool, exercise facilities, restaurant, private balconies, and more. Located less than 2 miles from the Texas A&M campus. $$.

The Villa at Messina Hof Bed and Breakfast. 4545 Old Reliance Rd., Bryan; (800) 736-9463, ext. 222; messinahof.com. One of Texas's most romantic bed-and-breakfast properties, guests enjoy an evening wine and cheese reception, a European-style champagne breakfast, and a winery tour. Featuring 11 antiques-furnished guest rooms, it is a place where couples can enjoy an evening alone in the vineyards at a romantic hideaway. Book early for this popular getaway on weekends and holidays. $$$.

east

day trip 01

east

sausage country:
manor, elgin, mcdade, giddings, serbin

Driving from Austin's eastern side, you'll notice an abrupt change as the suburban environment melts away within a few miles and you find yourself in small-town Texas. The area is a major hotbed of barbecue culture centered around the town of Elgin, home of Elgin hot sausage.

manor

Manor was named for settler James Manor, who came to the state with Sam Houston. Manor is primarily a bedroom community for the Austin area. To reach Manor, drive east from Austin on US 290.

elgin

Continue east from Manor on US 290 to Elgin. This city began as a railroad stop in 1872, named for the railroad commissioner. Often mispronounced (it rhymes with *again*), Elgin is known for two products: bricks and sausage. Red Elgin bricks are seen throughout Texas, and Elgin sausage is so prevalent that the city has been named by the Texas Legislature as the "Sausage Capital of Texas."

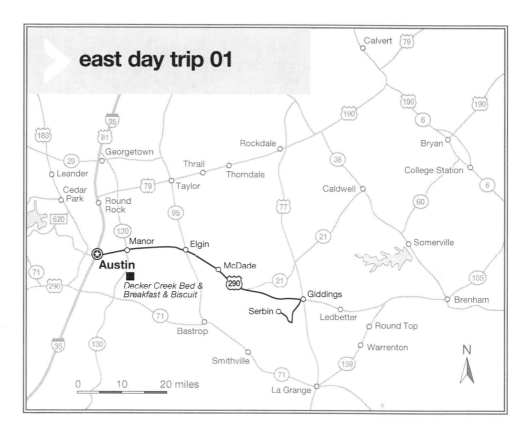

east day trip 01

Much of the city lies along US 290, but its real history is found off the highway in its historic downtown. Named a Main Street City for its preservation efforts, the downtown is home to several renovated buildings that now house shops.

If some of those historic buildings look familiar, you might have seen them in the movies. Thanks to its proximity to Austin and its genuine small-town look, Elgin has appeared in many Hollywood productions, including *Texas Chainsaw Massacre, What's Eating Gilbert Grape?, A Perfect World, Michael, Varsity Blues, The Alamo, Friday Night Lights,* and *The Transformers.*

where to go

Elgin Christmas Tree Farm. 120 Nature's Way, off Roy Davis Road; (512) 281-5016; elgin christmastreefarm.com. It doesn't have to be Christmas to plan a trip to the Elgin Christmas Tree Farm. Our favorite time of year to visit is the fall, when this farm comes alive with colorful pumpkins, hayrides, hay mazes, and more. At Christmas, much of the activity shifts to the fields as families work to find the perfect tree. The farm also features a small petting zoo with farm animals and a year-around Christmas store. Open seasonally. Fee for fall event.

Historic Tour. Pick up a copy of the free historic tour brochure at the chamber of commerce office (512-285-4515) at 114 Central Ave., or download a walking-tour brochure by visiting elgintx.com (see "Tourism Info"). This self-guided tour takes travelers past historic points such as the 1903 Union Depot, now home to the Elgin Depot Museum with information on the town's railroad history; the 1906 Nofsinger House, a Victorian home that now serves as Elgin City Hall; and past "ghost signs" that once advertised businesses such as Owl Cigars. Sixty-seven history structures are on the tour, many within walking distance, and others such as the original home of Southside Market, built in 1882, are farther afield.

Union Depot Museum. Depot Square at 14 Depot Square; (512) 285-2000; elgintx.com. Operated by the Elgin Historical Association, this historic Union Depot, built in 1903, now houses displays on the town's early days and the history of the railroad and includes a photo collection and archives. Open Wed through Sat, noon to 4 p.m. Free admission.

where to shop

Elgin General Store. 1155 Dildy Dr.; (512) 285-3210; elgin-generalstore.com. There's truth in advertising here, with a huge array of merchandise including clothing, gifts, hardware, horse tack and other livestock supplies and feed, and outdoor furnishings. Open daily.

hot guts

Yes, it's true; Elgin sausage is sometimes (make that often) referred to as Elgin Hot Guts. No, it's not an appetizing moniker. Nonetheless, this spicy sausage is the standard against which other Texas sausages are judged.

*The best-known of Elgin's smokin' stops is the **Southside Market & Barbeque** (1212 US 290 East; 512-281-4650; southsidemarket.com), probably one of the most recognized names in Texas barbecue lore. In business since 1882, the market is known for its sausage. The mainstay in many barbecue restaurants around the state, the Southside's product is what many people have in mind when they order sausage. Spicy but not hot, the concoction is all beef.*

For generations, Southside was located in a smoky den that spoke volumes about the history of barbecue. Sadly, the business outgrew its old home and now sits in a red tin building with a concrete floor—less atmospheric but now one of the largest barbecue restaurants in the state. The building may have changed, but the product remains the same. It's one we pick up fresh whenever we pass through Elgin; the smoky scent serves as a fragrant billboard long before you reach the Southside building.

G&M Drygoods. 20 N. Main St.; (512) 285-3547; elginowl.com. This new addition to Elgin's downtown features artisan-made gifts, gourmet foods, and candles as well as antique home decor accessories in a nicely restored historic building. Open Wed through Sun.

The Owl Wine Bar and Home Goods Store. 106 N. Main St.; (512) 284-3547; elginowl .com. Inspired by a "ghost mural" for Owl Cigars on a downtown Elgin wall, this shop offers an eclectic mix of old and new items including glassware, home furnishings, accessories, and gifts. The wine bar dispenses imported and domestic vintages and beers along with appetizers and desserts. Open Thurs through Sun.

where to eat

Aviator Pizza & Brew Company. 18810 US 290 East; (512) 827-3553; aviatorpizza.com. It may be sacrilegious to suggest anything to eat but barbecue in Elgin, but this slick, lively pizza place makes a great alternative. Besides an array of pizzas, the large menu includes pasta dishes, calzones, salads, wings, and grinders on sourdough buns. Lunch specials are offered daily. Open for lunch and dinner daily. $–$$.

Meyer's Elgin Sausage. 188 US 290; (512) 281-5546 or (800) MRS-OINK; cuetopiatexas .com. Since 1949 this sausage has been a regional favorite. The restaurant includes plenty of sausage as well as smoked turkey, ribs, and more. You can also purchase gift boxes of Meyer's sausage to go. Open daily. $.

Southside Market & Barbeque. 1212 US 290 East; (877) 487-8015 or (512) 281-4650; southsidemarket.com. This casual barbecue eatery has been the source of Elgin sausage since 1882. Although the market has moved from its original downtown location, the dining room is still filled with Formica tables, the smell of smoke, and happy customers. Open daily. $.

mcdade

About 8 miles outside of Elgin lies the small community of McDade. The town has always depended heavily on farming and ranching and is especially noted for its watermelon crop, but its claim to fame was its role in the TV miniseries *True Women*. An annual watermelon festival and the Sherwood Forest Faire are the big draws to the area. (See Festivals and Celebrations at the back of this book.)

giddings

From McDade continue east on US 290 to Giddings, the county seat of Lee County. The town began as a railroad community in the 1870s. At that time, most of the residents of Giddings were Wendish immigrants (Germans of Slavic descent); these founders later moved to the nearby community of Serbin. Today Giddings remains a quiet railroad town, although oil production has taken over as the major economic activity. For its size, Giddings boasts a respectable number of attractions, most relating to history and Texas culture.

where to go

Fireman's Park. 2 miles west of Giddings at 2495 US 290; (979) 542-2311. This park is notable mainly for its antique carousel, a memento of the 1930s when a traveling carnival visited Giddings and left it behind to repay a debt. The carousel has been restored and is used during special events such as the town's Fourth of July Celebration. The park also includes sports fields, picnic areas, and an RV park. Open daily during daylight hours. Free admission.

Giddings Post Office. 279 E. Austin St.; (979) 542-2456. One wall of the city post office contains a mural painted in 1939 by artist Otis Dozier, part of a federal plan to help artists during the Great Depression. The mural is titled *Cowboys Receiving the Mail*. Open Mon through Sat. Free admission.

Giddings Public Library & Cultural Center. 276 N. Orange St.; (979) 542-2716; giddings publiclibrary.org. This unassuming building contains one of the most extensive collections pertaining to Native Americans in Texas. The Arnold Smith Collection, compiled by local resident Arnold Smith, contains nearly 2,500 artifacts including tools, pottery, and weapons, some dating from the Paleo-Indian period. Another notable collection here is the Hilton Lee Smith Baseball Memorabilia Collection, named for a Giddings athlete who was a pitcher in the Negro Baseball League. Open Mon through Sat. Free admission.

Schubert-Fletcher Home. 173 E. Hempstead St.; (979) 542-2072. This historic structure dates from 1879 and is home to the Lee County Heritage Center. Exhibits describe the history of Lee County through photos, videos, and artifacts. Tours of the museum are arranged by appointment Mon through Sat. Free admission; donations accepted.

where to shop

The Grapevine. 790 E. Austin St.; (979) 542-1250; the-grapevine-boutique.myshopify .com. This shop offers jeans, boots, and other women's clothing and accessories, including a large selection of purses, along with home decor items. Open daily.

serbin

Turn south on US 77, then south again on FM 448, continuing for 5 miles. At the intersection with FM 2239, turn right and continue 2 miles to the hamlet of Serbin.

This town was settled by the Wends, who came to Texas in the 1850s and brought with them the Gothic architecture of their homeland. From 1865 to 1890 it was a thriving town, boasting dry goods, jewelry, music stores, a drugstore, three doctors, and two dentists. When Serbin was bypassed by the railroad, it quickly declined.

where to go

St. Paul Lutheran Church. Off FM 2239 at 1572 CR 211; (979) 366-9650; stpaulserbin .org. This historic church, a smaller version of the elaborate German cathedrals of the 18th and 19th centuries, was built in 1859 of native sandstone. St. Paul Lutheran is one of the famous painted churches of Central Texas. To replicate marble, the parishioners skillfully painted the interior plaster walls using turkey-feather brushes, creating a faux-stone effect. This church once had an unusual seating arrangement: Men sat in the balcony, and women and children took the pews on the floor. Today, St. Paul remains an active church and is considered the mother church of the Lutheran Church (Missouri Synod) in Texas. Open daily. Free admission.

Texas Wendish Heritage Museum. 1011 CR 212; (979) 366-2441; texaswendish.org. You'll find antique furniture and household items as well as photos of the early days in this local history museum, which traces the immigration of the Wends to Texas. Open Tues through Sun 1 to 5 p.m. Fee; under 14 free.

day trip 02

This day trip is an extension of East Day Trip 01, for travelers looking for a longer getaway. The trip is filled with early Texas history, including the location of the first Texas capital in Washington-on-the Brazos. Begin by taking US 290 East from Austin beyond Elgin and Giddings, following a route nicknamed the Presidential Corridor.

ledbetter

From Giddings drive east on US 290 for 9 miles to the tiny community of Ledbetter. The first town in the county to boast a railroad, its importance declined when nearby La Grange became a freight center.

where to go

Stuermer Store. 100 US 290 East; (979) 249-5642. This metal building has served as a general store since 1870. At one time the current owner's grandfather ran a saloon next door. Now the businesses are joined, creating a general store, museum, and soda shop all in one. A working museum exhibits the tools of the early grocery, from cheese cutters to coffee grinders. Today the wildest drink in the saloon is an old-fashioned malt. You can order up some local ice cream or fresh sandwiches at the fountain and listen to free tunes on a jukebox packed with oldies. Open Mon through Fri. Free admission.

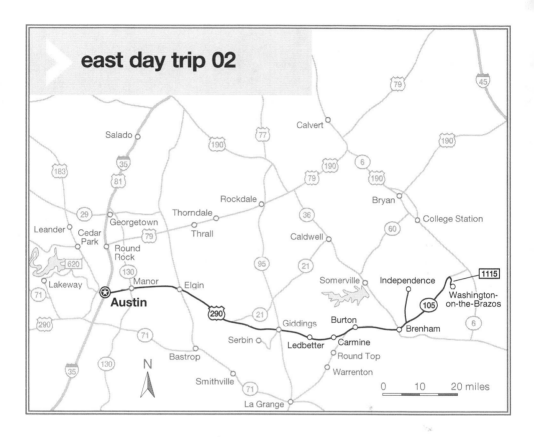

east day trip 02

carmine

Continue east on US 290 to the community of Carmine, covered in Southeast Day Trip 02 and best known for its participation in the Round Top area's Antiques Week sales.

burton

Follow US 290 to the tiny agricultural community of Burton, located just off US 290 on FM 390. With a population of 387, this town has a surprising number of shops and businesses, many open only on weekends.

Take some time to walk around the historic buildings before touring the Cotton Gin Museum.

where to go

Texas Cotton Gin Museum. 307 N. Main St.; (979) 289-3378; texascottonginmuseum .org. Arrange a 90-minute tour of this restored gin, a Texas Historic Landmark. You'll see the engine room, the mechanical floor, the ginning floor, and an old cobbler shop where harnesses were made for the horses that pulled the cotton wagons. Tours can be conducted in German. The site also includes the historic Wehring Shoe and Leather Shop, the Wehring House, and the Cotton Warehouse. Open Tues through Sat 10 a.m. to 4 p.m. Free admission; fee for tours.

brenham

Return to US 290 and continue east to Brenham. In this state, Brenham is synonymous with Blue Bell ice cream, one of the biggest independent ice-cream manufacturers in the country, selling more than 25 million half-gallon containers a year. It's as Texan as bluebonnets and two-stepping, and expatriates have been known to carry back picnic freezers full of Brenham's product.

Brenham has a host of other less-fattening attractions as well, including a historic downtown that's filled with antiques and specialty shops, and residential streets that showcase splendid antebellum and Victorian homes. A free visitors' guide of historic sites is available from the Washington County Chamber of Commerce, 314 S. Austin St. in Brenham; (888) BRENHAM or (979) 836-3695.

where to go

Blue Bell Creameries. Loop 577 off US 290 West; (800) 327-8135 or (979) 830-2197; bluebell.com. Blue Bell has been making ice cream since 1911, when it packaged its product in wooden tubs and delivered it by horse-drawn wagon. The "tasting room" here is an antique soda shop where visitors can choose from over 20 flavors. After a free dish of your personal favorite, you can have a look around the Country Store, where you can choose from Blue Bell T-shirts, mugs, kitchenware, toys, and other merchandise. Cameras are not permitted on tours. Call before planning your excursion. Open Mon through Sat. Tours conducted Tues through Fri; call for times. Free admission; fee for tours.

Brenham Heritage Museum. 105 S. Market St.; (979) 830-8445; brenhamheritage museum.org. This museum, housed in a historic post office building, features the history of Brenham and Washington County through permanent and rotating displays. Next to the museum a Silsby steam fire engine from the late 1800s is on display. Open Wed 1 to 4 p.m., Thurs through Sat 10 a.m. to 4 p.m. Free admission.

Flying Horses Carousel. Fireman's Park, 901 N. Park St.; (979) 337-7250; cityofbrenham .org. A classic vintage carousel housed in a 1935 WPA building has been the centerpiece of this 30-acre downtown park since it was purchased by the city in 1935. The carousel is open for rides on weekends from March through Oct. Children 12 years and younger can ride while adults and older children can stand beside the horses or ride on the gondolas. Fee.

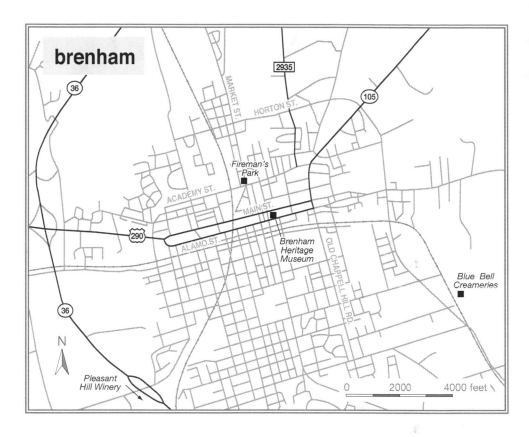

Heritage Home Tours. 2203 Century Circle; (979) 836-1690; giddingsstonemansion.com. Conducted by the Heritage Society of Washington County, tours visit three historic homes: the Ross Carroll Bennett House (1898), the Giddings Wilkin House Museum (1843), and the Giddings Stone Mansion (1870). All have been designated as Texas Historic Landmarks. Tours must be booked in advance. Fee.

Horseshoe Junction Family Fun Park. 2080 US 290 West; (979) 251-8701; horseshoe junction.com. This family fun park has activities ranging from miniature golf to go-karts to laser tag. The more adventurous will appreciate the three-story Cliffhanger Climbing Wall and the Slingshot Jumper. Hours vary with season. Fee.

Pleasant Hill Winery. 1441 Salem Rd., just south of US 290 and TX 36 intersection; (979) 830-VINE; pleasanthillwinery.com. Travel just a few hundred yards west and a hillside vineyard will appear. Free tours and tastings are offered inside the carefully reconstructed old barn at the top of the hill. Enjoy the spectacular view of the vineyard below. Spend some time studying the corkscrew collection and winery artifacts, or just enjoy the warmth and beauty of the barn's interior. The tour will take you through the path of the grape as it makes its transformation from vine to wine. Gift shop with Texas wines and souvenirs for sale.

Open Sat noon to 5 p.m. and Sun noon to 4 p.m. Groups may request other tour times by appointment. Free admission.

where to stay

The Brenham area is home to more than 25 bed-and-breakfasts, many located in historic homes or on local farms. The city also has several motels. For more information on accommodations, call (979) 337-7580; write Visit Brenham Texas, 115 W. Main St., Brenham, TX 77833; or visit visitbrenhamtexas.com.

Ant Street Inn. 107 W. Commerce St.; (800) 481-1951 or (979) 836-7393; antstreetinn .com. Located in the Ant Street Historic District, this historic structure includes 15 guest rooms. Each room features individual climate control, wireless high-speed Internet service, polished hardwood floors, and antique furnishings. $$–$$$.

Far View Bed & Breakfast. 1804 S. Park St.; (979) 836-1672; farviewbedandbreakfast .com. This stately home built in 1925 is a nice blend of vintage elegance and modern amenities like private baths, satellite TV, and in-room wireless Internet. The manicured grounds include a swimming pool and a lawn for croquet and horseshoe pitching. $$–$$$.

The Inn at Nueces Canyon Ranch. 9501 US 290 West; (800) 925-5058 or (979) 289-5600; nuecescanyon.com. This expansive equestrian center offers group activities on a working ranch. Guests can watch cutting horses at work, enjoy a hayride, and relax with a barbecue dinner. The center also hosts cutting-horse shows most weekends. Accommodations are available as well. Advance reservations are required for all tours and activities. $$.

independence

From Brenham head east on TX 105 then turn north on FM 50 to reach the community of Independence.

This historic town, founded in 1835, served as the original home to Baylor University; Sam Houston and his family also resided here. Today the town works hard to preserve its historic roots with many projects sponsored by the nonprofit Independence Preservation Trust. If you'd like to leave your car and tour Independence by bicycle, you'll also find a self-guided bike tour at independencetx.com that travels along rural roads to many of the community's historic sites as well as scenic views of the Brazos River Valley. On March and April weekends, the Independence Historical Society conducts free tours of some of the historical attractions in the town, including an early dogtrot cabin, a 1900 one-room schoolhouse, and the John P. Coles Home.

where to go

The Antique Rose Emporium. 10,000 FM 50 (head northeast from Brenham on TX 105, then turn north on FM 50 and continue for 9 miles); (800) 441-0002 or (979) 836-5548; antiqueroseemporium.com. This display garden showcases the many products of the emporium, and a nursery specializing in historic types of roses. You'll find varieties that once graced early Texas homes such as "Adam," considered the first of the tea roses and dating to 1838, and the even older "Archduke Charles," whose flowers change colors in the heat of the Texas sun. The display gardens include historic structures, cottage gardens, herb gardens, and more. Open daily. Free admission.

Independence General Store. 9400 Lueckemeyer Rd.; (979) 836-4211; independencetx .com/GeneralStore.htm. If the front of this stone structure looks familiar, you're right! The original wooden building was rebuilt in 1939 by owner Walter C. Lueckemeyer, who modeled it on that icon of Texas history, the Alamo. Current owners Mike and Brenda Bentke Meadows sell grocery items and gas here now and operate a lunch counter. Open daily.

Texas Baptist Historical Center-Museum. 10405 FM 50; (979) 836-2929; texasbaptist historicalmuseum.weebly.com. This Baptist church, once attended by Sam Houston, is one of the state's oldest Baptist churches as well as the birthplace of Baylor University. Open Tues through Sat 10 a.m. to 4 p.m. Free admission.

washington-on-the-brazos

To reach this community, also known as Washington, take TX 105 northeast of Brenham for 14 miles, then turn right on 1115.

The town dates to the days of a ferry landing on the Brazos River that operated at the site from 1822. Washington has become best known, however, as the birthplace of Texas. On a cold March day in 1836, founders gathered here and signed the Texas Declaration of Independence, establishing the state as a sovereign nation.

From 1842 to 1845, Washington served as the capital of the republic, also gradually becoming a commerce center on the busy Brazos. When the seat of government was moved to Austin, the town hung on, kept alive by its position on the river. Eventually, though, in the 1850s, Washington was bypassed by the railroads, and the community dwindled to a tiny dot on the map.

One of the hidden treasures of the Texas parks system is the Washington-on-the-Brazos State Historical Park. Today the park includes a visitor center and interpretive trails that introduce visitors to the importance of this site where the early Texans declared an independent and sovereign nation. Near the center, the Star of the Republic Museum, built in the shape of a star, highlights the history of the Republic of Texas with exhibits and special collections.

The park's interpretive trail winds from Independence Hall—a replica of the original building where the signing of the Texas Declaration of Independence took place—to the historic Washington town site. To reach Washington-on-the-Brazos State Historical Park from Brenham, take TX 105 northeast of the city for 14 miles, then turn right on FM 912 to reach the park. The facility is open daily from 8 a.m. to sundown.

where to go

Washington-on-the-Brazos State Historical Park. Between Brenham and Navasota off TX 105 on FM 105 at 23400 Park Rd.12; (936) 878-2214; wheretexasbecametexas.org. Located on the banks of the Brazos River, this quiet park is shaded by acres of walnut and pecan trees. This is a day-use park, with picnic tables along the river. Free admission to the park; admission for specific sites. Combination tickets for multiple sites at the park are available at any site or at the visitor center. Its main sections include the following points of interest:

Visitor Center. (936) 878-2214. Features interactive exhibits highlighting the historic attractions located within the park. Also includes the Washington Emporium gift shop. Tickets to the park's main attractions can be purchased here. Open daily 10 a.m. to 5 p.m.

Barrington Living History Farm. (936) 878-2214. This was once the home of Anson Jones, the fourth and last president of the Republic of Texas. A self-guided tour of the site includes a two-story home that has been relocated, an orchard, a demonstration garden, a carriage shed, a corn crib, a kitchen, and more. Open daily 10 a.m. to 4:30 p.m.

Independence Hall. (936) 878-2214. The original building where the signing of the Texas Declaration of Independence took place did not survive the 19th century. In 1901, a group of citizens erected a monument at the site. The simple frame building reconstructed here holds long, mismatched tables and unadorned chairs. Forty-minute guided tours are available; call to confirm tour times. Open daily (check the visitor center for tour times and prices).

Star of the Republic Museum. (936) 878-2461; starmuseum.org. Built in the shape of a five-pointed star, this museum covers the republic period of Texas history, 1836 to 1846. Visitors can start with the 20-minute film *Once a Nation* for an overview of the period. Upstairs, exhibits cover all aspects of commerce during the 19th century, including displays on the general store, steamboats, blacksmithing, and carpentry. Open daily 10 a.m. to 5 p.m.

southeast

day trip 01

southeast

lost pines:
cedar creek, bastrop, smithville, la grange

One of Texas's natural anomalies, the Lost Pines forest is the westernmost stand of loblolly pines in America. Scientists believe that these trees were once part of the forests of East Texas, but climatic changes over the last 10,000 years account for the farmland now separating the Lost Pines from their cousins to the east.

cedar creek

Originally a small town located 11 miles west of Bastrop, the Cedar Creek area has spread north, reaching TX 71. The town was first settled in the 1830s as a farming community tucked between piney woods and blackland prairies. Cedar Creek's early population peaked at around 600 in the late 1800s, when it became a shipping terminal for cotton and other agriculture. Although some petroleum deposits were discovered in the early 1900s, the town gradually declined until recent times when suburban development from Bastrop began to rapidly populate the Cedar Creek area.

where to go

The Dinosaur Park. 893 Union Chapel Rd.; (512) 321-6262; thedinopark.com. This attraction features—you guessed it—life-size dinosaur replicas in an outdoor setting that kids will enjoy. Other activities include a fossil dig, playground, picnic area, and the Dinosaur Store.

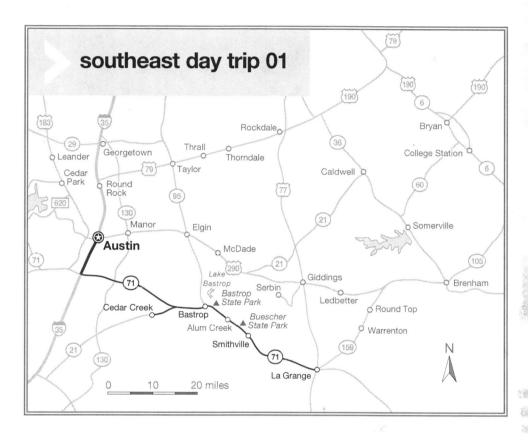

southeast day trip 01

Hours change with the seasons and public school schedules, varying from weekends only to daily. Fee.

McKinney Roughs Nature Park. 8 miles west of Bastrop at 1884 TX 71; (512) 303-5073; lcra.org. A favorite with both hikers and equestrians, this 1,100-acre park preserves several ecosystems as well as extensive riparian habitat along the Colorado River. Open daily 8 a.m. to 5 p.m. Fee.

where to shop

Berdoll Pecan Candy and Gift Company. 2626 TX 71 West; (800) 518-3870; berdoll pecanfarm.com. For over 30 years this unique shop on TX 71 has sold all things pecan, from the nuts themselves (grown in their own pecan orchards located nearby) to pies, candies, and myriad other items. If you happen by when they are closed, never fear, a vending machine on the front porch sells several of their items, including pecan pies! Open daily 9 a.m. to 5:30 p.m. Jan through mid-Mar; 9 a.m. to 7 p.m. mid-Mar through Dec.

where to stay

Hyatt Regency Lost Pines Resort and Spa. 575 Hyatt Lost Pines Rd. (13 miles east of Austin-Bergstrom International Airport on TX 71); (512) 308-1234; hyatt.com.This luxury destination resort, located near McKinney Roughs, offers 491 guest rooms and a distinctive Central Texas atmosphere. The hotel spans over 400 acres and offers an equestrian center, an Arthur Hills–designed golf course, rafting on the Colorado River, supervised children's programs, a full-service spa, and more. $$$.

bastrop

To reach Bastrop from Cedar Creek, continue east on TX 71. Unlike the juniper-dotted hills to the west or the rolling farmland to the east, the Bastrop area is surrounded by a pine forest called Lost Pines. Bastrop holds the honor as one of the oldest settlements in the state, built in 1829 along the Camino Real, a road also known as the King's Highway and the Old San Antonio Road. This was the western edge of the "Little Colony" established by Stephen F. Austin. Settlers came by the wagonload from around the country to claim a share of this fertile land and to establish homes in this dangerous territory. Even as houses were being built, Native American raids continued in this area for many years.

Bastrop is a popular day trip for Austinites looking for a chance to shop and savor some quiet country life in a historic setting. Outdoor-lovers can enjoy two nearby state parks as well as the Colorado River, which winds through the heart of downtown. Canoe rentals and guided trips along the river are available.

where to go

Bastrop Visitor Center. 904 Main St.; (512) 303-0904; visitbastroptx.org. Bastrop's visitor center is located in a historic 1930s building that has served as a fire station, jail, tax office, and city hall. Now it is the headquarters of the Bastrop County Historical Society and offers information on Bastrop attractions, accommodations, and events and houses the Bastrop County Historical Society Museum. Open 10 a.m. to 5 p.m. Mon through Sat. Free admission.

Bastrop County Historical Society Museum. 904 Main St.; (512) 303-0904; bastrop countyhistoricalsociety.com. For over 50 years the historical society has collected artifacts and documents that trace the history of Bastrop and Bastrop County, including Native American items. The museum is housed in the same building as the visitor center. Open 10 a.m. to 5 p.m. Mon through Sat. Free admission; donations accepted.

Bastrop Opera House. 711 Spring St.; (512) 321-6283; bastropoperahouse.com. Built in 1889, this building was once the entertainment center of town. Today the historic structure is the cultural center of Bastrop, the site for live theater ranging from mysteries to vaudeville. Call for information on group tours, which are available by appointment.

Bastrop State Park. 100 Park Road 1A (1.5 miles east of Bastrop); (512) 321-2101 or (512) 389-8900; tpwd.state.tx.us. Long a favorite among Texas state parks for its beautiful Lost Pines setting, a wildfire in 2011 affected much of the park's 3,500 acres. Reconstruction efforts have resulted in most of the park being reopened, including hiking trails, the golf course, campsites, and the park's iconic 1930s-built stone and cedar CCC cabins. (Unfortunately floods in 2015 destroyed the dam that formed the 10-acre fishing lake.) The cabins feature fireplaces, bathrooms, and kitchen facilities. Despite the fire's effects, the cabins remain very popular, so book well in advance. Open daily. Fee.

June Hill Pape Riverwalk. Enjoy this nature walk along the banks of the Colorado River. Opened in 1998, the half-mile trail features a variety of trees, native plants, and wildflowers. It is accessible from either Fisherman's Park (1200 Willow St.) or Ferry Park (502 Water St.). Free admission.

North Shore Park, Lake Bastrop. 603 FM 1441 (3 miles east of Bastrop via TX 95 and FM 1441); (800) 776-5272 or (512) 498-1922; lcra.org. Day travelers and overnight campers can use this Lower Colorado River Authority (LCRA) park on the 900-acre lake. Facilities include campsites, RV sites, group pavilions, a two-lane boat ramp, a fishing pier, playgrounds, trails, and more. Fishing for largemouth bass, catfish, and perch is a popular activity. Open daily. Fee.

South Shore Park, Lake Bastrop. 375 South Shore Rd. (east of Bastrop via TX 21 and FM 352); (800) 776-5272; lcra.org. This popular LCRA park on Lake Bastrop includes restrooms, showers, a group facility, hike/bike trails, picnic facilities, and a boat ramp. Open daily. Fee.

where to shop

Apothecary's Hall. 805 Main St.; (512) 321-3022. Shop in this downtown store for antiques ranging from collectibles to furniture. It is located in a historic building that dates to the 1830s. Open daily.

Buc-ee's. 1700 TX 71 East; (979) 230-2920; bucees.com. OK, it's not often that we consider a gas station and convenience store guidebook-worthy, but then Buc-ee's is no ordinary convenience store. This Texas-size convenience store / gift shop is an attraction in itself due to its sheer size. Not only filled with every kind of road-trip munchie you could imagine, the store also features all things Texas, from cookbooks to jewelry to gourmet gifts. Open 24 hours daily.

Sugar Shack. 114 TX-Loop 150; (512) 321-3777; sugarshackbastrop.com. Owned and operated by the Rogers family since 1995, Sugar Shack offers sweets and gifts to please youngsters and adults alike. Open daily.

where to eat

Maxine's Café & Bakery. 905 Main St.; (512) 303-0919; maxinescafe.com. Open for breakfast, lunch, and dinner, Maxine's has become a beloved fixture in downtown Bastrop. The restaurant is known for its griddle cakes, burgers, chili, and homemade pie. Open daily. $–$$.

where to stay

Bastrop State Park Cabins. 100 Park Road 1A (1.5 miles east of Bastrop); (512) 389-8900; tpwd.state.tx.us. These picturesque stone and cedar cabins were built in the 1930s by the Civilian Conservation Corps from native materials. They feature rustic fireplaces, bathrooms, and kitchen facilities. ***Note:*** Due to their popularity, cabins should be booked well in advance. $$.

Pecan Street Inn Bed and Breakfast. 1010 Pecan St.; (512) 988-1231; pecanstreetinn .com. Located just 2 blocks from downtown, this stately Victorian offers rooms and suites featuring antique furniture, heart-pine floors, and high ceilings. All have modern amenities, some with fireplaces. $$–$$$.

smithville

Continue east from Bastrop on TX 71 to Smithville, a small town built alongside the railroad tracks at the edge of the piney woods and home of Buescher State Park. Smithville was once a riverboat ferry stop on the Colorado. In the 1880s the railroad replaced the ferries as the main mode of transportation, and tracks were laid across town. Today the railroad still plays an important part in Smithville's economy.

Beginning with the Sandra Bullock movie *Hope Floats* in 1997, Smithville has been the backdrop for several Hollywood productions, including Terrence Malick's *Tree of Life* in 2011. In fact, this small town was the first Texas town honored as a Film Friendly Community by the Texas Film Commission.

where to go

Buescher State Park. 3 miles north of town at 100 Park Rd, via TX 71 and FM 2104, or access from Park Road 1; (512) 237-2241; tpwd.state.tx.us. Buescher (pronounced "BISH-er") neighbors Bastrop State Park, but the two boast different environments. Oaks and other hardwoods dominate this park, along with a few pines. The park is especially popular for its 30-acre lake. Visitors can enjoy ample campsites and screened shelters, as well as a playground and picnic area. Open daily 6 a.m. to 10 p.m. Fee.

James H. Long Railroad Park and Museum. 100 NW First St.; (512) 237-2313. Built beside the tracks, this park has two cabooses and a depot relocated here from West Point, a community east of town. The museum features exhibits of historical Missouri-Kansas-Texas Railroad artifacts and replicas of the Smithville Depot. The chamber of commerce office is housed adjacent to the depot as well. Open Mon through Fri 10 a.m. to 4 p.m. and Sat 10 a.m. to 2 p.m. Free admission.

Rocky Hill Ranch. FM 153, 2 miles northeast of Buescher State Park; (361) 548-5728; rockyhillranch.com. Beginner, intermediate, advanced, and expert trails tempt mountain bikers with more than 1,000 acres that include gentle slopes and challenging grades as well as stream crossings. More than 30 miles of trails are available for use by helmeted bicycle riders. The ranch is open for day use; or if you are staying longer, campsites and RV electric sites are available along small creeks and spring-fed water holes. Open daily. Fee.

Smithville Heritage House & Museum. 602 Main St.; (214) 673-2223. This 1908 Victorian home contains the Smithville archives and a museum of local memorabilia. Open Tues 10 a.m. to noon or by appointment. Free admission.

Vernon L. Richards Riverbend Park. 107 TX 71 West at the Colorado River, just north of Smithville; (512) 237-3282 for information or campsite reservations; smithvilletx.org. This LCRA park is operated by the City of Smithville and hosts many special events, including the Smithville Jamboree and the Smithville Music Festival. The park includes restrooms, a group facility, 19 RV hookups, hike/bike trails, kids' playground, picnic facilities, and a boat ramp. Open daily for day use and camping. Free admission.

Veterans Memorial Park. 311 NW Second St., (512) 237-3282; smithvilletx.org. This memorial honors military veterans, particularly local soldiers who gave their lives in service to their country, with bronze plaques and other sculptures. Open daily. Free.

where to shop

Bella's Cottage Antiques. 119 Main St.; (512) 237-2463; bellascottageantiquestx.com. This downtown shop features a large inventory of vintage items including furniture, jewelry, art objects, and household furnishings. Open daily.

la grange

Just 4 miles southeast of Smithville on the left side of TX 71 is a scenic overlook, an excellent place to pull over for a picnic. From here you can gaze at the miles of rolling hills and farmland that attracted many German and Czech immigrants a century ago.

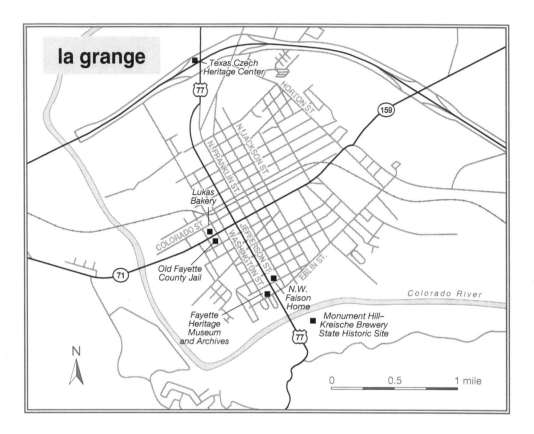

Continue on TX 71 to the somewhat infamous community of La Grange. For generations this was a quiet town in the center of a farming region. In the 1970s, however, La
Grange caught the attention of the public with the unveiling of the Chicken Ranch, a brothel
that became the subject of the Broadway musical and movie *The Best Little Whorehouse in
Texas*, not to mention the famous ZZ Top song "La Grange." The Chicken Ranch is gone
now, but La Grange still has other sights to see.

where to go

Fayette Heritage Museum and Archives. 855 S. Jefferson St.; (979) 968-6418 or (979)
968-3765; cityoflg.com/departments/library.php. Housed inside the Fayette Public Library,
this museum contains displays on the area's rich history, along with extensive genealogical
records. Open Tues through Sat; call for hours. Free admission.

LaGrange Visitor Center. 254 N. Jefferson St.; (979) 968-3017; visitlagrangetx.com.
Located in a historic casino built in 1881. Open daily. Free admission.

Lake Fayette Oak Thicket Park. 4819 W. TX 159 (about 7 miles east of La Grange on TX
159; turn right at the sign for Fayette County Lake); (979) 249-3504; camprrm.com/parks/

texas/lcra/oak-thicket-park. This 65-acre park offers plenty of family-oriented activities: a playground, fishing piers, and a good swimming area on Lake Fayette. Camping is available, as well as 8 cabins. Open dawn to dusk for day use. Fee.

Lake Fayette Park Prairie Park. 1250 Park Prairie Rd. (travel 10 miles east of La Grange on TX 159); (979) 249-3504; lcra.org. Located on 2,000-acre Lake Fayette, Park Prairie is another favorite with families, thanks to volleyball courts, plenty of picnic space, tent camping, and even some pelicans and gulls along the shores of the lake. Hikers can walk to Oak Thicket Park on a 3-mile trail. Other facilities include restrooms, showers, a group facility, and a boat ramp. Open dawn to dusk for day use. Fee.

Monument Hill & Kreische Brewery State Historic Site. 414 State Loop 92 (off US 77, 1 mile south of La Grange); (979) 968-5658; thc.texas.gov/historic-sites/monument-hill-state -historic-site. Located on a 200-foot bluff high above town, this site is home to two combined parks. Open daily 8 a.m. to 4:30 p.m. Fee.

Kreische Brewery State Historic Site recalls a far more cheerful time in Texas history. Heinreich Kreische, who immigrated here from Germany, purchased the hilltop and the adjoining land in 1849, including the burial ground of those Texas heroes, for his brewery site. Before closing the brewery in 1884, Kreische became the third-largest beer producer in the state. Stroll the grounds and enjoy the view high over the Colorado River, then follow the trail downhill to the site where the

the chicken ranch

La Grange drew international attention in 1973 when the story of what many believe was the country's oldest continuously run brothel was exposed by consumer affairs reporter Marvin Zindler from KTRK-TV in Houston. The report would inspire a Broadway musical and movie as well as lot of curiosity about the site, which was located on 11 acres outside of La Grange. The house, which was added on to many times as the number of women increased, was nicknamed the Chicken Ranch during the Great Depression. When customers grew more scarce, the proprietor, a woman known as Miss Jessie, began allowing men to pay in chickens. Soon the ranch was overrun with both poultry and eggs, both of which they sold locally.

As economic times improved, the ranch returned to a cash basis. Ownership changed in 1952 to Edna Milton, a madam who become one of La Grange's largest philanthropists.

When the Chicken Ranch closed, the building was moved to Dallas and, for a while, became a chicken restaurant.

brewery once stood. Guided tours of the brewery and the Kreische house are conducted seasonally; call for tour times.

Monument Hill Historical Park is the burial site for the Texans who died in the Dawson Massacre and the Mier Expedition, two historic Mexican conflicts that occurred in 1842, six years after the Texas Revolution. The Dawson Massacre took place near San Antonio when La Grange citizen Nicholas Dawson gathered Texans to halt continual Mexican attacks. Dawson's men were met by hundreds of Mexican troops, and 35 Texans were killed. The Mexican village of Mier was attacked in a retaliatory move, resulting in the capture of Texas soldiers and citizens by Mexico's General Santa Anna, who ordered every tenth man to be killed. The Texans were blindfolded and forced to draw beans: 159 of them white and 17 black. Men who drew white beans were imprisoned; those who drew black ones were executed.

Muster Oak. Northeast corner of Courthouse Square; tfsweb.tamu.edu. Beneath this historic oak tree, Captain Dawson gathered 53 troops to join the Texas-Mexican Revolution in 1842. Muster Oak is designated as one of the "Famous Trees of Texas" by Texas A&M University.

N. W. Faison Home. 822 S. Jefferson St.; (979) 968-5756; faisonhouse.org. N. W. Faison was a survivor of both the Dawson Massacre and the Mier Expedition. The Faison family resided in this home for more than 20 years, and today it contains the family's furniture as well as exhibits from the Mexican War. Open for tours noon to 4 p.m. Sat and by appointment. Fee.

Texas Czech Heritage and Cultural Center. 250 W. Fairgrounds Rd.; (888) 785-4500 or (979) 968-9399; czechtexas.org. Located next to the Fayette County Fairgrounds, this cluster of restored historic buildings house perhaps the most comprehensive collection of materials related to the Czech experience in Texas. The 70-acre compound includes exhibits of genealogical records in the Melnar Library and the Hoelscher House, which houses the Polka Lovers Club of Texas Museum. The Texas Czech Village is composed of numerous farmhouses and buildings. Much of the signage is in both English and Czech. Open Tues through Sat. Free admission.

Texas Heroes Museum at Old Fayette County Jail. 171 S. Main St. This historic building once housed the Fayette County Jail, serving in that role for a century. Free admission.

White Rock Park. 940 Mode Ln. (US 77 south to Elbin Road, continue about 0.75 mile to Mode Lane/CR 134, then take a right on Mode Lane and travel about 0.25 mile); (979) 968-5805; cityoflg.com/departments/parks.php. On the east bank of the Colorado River, this 24-acre day-use park includes restrooms, hike/bike trails, picnic facilities, a fishing pier, and a canoe launch. The park was developed by the LCRA but is operated by the City of La Grange. Open dawn to dusk. Free admission.

where to eat

Las Fuentes. 658 S. Jefferson St.; (979) 968-8957; lasfuentesmexicanrestaurant.net. This restaurant located near the courthouse square serves up authentic Mexican dishes for lunch and dinner. You'll find most of your favorite Tex-Mex combinations here as well as some unique specialties like grilled quail and red snapper a la plancha, an 8-ounce fillet cooked in garlic and butter. Las Fuentes also offers daily lunch specials and a separate children's menu. Open daily. $$.

Lukas Bakery. 135 N. Main St.; (979) 968-3052. Since 1947 this landmark bakery has been turning out fragrant delights like bread, kolaches, and pigs in a blanket. Open Mon through Sat 5 a.m. to 1 p.m. $.

Weikel's Bakery. 2247 W. TX 71; (979) 968-9413; weikels.com. The Czech pastry specialties for which this region is known make up many of the offerings at this highway-side bakery. Kolaches and pigs in a blanket are top items; kolaches come in a range of flavors, from pineapple to poppy seed to prune. The bakery may not look like much from the outside (well, actually, it looks like a gas station), but it was named one of America's top 10 bakeries by foodies Jane and Michael Stern, and for good reason. Open Mon through Wed 5 a.m. to 9 p.m. and Fri through Sun 5 a.m. to 10 p.m. Closed Thurs. $.

day trip 02

southeast

petite getaway:
carmine, round top, winedale, shelby,
fayetteville, warrenton

This day trip can be reached from Southeast Day Trip 01 via La Grange or East Day Trips 01 and 02, which take you through Elgin and Giddings, turning south in Carmine.

While these towns may be petite in terms of population, they pack a wallop when it comes to drawing vacationers, especially during "Antiques Week," traditionally scheduled for the first full weekend in April (although this can vary with the timing of Easter) and October. During Antiques Week, dozens of antiques shows dot the countryside, featuring thousands of vendors and tens of thousands of shoppers from across the country.

If you think you might want to expand your day trip into a multiday shop-a-thon, book accommodations months in advance. Lodging can be very hard to come by for these prime weekends. You'll find a lodging request form on the Round Top Area Chamber website, round-top.org; they'll send your lodging request to member accommodations to check for availability.

carmine

Located on busy US 290, tiny Carmine is easy to miss during most of the year, but during Antiques Week in the spring and fall, it becomes the first shopping stop for many Austin travelers.

where to shop

Hourglass Trading Company. 248 Centennial; (979) 278-4040. This shop is located in the old Carmine lumberyard and offers wares from over 30 different dealers. Some of the

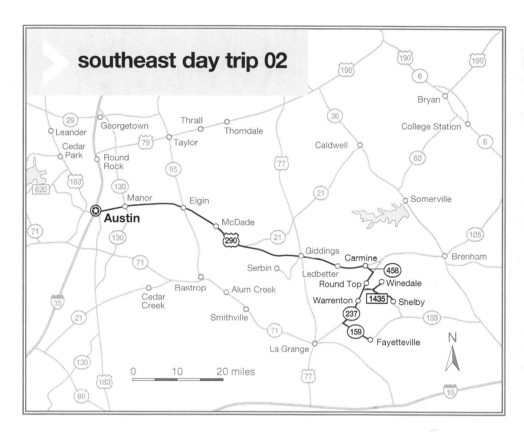

southeast day trip 02

inventory here includes furniture, vintage apparel, glassware and china, and other home decor. Open Thurs through Sun.

During **Antiques Week** in the spring and fall, Carmine hosts several large events:

County Line Antique Show. Intersection of Spur 458 and TX 237; (760) 587-1300. This antiques show takes place in several historic buildings that are themselves part of the fun. Shop in a former gas station, an old sausage company, and even an air-conditioned building as well as open-air tents during the twice-annual event.

La Bahia Antiques Show. TX 237, north of where Spur 458 intersects with the highway; (979) 289-2684. This antiques show takes place in a historic community center. Free admission.

The Original Round Top Antiques Fair at the Carmine Dance Hall. 2 blocks north of US 290 at highway crossover sign; (512) 237-4747; roundtoptexas antiques.com. One of four venues offered by this very popular company, one ticket offers admission to all four sites. Many consider this market, held at an authentic old-time dance hall, one of the best.

round top

From Carmine take Spur 458 south to TX 237, turning south on TX 237 to continue to Round Top. Officially founded in 1835 by settlers from Stephen F. Austin's second colony, this town is filled with restored homes, log cabins, and country stores.

Round Top is also home to a world-class music facility. The International Festival Institute, located just outside of town, offers performances by visiting symphony orchestras under the summer stars.

"Downtown" Round Top consists of several blocks flanking the old courthouse. Today the county seat is located in nearby La Grange, but the lawn of the Round Top courthouse is still faithfully maintained by the DYD (Do Your Duty) Women's Club, as it has been since the 1930s.

where to go

Round Top Family Library. 206 W. Mill St.; (979) 249-2700; ilovetoread.org. Serving as a traditional lending library for the residents of Round Top, this facility is also the home of the Bybee Texas Heritage Collection, focusing on Texas history, furniture, decorative arts, and architecture as well as oral histories of the pioneers who settled this region. The library is housed in the 1925 Hope Lutheran Church, a Gothic structure moved to Round Top from Milam County. Open 1:30 to 5:30 p.m. Mon through Fri and 10 a.m. to 2 p.m. Sat. Free admission.

Round Top Festival Institute. 248 Jaster Rd. (off TX 237, 5 blocks north of Henkel Square); (979) 249-3129; festivalhill.org. This music and theater center was founded by noted pianist James Dick. During the school year, the Institute presents monthly concerts. In the summer, the center hosts students from around the world who entertain guests with musical performances. The center is housed in historic buildings, including an 1870 farmhouse and a former school for African Americans. The focal point of this site is the Festival Concert Hall, a limestone structure fitted with 1,000 seats. In its grandiose scale and its dedication to craftsmanship, the concert hall rises from its rural surroundings like a grand cathedral.

Even if you don't have the opportunity to attend a concert here, call to schedule a tour. Your look at the Institute can include the David Guion Museum Room, housing a collection of belongings and music of this Texas composer, and the Oxehufwud Room, a collection of Swedish decorative arts that recall the life of a Swedish noble family whose final member retired in La Grange. Bring a picnic lunch and enjoy the 100-acre grounds, which are planted with thousands of trees and include walking trails and a stonework bridge, constructed to resemble a Roman footbridge. Fee.

where to shop

Antiques Fairs. Round Top holds antiques fairs like no place else in the state. These events draw collectors from across the country for staggered antiques shows that range over a one-week period (deemed "Antiques Week") in both the spring and fall, with limited shows in June as well.

Marburger Farm Antique Show. TX 237 between Round Top and Warrenton; (800) 947-5799; roundtop-marburger.com. This show, which has been featured in top magazines such as *Country Living*, offers indoor and outside stalls spanning 10 large tents and 12 historic buildings with more than 300 dealers. The 27 acres of parking gives you an idea of how popular this show is, which offers, for a higher fee, an early bird sales day.

The Original Round Top Antiques Fairs. At the Big Red Barn on TX 237; (512) 237-4747; roundtoptexasantiques.com. These megafairs draw antiques lovers from around the state to more than 300 booths. In addition to spring and fall Antiques Fairs, the company also presents a Winter Antiques Show.

Texas Rose Antique Show. 2075 S. TX 237; (256) 390-5337; texasroseshow .com. Collectibles, not flowers, are the hallmark of this show held in Mar and Oct. Vendors display their wares over 5 acres and within a 36,000-square-foot building. Free admission (and free parking).

Henkel Square Market. 201 N. Live Oak St.; (979) 249-5840; henkelsquareroundtop.com. A cluster of restored pioneer buildings now house a collection of shops selling arts and crafts, home and yard furnishings, and apparel. The visitor center of the Round Top Area Chamber of Commerce is also located in the square. Open Wed through Sun.

where to eat

Royers Round Top Cafe. 105 Main St., on the square; (979) 249-3611; royersroundtop cafe.com. You wouldn't expect to find grilled rack of lamb, fresh red snapper in Cajun sauce, or grilled quail stuffed with shrimp at a small-town diner, but here it is. This lively joint serves up some of the best cooking in Central Texas in a fun atmosphere that's popular with locals and visitors alike. It's all topped off with homemade pies that include key lime chess, buttermilk, and that Texas favorite, pecan. Royers operates a mail-order and wholesale business, featuring meat seasonings, mesquite mustard, peach 'n' pepper preserves, and applesauce butter. Open Wed through Sun. $–$$.

The Stone Cellar. 550 N. Washington St.; (979) 249-3390; stonecellarwines.com. An array of gourmet pizzas are the order of the day here as well as salads and nachos. A bar offers wines and over 20 beers on tap. You can catch live music on Fri and Sat evenings. Open Thurs through Sat. $$.

winedale

If you're continuing on a collectibles hunt during Antiques Week, skip Winedale and continue on to Shelby. Otherwise, make time to detour to historic Winedale.

To reach the tiny burg of Winedale, head east of Round Top on FM 1457, then north on FM 2714. This town does not appear on the official Texas State Map, but it's definitely on the map for Shakespeare buffs, thanks to the University of Texas productions here.

Winedale started out in 1870 as a German community named Truebsal. Eventually the community relocated slightly and, thanks to a grape crop from area farmers, got a post office with the official name of Winedale. Today the area is best known as the home of the Winedale Historical Center, part of the University of Texas's Dolph Briscoe Center for American History. Winedale's preservation dates back to the early 1960s, when conservationist Miss Ima Hogg worked to preserve the old Samuel Lewis homestead here, later donating it to the university.

where to go

Things are pretty quiet in Winedale for most of the year, except during the Shakespeare at Winedale events and in mid-December during the Christmas at Winedale celebration.

Shakespeare at Winedale. 3738 FM 2714 (4 miles east of Round Top via FM 1457, then north on FM 2714); (512) 471-4993 or (512) 471-4726; liberalarts.utexas.edu/winedale/. Operated by the University of Texas at Austin, this center hosts annual Shakespeare productions that draw visitors from across the state. Students from assorted disciplines have come to Winedale every summer since 1970 to perform the works of the Bard in an old hay barn that has been refitted as an Elizabethan-style theater. For 15 to 18 hours a day, the students make costumes, prepare lighting, and rehearse. Check the schedule for public performances. Reservations for the performances are highly recommended. Fee.

Winedale Historical Center. 3738 FM 2714 (4 miles east of Round Top via FM 1457, then north on FM 2714); (979) 278-3530; cah.utexas.edu. Although Shakespeare at Winedale is a limited activity, the center is a year-around attraction. The 225-acre complex is home to a collection of eight historic structures, a research center, a nature trail, and a picnic area. Tours (by appointment only) take visitors through homes furnished with period antiques and details such as stenciled ceilings that recall the area's German heritage. Open Mon through Fri 9 a.m. to 5 p.m. Fee.

shelby

To reach Shelby, head 6.1 miles east from Round Top on FM 1457. If you've made the Winedale detour, return to FM 1457 by retracing your steps on FM 2714, then turn east on FM 1457.

The small community of Shelby is old by Texas standards, first getting a post office in the 1840s. The post office closed in the early 20th century, but Shelby still brings many visitors during Antiques Week, thanks to several shows held in this burg.

fayetteville

This scenic little community dates back to Texas's early days. It was settled by three families from Stephen F. Austin's Old Three Hundred, the first colony settlers who received land grants. They were soon followed by Czech, German, and other immigrants who through the years named and renamed the community. Its most interesting moniker? Lick Skillet. The name came from the days when free meals were distributed and those who arrived too late were told to "lick the skillet."

Today the town recalls that heritage with an October Lick Skillet Festival. The town also participates in Antiques Week (although you'll find antiques shops open year-round). Downtown, don't miss the 1880 precinct courthouse, built to help residents avoid the journey to the county courthouse in La Grange. The precinct courthouse also has a chiming clock, donated by the women's Do Your Duty Club, making Fayetteville the world's smallest town with a clock of that type.

Things are generally very quiet in Fayetteville, with limited hours at some shops and restaurants. During Antiques Week in the spring and fall, however, look for extended hours (and larger crowds).

where to go

Fayetteville Area Heritage Museum. 119 N. Washington St.; (979) 249-6249; fayetteville txmuseum.org. Located on Fayetteville's town square, this museum traces the history of the town. Don't miss the displays on the Baca (pronounced "Batcha") Band, a Czech family band that started in the late 1800s and became one of Texas's top musical acts. Open Sat 11 a.m. to 2 p.m. or by appointment. Free admission; donations accepted.

Walking Tour of Historic Town Square. Fayetteville's status as a true historical treasure is emphasized by the fact that a total of 345 buildings here are listed on the National Register of Historic Places. Fayetteville's town square is filled with fine examples of 19th-century architecture. The chamber of commerce offers a "Historic District Walking Tour Guide," which can be downloaded at their website, greaterfayettevillechamber.org. The Greater Fayetteville Chamber of Commerce is located at 124 N. Washington St.; (713) 598-6331.

where to eat

Joe's Place. 120 N. Live Oak St.; (979) 378-9035; joesplacetx.com. A fixture on Fayetteville's square, Joe's serves Texas favorites like chicken-fried steak, barbecue, steaks, and seafood. Its century-old shotgun-style interior is packed at lunchtime with locals who show up for the daily specials. Open Wed through Sun. $–$$.

Orsak's Cafe. 121 W. Fayette St., on the square; (979) 378-2719. Country food is the order of the day at this Fayetteville favorite for breakfast, lunch, and dinner. Catfish is tops, as are chicken-fried steak and burgers, but save room for the ice cream. Open Sun through Thurs 8 a.m. to 9 p.m. and Fri and Sat 8 a.m. to 10 p.m. $.

warrenton

From Fayetteville head west on FM 1291 to Warrenton, best known as the home of the smallest Catholic church in the world.

where to go

St. Martin Catholic Church. West side of TX237 north of town at 3490 TX-237; (979) 378-2277. Billed as the world's smallest Catholic church, St. Martin's is a simple white frame building. Inside the Lilliputian house of worship, plain wooden benches serve as pews before an ornate altar. Step inside for a look; visitors are welcome. Free admission.

where to shop

Like nearby Round Top, Warrenton is home to several antiques shows in both the spring and fall. Many of the Warrenton booths open days before the Round Top booths.

Cole's Antique Show. TX 237 at intersection with FM 954; (281) 229-5877; colesantiqueshow.com. This antique show spills out of a massive, air-conditioned building into tented booths with 10 acres of parking. Over 250 vendors are represented here.

The Zapp Hall Antique Show. 4217 TX 237; (713) 824-1157; zapphall.com. With a motto of "Come for the antiques, stay for the atmosphere," this market is known not only for its fine antiques but also for its other activities, including free live music, a beer garden, and even an annex of Round Top's famous Royer's Round Top Cafe. The whole event takes place in a historic dance hall.

To head back to Austin from Warrenton, continue west on FM 1291; the road continues through the agricultural community of Walhalla before turning north and continuing to Ledbetter. At Ledbetter, you'll intersect with US 290; turn west and continue to Austin.

You can also choose to head south to La Grange on TX 237, continuing as it becomes TX 159. This will take you through the community of Oldenburg, then to La Grange, where you can join Southeast Day Trip 01 and return home via La Grange, Smithville, Bastrop, and Cedar Creek.

south

day trip 01

south

barbecue trail:
mckinney falls state park, lockhart, luling

Fragrant smoke from famous Texas barbecue restaurants pervades the region along US 183 south from Austin. Barbecue enthusiasts from all over the world converge on Lockhart and Luling to sample the smoky delights.

mckinney falls state park

McKinney Falls State Park. 5808 McKinney Falls Pkwy., Austin (13 miles southeast of downtown Austin off US 183); (512) 243-1643; tpwd.texas.gov. A favorite with those looking for a quick getaway from the city, this park includes plenty of chances to view the area's wildlife, including white-tailed deer, raccoons, squirrels, and armadillos. Campers can choose from several types of sites as well as screened shelters. Swimming in a scenic portion of Onion Creek is a popular attraction here, too. Fee.

lockhart

Lockhart is a conglomeration of the stuff of Texas legends: battles, cattle drives, cotton, and oil. This small town, located 23 miles south of Austin on US 183, contains a state park and lots of history.

The biggest event in Lockhart's past was the Battle of Plum Creek in 1840. More than 600 Comanches raided the community of Linnville and were on their way home when they

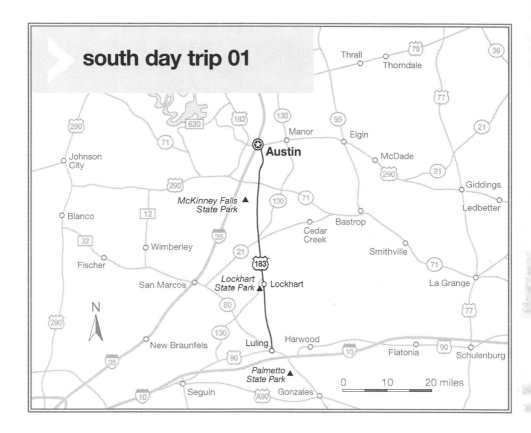

passed through this area. A group of settlers joined forces with the Tonkawa tribe to attack the Comanches, driving them farther west and ending attacks from Native Americans in the region. This battle is reenacted every June at the Chisholm Trail Roundup.

Lockhart is also well known as the home of Mebane cotton. Developed by A. D. Mebane, this strain is resistant to the boll weevil, an insect that can demolish not only whole fields but also entire economies.

where to go

Caldwell County Museum. 315 E. Market St.; (512) 398-5796; caldwellcountyhistorical commission.org. You can't miss this old building—just look for the five-story redbrick castle. Built in 1908 as the county jail, this imposing structure was designed with Norman-style castellations, giving it almost a fairy tale look. Today the building, which houses items detailing the settlement and history of the region, is operated by the Caldwell County Historical Commission and is open to the public on Sat and Sun from 1 to 5 p.m. Other times by appointment. Fee.

lockhart meets hollywood

While its reputation as the barbecue capital of Texas has made Lockhart legendary among foodies, its historical architecture and small-town charm has secured this Hill Country community a place in Hollywood history. The Muldoon Blue sandstone facade of the Caldwell County Courthouse played a starring role alongside Johnny Depp in a scene from the 1993 drama What's Eating Gilbert Grape? *and the 19th-century structure also appears in the cult comedy favorite* Waiting for Guffman. *Locals lined the bleachers at the high school football field in 1998 for the sci-fi flick* The Faculty, *and residents shop in the same aisles of the Walmart that actress Natalie Portman wandered in 2000 when she filmed the screen adaptation of the best-selling novel* Where the Heart Is.

Dr. Eugene Clark Library. 217 S. Main St.; (512) 398-3223; clark-library-lockhart.org. Built in 1889, this is the oldest continuously operating library in Texas. Modeled after the Villa Rotunda in Vicenza, Italy, the Classical Revival building has stained-glass windows, ornate fixtures, and a stage where President William Taft once spoke. Open Mon through Sat. Free admission.

Lockhart State Park. 2012 State Park Rd. (1 mile south of Lockhart on US 183 to FM 20, head southwest for 2 miles to Park Road, continue 1 mile south); (512) 398-3479; tpwd .texas.gov. This 263-acre park has a 9-hole golf course, fishing on Plum Creek, picnic areas, a swimming pool, and campsites for both tents and trailers. Many of the facilities were built by the Civilian Conservation Corps in the 1930s. Open daily 6 a.m. to 10 p.m. Fee.

where to shop

Manny Gammage's Texas Hatters. 911 S. Commerce St.; (800) 421-4287 or (512) 398-4287; texashatters.com. Formerly in Buda, this store's founder, the late Manny Gammage, was "Texas's Hatmaker to the Stars." His custom hats topped the heads of Roy Rogers, Willie Nelson, Ronald Reagan, Burt Reynolds, and many other celebrities whose pictures decorate the shop walls. Besides the obligatory cowboy hats, this store also sells hand-blocked high rollers, Panamas, and derbies. Open Tues through Sat 9:30 a.m. to 5:30 p.m.

where to eat

Black's Barbecue. 215 N. Main St.; (512) 398-2712; blacksbbq.com. This cafeteria-style restaurant is reputedly the oldest barbecue joint in Texas under the same continuous family ownership. Beef brisket is the specialty of the house, along with sausage, ribs, chicken, and ham. There's also a fully stocked salad bar. Open daily. $–$$.

Kreuz Market. 619 N. Colorado St.; (512) 398-2361; kreuzmarket.com. For generations, Kreuz (pronounced "Krites") Market was the stuff of legend. The menu at this meat-lover's paradise features brisket, beef shoulder clod, spicy sausage, pork loin, prime rib, and pork ribs, all served on butcher paper without forks and without a drop of barbecue sauce. Open daily. $–$$.

Smitty's Market. 208 S. Commerce St.; (512) 398-9344; smittysmarket.com. Since 1900 this store was part of Kreuz Market, the no-frills barbecue joint and Texas legend. "Smitty" Schmidt bought the restaurant from its original owner in 1948 and devised the huge pit system for barbecuing. The smokehouse was run first by Schmidt, then by his two sons until 1999, when the family divided the business: Sister Nina Schmidt Sells took the building and brother Rick took the name, moving it to a newer building that houses Kreuz Market. Today the original brick building is home to Smitty's Market, which still operates much as the original did. The specials include brisket, pork chops, sausage, and pork ribs. Side dishes are also sold here, including potato salad, coleslaw, and beans. Open daily. $–$$.

luling

Continue south on US 183 for 17 miles to the oil town of Luling. Oil was discovered here in 1922, and fields pumping this "black gold" can still be seen throughout the Luling area. Even before that time the town had a reputation as the toughest town in Texas, frequented by gunfighters like John Wesley Hardin and Ben Thompson. Luling was also a cattle center and one end of a railroad line to Chihuahua, Mexico.

When oil was discovered, the economy of the town shifted to this profitable industry. As part of a beautification effort, the chamber of commerce commissioned an artist to transform several of Luling's pump jacks into moving sculptures in the shapes of cartoon characters. There's even a Santa Claus and a butterfly to brighten up the streets. Maps to these whimsical pump jacks are available from the chamber of commerce office at 421 E. Davis Street; (830) 875-3214; lulingcc.org.

where to go

Central Texas Oil Patch Museum & Luling Chamber of Commerce Visitors' Center. 421 E. Davis St.; (830) 875-3214; lulingoilmuseum.org. Luling's oil businesses, starting with Rafael Rios No. 1 (an oil field 12 miles long and 2 miles wide), are explored in this museum. Displays include oil well drilling tools, photos, and documents. Open Mon through Sat. Free admission.

Luling Zedler Mill Paddling Trail. 5 miles west of Luling, where US 90 crosses the San Marcos River; tpwd.texas.gov/fishboat/boat/paddlingtrails/inland/luling. In the 1870s both a gristmill and cotton mill were built at this site to harness the power of the San Marcos River. The cotton gin was destroyed by flash flood, then rebuilt, only to become an electric plant.

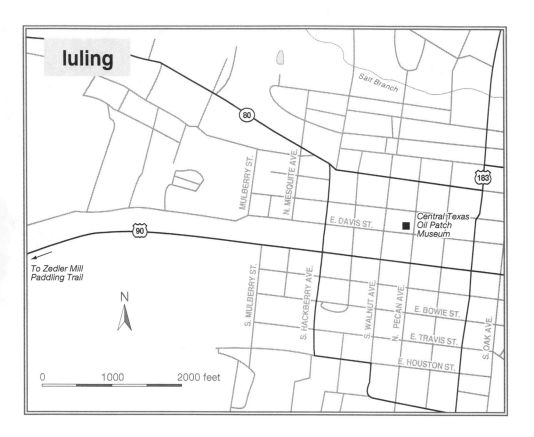

This site became part of Texas's first paddling trail, operated by Texas Parks and Wildlife. You'll put into the river 6 miles upstream, then come out at Zedler Mill, located within city limits. (There's a dam beyond the mill, so be careful not to go beyond the mill.) Check the website for information on local canoe rentals, shuttles, and even GPS coordinates along the river. Free admission.

Palmetto State Park. 78 Park Road 11 South (6 miles southeast of town on US 183, then southwest on Park Road for 2 miles); (830) 672-3266; tpwd.texas.gov. Along the banks of the San Marcos River, Palmetto State Park is a topographical anomaly amid gently rolling farm and ranch land. According to scientists, the river shifted course thousands of years ago, leaving a huge deposit of silt. This sediment absorbed rain- and groundwater, nurturing a marshy swamp estimated to be more than 18,000 years old. Now part of the state park, the swamp is filled with palmettos as well as moss-draped trees, 4-foot-tall irises, and many bird species. Nature trails wind through the area. The park has full hookups and tent sites. There's also picnicking, but bring along mosquito repellent during the warmer months. Open daily. Fee.

where to eat

Luling City Market. 633 Davis St.; (830) 875-9019. This is small-town barbecue the way it ought to be: served up in a no-frills meat market, with ambience replaced by local atmosphere. The Luling City Market turns out smoked brisket, sausage, and ribs. Open Mon through Sat. $.

day trip 02

south

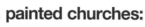

>>> **painted churches:**
flatonia, praha, schulenburg, dubina,
ammannsville, hostyn, high hill

This day trip continues the journey of South Day Trip 01 on US 90, traveling east of Luling to the small German and Czech communities where the largest building in town is often a historic church. These are called collectively the Painted Churches of Texas, known for their elaborately painted interiors and faux details such as marbleized columns, all reminders of the homelands left behind.

The churches on this tour are open occasionally, but, if you drive by, it's worth a stop to see if you might be able to take a peek at the beautiful interiors. The Schulenburg Chamber of Commerce (618 N. Main St.; 979-743-4514; schulenburgchamber.org) offers guided group tours with prior arrangement and also offers maps to the locations. You'll also find more details about these churches in the PBS documentary *The Painted Churches of Texas* and its accompanying website, klru.org/paintedchurches.

flatonia

Return to US 90 and continue east to the small town of Flatonia. This community was settled by English, German, Bohemian, and Czech immigrants, many of whom came to the US in the 1850s and 1860s to avoid Austro-Hungarian oppression.

Flatonia is famous for Czhilispiel, a huge celebration each October that draws thousands of visitors with chili and barbecue cook-offs and live entertainment.

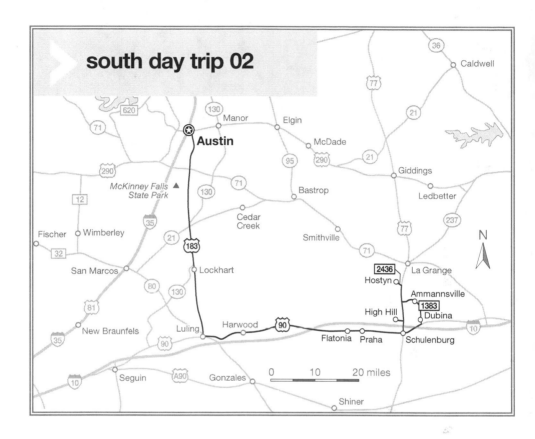

south day trip 02

where to go

E. A. Arnim Archives and Museum. 101 E. North Main St.; (361) 865-3455; arnimmuseum .org. This local history museum contains exhibits on Flatonia's early days and its settlement by many cultural groups. Open Thurs through Sat and by appointment. Free admission.

Flatonia Photo Pavilion. Penn and Main Streets at 422 E. Main St. This simple park is primarily of interest to train buffs. Flatonia holds a special place in the hearts of train lovers thanks to its position along north–south and east–west cross rails. This elevated, open-air pavilion, located by the cross rails, provides a safe place for train viewing. Free admission.

Railroad Tower. Downtown at 104 E. Main St.; (361) 865-3920; flatoniachamber.com. Train buffs also can enjoy a view of the old Railroad Tower, one of the longest-standing switch towers in the state. The switch was manually operated until 1997; previously open for touring, it was damaged by a car in 2014. Surrounding the tower, though, you'll find a long park that follows the rails, a nice place for viewing the trains or just taking a small-town stroll. Free admission.

praha

Three miles east of Flatonia on US 90 is Praha (the Czech spelling for "Prague"). Named for its European counterpart, Praha holds a predominantly Czech population, descendants of immigrants who came here in 1855.

where to go

Assumption of the Blessed Virgin Mary Church. 821 FM 1295 (2 miles east of US 90); (361) 596-4674; stmaryspraha.org. The main structure in Praha is the Assumption of the Blessed Virgin Mary Church, often called St. Mary's. Built in 1895, it is one of a half-dozen painted churches in the area. Although few examples remain today, they were not unusual in the 19th century.

St. Mary's has a beautifully painted vaulted ceiling, the work of Swiss-born artist Gottfried Flury. Never retouched, the 1895 murals on the tongue-and-groove ceiling depict golden angels high over a pastoral setting. This Praha church, as well as ones in High Hill and Ammannsville, are listed on the National Register of Historic Places. Free admission.

schulenburg

Continue east on US 90 to the agricultural community of Schulenburg (meaning "school town" in German). The Carnation milk company's first plant was built in Schulenburg in 1929, and even today dairy products generate a major source of income for the area. Schulenburg is known as the "home of the painted churches," although the elaborately painted structures are actually located in nearby small communities.

where to go

Painted Churches Tour. With two- or three-week notice, the Schulenburg Chamber of Commerce (866-504-5294 or 979-743-4514; schulenburgchamber.org) provides guides for tour groups of 10 or more. The guided tour includes many of the churches found in this chapter: Praha's Assumption of the Blessed Virgin Mary Church, Dubina's Saints Cyril and Methodius Catholic Church, Ammannsville's St. John the Baptist Catholic Church, and High Hill's Nativity of the Blessed Virgin Mary Church. You can always enjoy a self-guided tour; maps of the church locations are available at the Schulenburg chamber office at 618 N. Main St.

where to eat

Oakridge Smokehouse Restaurant. I-10 and US 77 at 712 US 77; (800) 320-5766 or (979) 743-3372; oakridge-smokehouse.com. Hungry travelers between San Antonio and Houston know all about Oakridge Smokehouse. In business since the 1940s, this family-owned company churns out barbecue and sausage to please travelers and mail-order customers. The comfortable restaurant is popular with families, not just for its extensive menu, but also for its large gift shop up front. $–$$.

dubina

From Schulenburg, head northeast on US 90 to the intersection with FM 1383. Turn north on 1383 and continue just over 2 miles to the community of Dubina. Nicknamed the "Mother of Czechs in Texas," Dubina holds the title as the first Czech settlement in the Lone Star State. Even its name—derived from the term for an oak grove—harkens back to its Czech roots.

where to go

Saints Cyril and Methodius Catholic Church. FM 1383; (979) 725-6714. Built in 1909, this church is home to spectacular murals. Covered over during a 1952 remodel, the paintings were uncovered in 1981 and renovated by a local parishioner. The murals depict winged angels and elaborate stenciling. Mass is held here Sun at 9 a.m. Free admission.

ammannsville

From Dubina continue north on FM 1383, turning west as FM 1383 intersects with FM 1965 and continues as FM 1383. Ammannsville was settled by both German and Czech immigrants in the 1870s, growing by 1900 to include multiple stores, blacksmiths, a physician, and two gins. Eventually the population of this agricultural community dwindled, though, and today only about 40 or so residents call Ammannsville home.

where to go

St. John the Baptist Catholic Church. 7745 Mensik Rd.; (979) 743-3117. Originally built along with a school in 1890, the first church was destroyed by a hurricane in 1909 and the rebuilt church burned a few years later. Designed by architect John Bujnoch, the church was again rebuilt in 1918. This painted church has stained-glass windows illustrating the Czech history of the parish. Mass is still held here on Sun. Free admission.

hostyn

From Ammannsville continue west on FM 1383 to the intersection with US 77, turning north to the intersection of FM 2436. Turn left on FM 2436 and continue 1 mile to the community of Hostyn.

It's easy to see why this town was first named Bluff; the town overlooks the Colorado River. Settled by Germans in the 1830s and joined by Czech settlers 20 years later, the name was later changed to Hostyn after a Moravian city.

where to go

Hostyn Grotto. 936 FM 2436. This grotto, a replica of France's Grotto of Lourdes, was constructed in 1925 in thanks for the end of the 1924–25 drought. The grotto is located at the Holy Rosary Catholic Church; the grounds are also home to an adjoining cemetery. The cemetery is of interest not only for its Czech tombstones but also for the graves of a father and son buried side by side—although they fought on opposing sides during the Civil War. Open during daylight hours. Free admission.

high hill

From Hostyn return to US 77 and head south just over 5 miles to the intersection with FM 956. Turn right and head west on FM 956 for slightly more than a mile to the intersection with FM 2672. Turn left and drive south for 2.7 miles to the community of High Hill.

This town was once a thriving community on a stagecoach line but, when bypassed by the railroad in 1874, the population began dwindling—but not before the construction of the Nativity of the Blessed Virgin Mary Church, also known as St. Mary.

where to go

Nativity of the Blessed Virgin Mary Church. 2833 FM 2672; stmary-highhill.com. Also called St. Mary, this structure was built in 1906 and painted six years later. The Gothic-style redbrick building designed by Texas architect Leo Dielmann is noted for its wooden columns painted to resemble marble, stained-glass windows, and religious statuary. The church also has a history of a European-style seating arrangement, with women on the left and men on the right. Mass is held Sat at 6:30 p.m. and Wed at 7 a.m. Free admission.

day trip 03

south

>>> **texas history:**
gonzales, shiner, yoakum

This history-filled day trip offers a look at a historic battleground, one of Texas's most popular breweries, and one of the world's biggest leather producers. To begin this trip, head south on US 183 through Lockhart and Luling (see South Day Trip 01 for information on attractions in those cities).

gonzales

Continue south on US 183 for 13 miles to Gonzales, one of Texas's most historic cities. This is the "Come and Take It" town where the Texas Revolution began in 1835.

Plagued by constant attacks by Native Americans, Gonzales's citizens received a small brass cannon for protection sent by the Mexican government in 1831. Four years later, when relations between Texas and Mexico soured, more than 150 Mexican soldiers staged a battle to retrieve the weapon. The soldiers were faced with 18 Gonzaleans, who stalled the army while other citizens rolled out the small fieldpiece and prepared for action. Meanwhile, other townsfolk sewed the first battle flag of Texas, which pictured a cannon beneath the words "Come and Take It," a motto by which Gonzales is still known. The Texans fired a shot and the Mexican troops retreated. Although the confrontation was brief, it set off the Texas Revolution.

The site of this historic first conflict is marked by a monument located 7 miles southwest of Gonzales on TX 97. The first shots were fired a half mile north of the present monument.

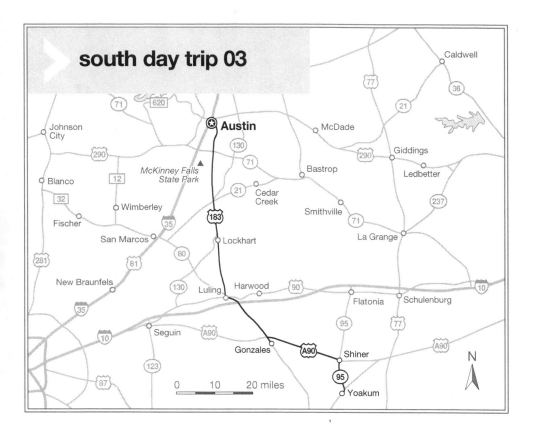

where to go

Gonzales Chamber of Commerce & Agriculture. 414 St. Lawrence St.; (888) 672-1095; gonzalestexas.com. Located in the Old Jail Museum, this office has brochures on local attractions and events. Open daily.

Gonzales Memorial Museum. 414 Smith St.; (830) 672-6350; gonzales.texas.gov. This museum is dedicated to the history of Gonzales and honors "The Immortal 32," members of the Gonzales Rangers who died defending the Alamo. Exhibits include the original "Come and Take It" cannon. Open daily. Free admission.

Old Jail Museum. 414 St. Lawrence St.; (830) 263-4663; gonzalestexas.com. This unusual museum is housed in the old Gonzales jail, built in 1887 and used until 1975. Downstairs you can tour the room where female prisoners and mentally ill persons once were incarcerated together. Exhibits include jail weapons created from spoons and bedsprings.

The walls of the second floor are chiseled with graffiti of past residents. The large room is rimmed with iron cells, all overlooking a reproduction of the old gallows that carried off its last hanging in 1921. According to legend, this prisoner continually watched the clocks on the adjacent courthouse, counting the hours he had left to live. He swore that he was innocent and said that if he were hanged, the clocks would never keep accurate time again. Although the four clock faces have been changed since then, none of them has ever kept the same time again. Open Tues through Sat. Free admission.

Pioneer Village Living History Center. 2122 N. St. Joseph St. (0.5 mile north of town on US 183); (830) 672-2157; texasindependencetrail.com. This center takes visitors back to Gonzales's frontier days. The village is composed of log cabins, a cypress-constructed house, a grand Victorian house, a smokehouse, a blacksmith shop, and a church. The village also stages reenactments, including the "Come and Take It" battle reenactment in Oct. Open 1 to 5 p.m. Tues through Sun; group tours by appointment. Fee.

shiner

Take US 90A east of Gonzales for 18 miles to the tiny town of Shiner, best known as the home of Shiner Beer. If you make the trip during the week, stop by the Spoetzl Brewery for a free tour and a sample of the hometown product.

where to go

Cigar Factory and Green Cabin Museums. 817 N. Avenue E (Highway 90-A); (361) 594-4180; shinertx.com. Two historic buildings grace Shiner's downtown. The Louis Ehlers Cigar Factory opened in 1895, and their products once enjoyed widespread popularity in the area. The Green Cabin Museum preserves the home of prominent local businessman William Green Jr. The cabin was built in 1853. The Shiner Chamber of Commerce office is next door, offering visitors guides and maps. Open Mon through Wed and Fri. Free admission.

Edwin Wolters Memorial Museum. 306 S. Avenue I (off TX 95 South); (361) 594-3774. This museum is filled with home implements, weapons, fossils, and even a country store representing the community's early days. Open Wed through Sat. Free admission.

The Gaslight Theatre. 207 E. Seventh St.; (361) 594-2079; shinergaslight.org. Shiner's Gaslight Theatre's graceful facade has been a downtown landmark since 1895 and was the town's social center for many years. Now restored and modernized, it hosts amateur stage productions several times a year. Call for information on group tours, which are available by appointment.

Spoetzl Brewery. 603 E. Brewery St. (off TX 95 North); (361) 594-3852; shiner.com. This tiny but historic brewery was founded in 1909 by Kosmos Spoetzl, a Bavarian brewmaster. Here several Shiner beers are produced in one of the smallest commercial brew kettles in the country and the oldest independent brewery in Texas. Across the street, a museum and gift shop overflow with Shiner memorabilia, antiques, and photos of Spoetzl's early days. Brewery tours are conducted on weekdays every half hour starting at 10:30 a.m. on Mon through Sat and 12:30 p.m. on Sun. Last tour is at 4:30 p.m. every day.

Welhausen Park. 802 N. Avenue E (Highway 90-A); (361) 594-3362; shinertexas.gov. This park occupies a full city block just west of downtown. Beneath its large shade trees, you'll see an old-time bandstand, children's playscape, and several granite markers each commemorating historic events in the city's past. It's a good spot for a picnic. Free admission.

where to stay

The Old Kasper House Victorian Inn. 219 Avenue C; (361) 594-4336; oldkasperhousetx .com. This bed-and-breakfast is located in the former home of a cotton ginner and his wife from eastern Europe who was best known as a relative of Gregor Mendel, discoverer of genetic information (remember those Mendel pea models in Biology I?). Today the two-story house is a great small-town getaway, offering five rooms with private baths as well as several separate cottages on the property. $–$$.

yoakum

From Shiner drive south on TX 95 for 8 miles to US 77A. Turn right and continue for 2 miles. Yoakum was the starting point of many cattle drives along the Chisholm Trail, and in 1887

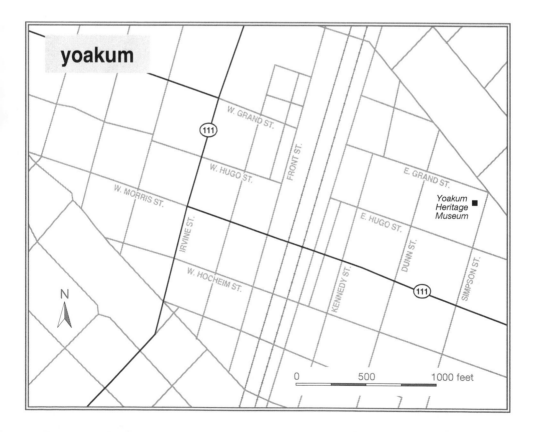

it became the junction for the San Antonio and Aransas Pass Railroad. When the railroad came to town, meatpacking houses followed.

In 1919 the first tannery opened, producing leather knee pads for cotton pickers. Soon other leather businesses arrived, and eventually Yoakum earned its title as "Leather Capital of the World." Today many of these leather manufacturers sell primarily to distributors and through online catalogs, such as Double J Saddlery, doublejsaddlery.com.

where to go

Yoakum Heritage Museum. 312 Simpson St.; (361) 293-7022. This two-story Victorian home dates from the early 1900s and is filled with Yoakum memorabilia, from railroad paraphernalia to household items. The most interesting exhibit area is the Leather Room, with its displays on the town's leather industry and featuring ornate handmade saddles. Open Sun, Tues, and Thurs 1 to 4 p.m. and 10 a.m. to 4 p.m. on Fri. Free admission.

Return home from Yoakum by retracing your steps or by heading north on TX 95 to Flatonia. From here go west on either I-10 or US 90.

day trip 04

south

shop 'til you drop:
buda, san marcos

Bring your credit card on this day trip, as it leads to some of Texas's finest outlet shopping destinations. Ever-expanding outlet malls featuring world-famous labels line I-35 as you head south to Buda and San Marcos.

buda

Head south from Austin on I-35 to the small town of Buda, located on Loop 4 to the west of the highway. This sleepy railroad town is a busy spot on weekends, when shoppers come to hunt antiques.

Buda is one of the most mispronounced communities in Texas (and with names like Gruene, Leakey, and Boerne around, that's saying a lot). To sound like a local, just say "b-YOU-da." The name has caused more than one visitor to come here expecting an Old-World Hungarian settlement. Though possibly a reference to Budapest, it's more likely of Spanish origin. According to legend, several widows cooked in the local hotel restaurant that was popular with employees of the International–Great Northern Railroad. The Spanish word for "widow" is *viuda*. Since the *v* is pronounced as a *b* in Spanish, Buda may be a phonetic spelling for *viuda*.

Buda is still a railroad town, with double tracks running parallel to Main Street.

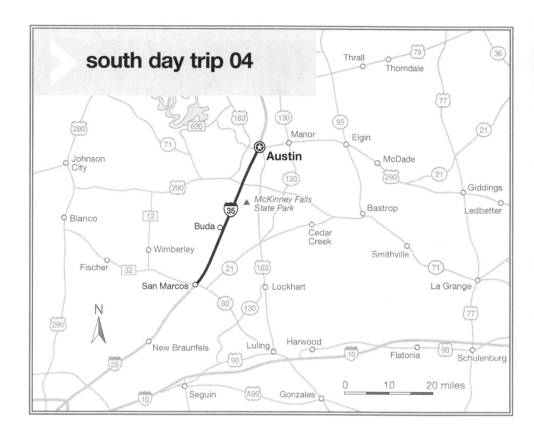

south day trip 04

where to shop

Buda's historic downtown is full of shops and boutiques selling antiques, fashions, home decor, and gourmet foods. Many of these are located in a 2-block stretch of Main Street.

Cabela's Buda. 15570 I-35; (512) 295-1100; cabelas.com. This Texas-size sporting goods store is an attraction for everyone. The 185,000-square-foot store features a large freshwater aquarium as well as a large "mountain" exhibit dotted with trophy animals of all types. The store also has an indoor archery range, dog kennels, a restaurant, live bait, and RV parking. Open daily.

san marcos

Head south on I-35 to San Marcos, the home of Texas State University, two Texas-size outlet malls, and the crystal-clear San Marcos River. Like the neighboring community of New Braunfels, San Marcos is best known for its pure spring waters. The San Marcos River, used by humans for more than 13,000 years, flows through town, providing the city with beautiful

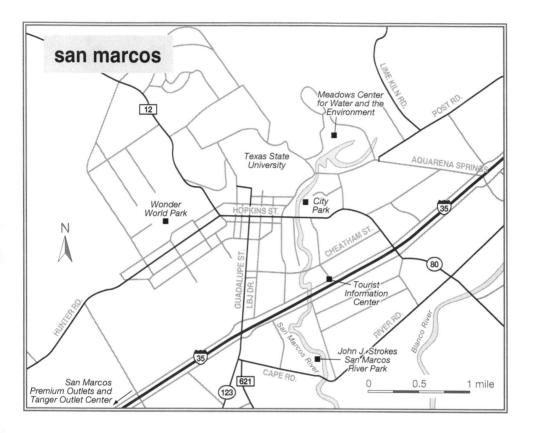

swimming and snorkeling spots and a family education park. The campus of Texas State University is located along a portion of the river as well.

Blessed with natural beauty, this city of 63,220 is a popular tourist town. One of the best-known attractions is the Meadows Center for Water and the Environment, which features the ecological and archaeological riches of the region. Nearby, another park offers a look at San Marcos's natural attractions both above and below the ground. Scientists believe Wonder Cave was created during a violent earthquake 30 million years ago.

There's no better way to see San Marcos during warm weather than from the river. Across from Texas State University, the Lions Club (512-396-5466; tubesanmarcos.com) rents inner tubes from May through September so that you can float down the San Marcos Loop. The floating excursion, in 72°F water, takes about an hour and a half. Snorkeling is popular here as well, and you might see a freshwater prawn (which can reach 12 inches in length), the rare San Marcos salamander, or some of the 52 species of fish.

Of course, not all of San Marcos's attractions are natural. Downtown, shops are encouraged to feature Texas-made items. While you're downtown, you'll notice the city's fresh face, thanks to more than $16 million in renovations in the last decade, transforming it into a shopping and dining area. Every Saturday the San Marcos Farmers Market takes place near the courthouse at 155 E. San Antonio St. Shop for arts and crafts, antiques, and specialty food and gift items at this old-fashioned outdoor market.

The Texas theme even carries into a popular downtown bed-and-breakfast. The Crystal River Inn offers accommodations in rooms named for Texas rivers. It also offers popular murder mystery weekends.

where to go

Tourist Information Center. 617 I-35, on the northwest side of town at exit 204B (C. M. Allen Parkway); (512) 393-5930; toursanmarcos.com. Traveling from the north, take exit 204B. From the south, take exit 205. Stop here for brochures on area attractions and accommodations, as well as free maps. Open Mon through Sat. Free admission.

Calaboose African American History Museum. 200 W. Martin Luther King Dr.; (512) 393-8121; calaboosemuseum.com. Housed in the 1873 building that served as Hays County's first jail, this museum preserves the history of the African Americans of San Marcos. Along with an extensive collection of books and artifacts, the museum also schedules frequent educational programs and public events. Open Sat 10 a.m. to 3 p.m. and by appointment. Donation.

Central Texas Wing Museum. 1841 Airport Dr.; (512) 396-1943; centraltexaswing.org. Operated by the Central Texas Wing of the Commemorative Air Force, the museum is housed in a vintage wooden hangar at the San Marcos Municipal Airport. This collection contains World War II artifacts and several historic aircraft. A unique display is a replica of the CAF Japanese "Kate," built for the movie *Tora! Tora! Tora!* Open Mon, Wed, Fri, and Sat 9 a.m. to 4 p.m. Donation of $10 suggested.

John J. Stokes San Marcos River Park. From TX 80 turn right on River Road for about 1 mile; turn left on County Road to the island where the park is located at 600 Cape St. Operated by the City of San Marcos, this day-use park is also known as Thompson's Island and is located across the river from the A. E. Wood State Fish Hatchery. The park offers river access but no facilities. Free admission.

Lyndon Baines Johnson Museum of San Marcos. 131 N. Guadalupe St. (across from the courthouse); (512) 353-3300; lbjmuseum.com. This museum features LBJ's educational ties to the region, from his years at Texas State University to his teaching days in Cotulla to the signing of the Education Bill. Open Thurs through Sat 11 a.m. to 5 p.m. Free admission.

The Meadows Center for Water and the Environment. 201 San Marcos Springs Dr.; (512) 245-9200; meadowscenter.txstate.edu. This former resort dates to 1928, when A. B. Rogers purchased 125 acres at the headwaters of the San Marcos to create a grand hotel. He added glass-bottom boats to cruise Spring Lake, which is fed by more than 200 springs that produce 150 million gallons of water daily. This 98-percent-pure water is home to many fish (including white albino catfish) and various types of plant life. Today visitors can still enjoy a cruise in the glass-bottom boats and will see the site of an underwater archaeological dig that unearthed the remains of Clovis Man, one of the hunter-gatherers who lived along the river more than 13,000 years ago.

Formerly Aquarena Springs (then Aquarena Center), a commercial amusement park, the Meadows Center is now part of Texas State University and focuses on ecotourism, with exhibits and activities aimed at introducing visitors of all ages to the natural history and attractions of this region. In addition to the glass-bottom boat rides, the park features an endangered species exhibit and plenty of educational fun. Open daily, although hours change seasonally. Free admission; fee for glass-bottom boat rides.

Wittliff Collection at the Alkek Library. 601 University Dr., Texas State University; (512) 245-2313; thewittliffcollections.txstate.edu. Located on the seventh floor of the Albert B. Alkek Library, the gallery traces the history of photography from the 19th century through today in both Mexico and the southwestern US. Also includes the Southwestern Writers Collection. Open daily; hours change with university schedule. Free admission.

Wonder World Park. 1000 Prospect St. (exit at Wonder World Drive on the south side of San Marcos and follow signs for about a mile); (512) 392-6711; wonderworldpark.com. A guided tour lasting nearly 1.5 hours covers the entire park, including the 7.5-acre **Texas Wildlife Petting Park,** the state's largest petting zoo. A miniature train chugs through the animal enclosure, stopping to allow riders to pet and feed white-tailed deer, wild turkeys, and many exotic species.

The next stop on the tour is **Wonder Cave,** created during a 3.5-minute earthquake 30 million years ago. The same earthquake produced the Balcones Fault, an 1,800-mile line separating the western Hill Country from the flat eastern farmland. Within the cave is the actual crack in the two land masses, where huge boulders lodged in the fissure. At the end of the cave tour, take the elevator ride to the top of the 110-foot **Tejas Tower,** which offers a spectacular view of the Balcones Fault and the contrasting terrain it produced.

The last stop is the **Anti-Gravity House,** a structure employing optical illusions and a slanted floor to create the feeling that you're leaning backward. In this house, water appears to run uphill. Open daily. Fee.

where to shop

San Marcos Premium Outlets. 3939 I-35 South, #900 (exit 200 from I-35); (512) 396-2200; premiumoutlets.com. This open-air mall, designed in Venetian style, ranks as one of the state's top tourist destinations. Luggage, shoes, leather goods, outdoor gear, china, kitchen goods, and other specialties are offered for sale. Chartered buses from as far as Dallas and Houston stop here regularly. For many travelers, this mall with more than 145 stores ranks as a day trip in itself (and many opt to extend with an overnight stay at one of the limited service accommodations in the area). Open daily.

Tanger Outlet Center. 4015 I-35 South (exit 200 from I-35); (800) 408-8424 or (512) 396-7446; tangeroutlet.com/sanmarcos. Shops feature name-brand designers and manufacturers in this open-air mall. Housewares, footwear, home furnishings, leather goods, perfumes, and books are available. Open daily.

where to stay

Crystal River Inn. 326 W. Hopkins St.; (888) 396-3739 or (512) 396-3739; crystalriverinn .com. The Crystal River Inn has elegant Victorian accommodations in rooms named for Texas waterways. Owners Cathy and Mike Dillon provide guests with a selection of special packages, including tubing on the San Marcos River and popular murder mystery weekends where costumed guests work to solve a mystery using clues based on actual events in San Marcos history. $$–$$$.

day trip 05

south

concrete city:
seguin

Many towns boast nicknames, from Austin's "River City" to San Antonio's "Alamo City." Seguin, though, has one of the most unusual: "The Mother of Concrete Cities." A Seguin chemist held several concrete production patents, which accounts for the use of the material in more than 90 area buildings by the end of the 19th century.

seguin

You can reach Seguin (pronounced "se-GEEN") by driving south on I-35 from Austin through San Marcos (see South Day Trip 04 for city attractions). It's a 36-mile trip to this town on the Guadalupe River named for Lieutenant Colonel Juan Seguin, a hero of the Texas Revolution. Prior to the Mexican invasion of 1837, Seguin was ordered by his superiors to destroy San Antonio. He refused, thus saving the city.

The most beautiful area of Seguin is Max Starcke Park. It offers picnic tables under huge pecan, oak, and cypress trees, and a winding drive along the Guadalupe River. Seguin is known for its huge pecan trees and boasts what was once the "World's Largest Pecan" on the courthouse lawn at Court Street.

where to go

Seguin Tourist Information Center. 116 N. Camp St.; (830) 379-6382; visitseguin.com. Stop here for brochures and maps. Open Mon through Fri.

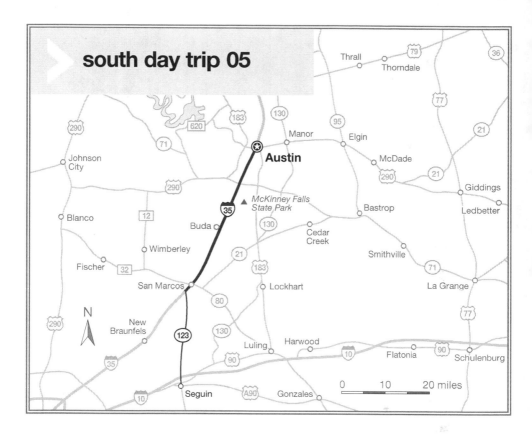

south day trip 05

Max Starcke Park. South side of town, off TX 123; (830) 401-2480; seguintexas.gov. Make time for this pleasant park, where visitors can enjoy golf, tennis, and baseball as well as many riverside picnic spots. A large wave pool is open seasonally. Free admission; fee for wave pool.

Sebastopol House. 704 Zorn St.; (830) 379-4833; seguintexas.com. This is one of the best examples of the early use of concrete in the Southwest. Sebastopol was once a large home constructed of concrete with a plaster overlay. Today it is open for tours and contains exhibits illustrating the construction of this historic building and its restoration in 1988. Guided tours given hourly Thurs through Sun 9 a.m. to 4 p.m. Free admission.

The Seguin–Guadalupe County Heritage Museum. 114 N. River St.; (830) 372-0965; heritagemuseum.net. This local history museum is housed in a former grocery store. Exhibits trace the multicultural heritage of Seguin's early settlers. Open Tues, Thurs, and Sat from 10 a.m. to 3 p.m. Free admission.

Seguin's Lakes. Seguin is surrounded by four lakes on the Guadalupe River that offer bass, crappie, and catfish fishing, including lighted docks for night fishing. RV facilities are available

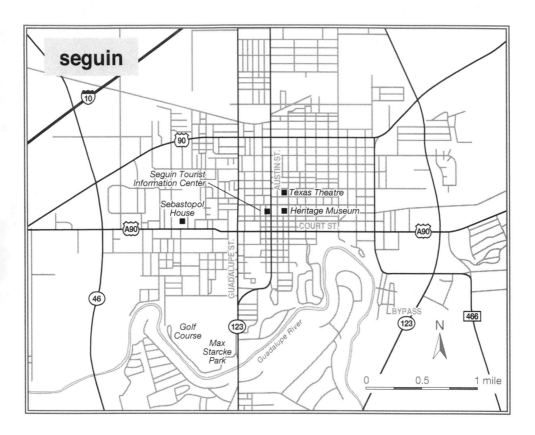

as well. The lakes include Lake Dunlap (I-10 to TX 46 exit west of Seguin, then 8 miles on TX 46); Lake McQueeney (I-10 to FM 78 exit, then west for 3 miles to FM 725, then turn right and continue for 1 mile); Lake Placid (I-10 to FM 464 exit, stay on access road); and Meadow Lake (I-10 to TX 123 bypass, then south for 4 miles).

The Stephen & Mary Birch Texas Theatre. 425 N. Austin St.; (830) 372-6168; thetexas .org. This 1931 theater has been used for scenes in two movies: *Raggedy Man* and *The Great Waldo Pepper*. Now a fully restored theater for the performing arts, it still sports its original marquee and recalls the old days of small-town Texas theaters. Although group tours are available by appointment, feel free to knock on the door and, if volunteers are working, you may score a free look inside.

True Women Tours. Fans of Janice Woods Windle's *True Women* can take a guided tour of the sites mentioned in this bestseller and seen in the television miniseries. Led by local docents, the tours take a look at sites that play an important role in the historical novel by the Seguin native: the live oak–shaded King Cemetery, the old First Methodist Church where two *True Women* characters were married, and the river where horses were daringly rescued in the tale.

flower power

*Is it spring? Grab the car keys in one hand, your camera in the other, and get ready for a bloomin' good time! Starting in late March and extending into early summer, wildflowers line the roadways throughout central and south Texas. The best way to find the top fields is with a quick call to the **Texas Department of Transportation's wildflower hotline** (800-452-9292). The hotline is active from mid-March until early May, and you can request information by region (Central Texas and Hill Country covers most of this book's scope).*

One of the most memorable stops is the Bettie Moss King Home, near the King Cemetery. The home, with its wraparound porch and shady lawn, was where several generations of the King family were raised and was also the childhood home of author Janice Woods Windle. For tours or a printed guide for a self-driving tour, contact the visitor center at (830) 401-0810. Fee for guided tour.

Wave Pool & Aquatic Center. Max Starcke Park East; (830) 401-2480. In this Texas-size pool, youngsters can cool off under the Mushroom Shower or splash in the simulated waves. Nearby, the sprawling Kids Kingdom Playscape makes an excellent stop for energetic young travelers as well. Open seasonally. Fee.

southwest

day trip 01

southwest

>>> **the alamo city:**
san antonio

Famous humorist Will Rogers once dubbed San Antonio "one of America's four unique cities," and it's easy to agree with the sentiment as you experience the city's gloriously multicultural atmosphere. No recent upstart among Texas cities, San Antonio was an important cultural and commercial crossroads long before the Texans' desperate struggle for independence. The city's history still lives as you walk its winding streets or take a river taxi through quiet canals.

san antonio

San Antonio has the reputation of a fun-loving town. Located 80 miles south of Austin on I-35, the city always has something going on to attract visitors. No matter when you choose to visit, you can bet that somebody, somewhere, is hosting a festival. Perhaps it has something to do with the sunshine or the fresh air, but whatever it is, you can feel it. It sizzles up like fajitas out of the city's Latino heritage, which abounds with colorful traditions and vivid memories.

San Antonio's rich cultural past dates to the early Native Americans who settled the area. They were followed by the 17th-century Spaniards, who came here in search of wealth. Later a group of Franciscan friars established a chain of missions designed to convert the tribes of the Southwest to Christianity. In 1718 Mission San Antonio de Valero (better known as the Alamo) became the first of five such structures in the city.

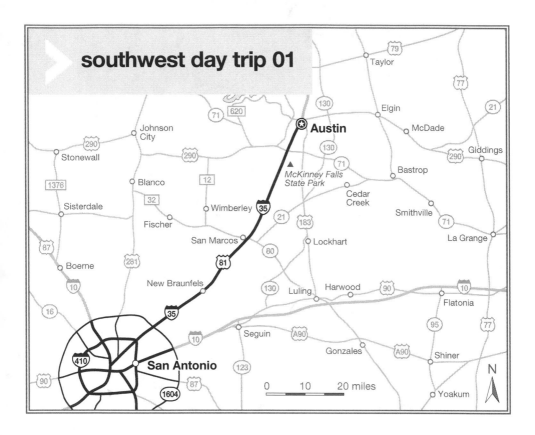

southwest day trip 01

Except for the Alamo, the missions are found in the San Antonio Missions National Historical Park, located within the city limits. The National Park Service has assigned interpretive themes to each of the four—the active parish churches of Mission Concepción, Mission San Juan Capistrano, Mission San Francisco de la Espada, and Mission San José. The latter, established in 1720, hosts a colorful "Mariachi Mass" each Sunday at noon.

San Antonio is also a foodie's paradise. This is the city that heralded the birth of fajitas—strips of marinated charcoal-grilled skirt steak. Here you'll also find to-die-for guacamole, pico de gallo (a Mexican condiment of onions, tomatoes, and chiles), and fresh flour tortillas.

With two excellent theme parks, a world-class zoo, and wonderful museums, San Antonio offers much more to see and do than this book can possibly list. For a complete rundown of possibilities, contact the San Antonio Convention and Visitor Bureau, visitsanantonio.com, (210) 244-2000. Stop in the Official Visitor Information Center at 317 Alamo Plaza (across from the Alamo), where you can pick up information. Open daily.

downtown: river walk area

San Antonio's River Walk is a centerpiece of the city and a must-see for visitors. The Paseo del Rio, as it's also called, is a European-style river walk that lies below street level. Part of an urban renovation project that began in 1939, the River Walk is now a top San Antonio attraction. Its winding sidewalks, which follow an arm of the San Antonio River, are lined with two-story specialty shops, sidewalk cafes, luxury hotels, art galleries, and bars. Like New Orleans's Bourbon Street, this area of San Antonio has an atmosphere all its own. Arched bridges connect the two sides of the walk, so visitors never have to venture up to street level.

One of the busiest sections of the Paseo del Rio extends from the Hyatt Regency Riverwalk at Crockett Street to the Hilton Palacio del Rio Hotel at Market Street. This stretch of walk boasts most of the sidewalk restaurants and shops. From Commerce Street, you can head up to the Henry B. Gonzales Convention Center and the Rivercenter Mall.

where to go

The Alamo. 300 Alamo Plaza, between Houston and Crockett Streets; (210) 225-1391; thealamo.org. Located in the very heart of San Antonio, the Alamo was once surrounded on all sides by the forces of Mexico's General Santa Anna. Now it's enveloped by high-rise office structures and a central plaza.

This "Cradle of Texas Liberty," situated on the east side of Alamo Plaza, is probably the most famous spot in Texas. Established in 1718 as the Mission San Antonio de Valero, it plunged into history on March 6, 1836, when 188 men died after being attacked by Santa Anna's Mexican forces. Among the most famous defenders were Jim Bowie, William B. Travis, and Davy Crockett.

A symbol of the state's independence and courage, the Alamo draws continuous crowds throughout the year. Visitors entering the main building, the Shrine, can see exhibits such as Bowie's famous knife and Davy Crockett's rifle, "Old Betsy." Various guided tours are also available, such as the After Hours Tour, Victory or Death Audio Tour, and Young Texans Tour. Those interested also can take a self-guided tour of the museum, the Long Barracks, and the beautiful courtyard. Open daily except Christmas Eve and Christmas Day. Free admission.

AMC Rivercenter 11 with Alamo IMAX. 849 E. Commerce St. (Rivercenter Mall); (888) AMC-4FUN or (210) 228-0351; amctheatres.com/movies/alamo-the-price-of-freedom. This theater features *Alamo . . . The Price of Freedom*, a 45-minute movie about the battle of the Alamo. The six-story screen and six-channel sound immerses you in the glory of the struggle, and it's a good thing to see before visiting the historic site. The theater alternates this movie with other IMAX features, so call for showtimes. Open daily. Fee.

The DoSeum. 2800 Broadway St.; (210) 212-4453; thedoseum.org. Formerly the San Antonio Children's Museum, this attraction features a state-of-the-art building containing

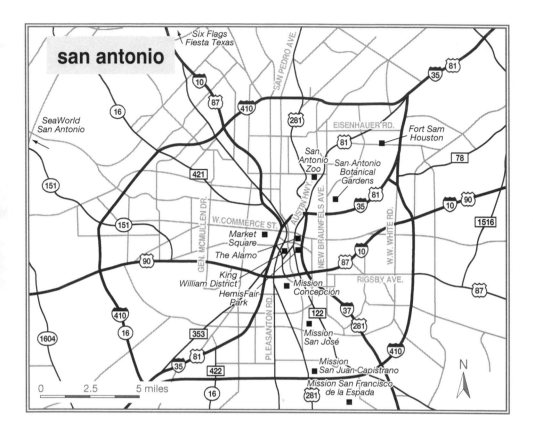

unique interactive exhibits designed to challenge and entertain children and teach problem-solving skills. Open daily. Fee.

Go Rio San Antonio Cruises. 2202 E. Nueva St., and with stops along the River Walk; (210) 227-746; goriocruises.com. If you only have a chance to do one thing in downtown San Antonio, consider a short river cruise. One of the most pleasurable and inexpensive attractions in town, these open barges take passengers on narrated cruises through the heart of San Antonio from morning until late evening. Special dinner cruises afford a romantic look at the city and are arranged by River Walk restaurants. Open daily; hours change seasonally. Fee.

Louis Tussaud's Waxworks. 301 Alamo Plaza; (210) 224-9299; ripleys.com/sanantonio. This attraction has wax figures of movie and TV celebrities as well as a theater of horrors. The "Heroes of the Lone Star" section is interesting, with realistic scenes depicting the fall of the Alamo. Ripley's Believe It or Not! and the 4D Moving Theater are located in the same building, and you can buy separate or combination tickets to the attractions. Open daily. Fee.

Steves Homestead. 509 King William St.; (210) 224-6163; saconservation.org. This grand home was built in 1876 and reflects the splendor of the King William district, which was settled by wealthy German residents of the period. The Victorian mansion's interior is filled with original furniture, and the grounds include several antique carriages and the gardener's quarters, now a visitor center. Both self-guided and guided tours of the home are available. Open daily. Fee.

Tower of the Americas. 739 E. Cesar E. Chavez Blvd.; (210) 223-3101; toweroftheamericas .com. San Francisco has its Golden Gate Bridge, St. Louis has the Arch, and since the 1968 World's Fair, San Antonio has had the Tower of the Americas. From ground level, it's the most recognizable landmark in the San Antonio skyline. At 750 feet, the tower's observation deck and revolving Chart House top-floor restaurant offer an unbeatable view of the city. If

king william

Imagine San Antonio without the River Walk. Without the Tower of the Americas. Without the bustling business that fills this modern metropolis.

It is the late 1800s. Texas is still a frontier, gaining statehood after its years as an independent republic and a territory of Mexico. After years of subsistence on a rugged frontier, San Antonio residents are finally ready for comforts, culture, and a community spirit that emphasizes education, music, and the language of their homeland.

*With these goals in mind, the **King William district** was born. Started by the founder of the utopian community Comfort (see Southwest Day Trip 04), this elegant neighborhood on the banks of the San Antonio River soon attained the status of a superior neighborhood. Going back to the mid-1800s, when this district was populated by the Alamo City's most successful businessmen and their families, many of these frontier citizens were German immigrants with names like Guenther, Wulff, and Heusinger. With their wealth gained in merchandising and investing, they set about building the most lavish homes in the city, most in the grand Victorian style.*

For visitors seeking a romantic getaway in San Antonio, a place to enjoy historic elegance in a quiet neighborhood that's within easy walking distance of the River Walk, King William is an ideal destination. Tucked in a quiet neighborhood beneath towering live oak trees, this area is home to numerous bed-and-breakfast establishments. Ranging from country comfort to antebellum elegance, there's a bed-and-breakfast for every taste.

those don't offer thrills enough for you, check out the Skies Over Texas 4-D Theater Ride (yep, get ready for the 3-D glasses!). Open daily. Fee.

University of Texas Institute of Texan Cultures at San Antonio. 801 E. Cesar Chavez Blvd. at HemisFair Park; (210) 458-2300; texancultures.utsa.edu This fascinating museum features exhibits and a multimedia presentation showcasing the 26 different ethnic groups who came here from around the world to settle the new frontier called Texas. Open daily. Fee.

where to shop

La Villita Historic Arts Village. 418 Villita St. (exit through Hilton Hotel, then 1 block right on S. Alamo Street); (210) 207-8614; lavillitasanantonio.com. This area on the east bank of the San Antonio River was developed in the mid to late 18th century by Mexican settlers who lived, without land title, on the outskirts of the Alamo mission. Today La Villita is San Antonio's finest crafts area, filled with weavers, glassblowers, sculptors, and even boot makers. Within the restored buildings, shops sell everything from woven wall hangings to silver jewelry, and the historic Little Church is often the site of weddings. Most shops open daily. Free admission.

Rivercenter Mall. 849 E. Commerce St.; (210) 225-0000; shoprivercenter.com. Bounded by Commerce, Bowie, Crockett, and Alamo Streets, this three-story mall is home to several anchor stores as well as specialty shops and restaurants. On the enclosed bridge over the river, vendors sell crafts and specialty items. The River Walk makes a U-turn in an outdoor dining area. Open daily.

where to eat

Bliss. 926 S. Presa St.; (210) 225-2547; foodisbliss.com. The perfect name for this chef-owned and -operated restaurant where food is bliss. Serving upscale contemporary America cuisine with an emphasis on season and fresh local ingredients, Bliss offers a menu that changes frequently plus a nice choice of beer and an award-winning wine list. The dining room seats 52, a chef's table in the kitchen seats 10, and a private event dining room serves up to 30 guests. Bliss also offers seasonal outdoor dining on a lovely back patio of the lovingly restored former filling station. $$$

Boudro's. 421 E. Commerce St.; (210) 224-8484; boudros.com. Ask many San Antonians for their favorite River Walk eatery, and you'll hear this name. This steak and seafood restaurant offers the finest in Southwestern cuisine, usually with a twist that makes it unique even among San Antonio's plethora of excellent restaurants. Start with a cactus margarita, a frozen concoction with a jolt of red cactus liqueur. Follow that eye-opener with an appetizer of blue crab seacakes or chili-fried oysters. Save room, though, for Boudro's specialties—coconut shrimp, wood-grilled fish fillet, and the specialty of the house, blackened prime rib. Seating is available on the River Walk or in the dining room. Open daily. $$$.

Schilo's. 424 E. Commerce St.; (210) 223-6692; schilos.com. This restaurant is located up on street level, not on the River Walk, but what it lacks in atmosphere it definitely makes up for in history. Papa Fritz Schilo, a German immigrant, opened a saloon in 1917, but when Prohibition came along, he converted the operation to a deli. It was a lucky break for diners; mere suds could never match the subs and sandwiches that continue to keep this spot packed with locals. Try a Reuben or a ham and cheese, or for dinner go all out with entrees like wiener schnitzel or bratwurst. Open daily 8:30 a.m. to 2 p.m. $.

where to stay

The Emily Morgan Hotel. 705 E. Houston St., next to the Alamo; (800) 824-6674 or (210) 225-5100; emilymorganhotel.com. General Santa Anna was enamored with a mulatto slave named Emily Morgan, who acted as a spy for the Texas army. Thanks in part to her efforts, Sam Houston's troops defeated Santa Anna's men at San Jacinto on April 21, 1836, winning the Texas Revolution. Emily Morgan came to be known as "the Yellow Rose of Texas" and is the namesake of this 177-room hotel. The rooms overlook the Alamo courtyard or Alamo Plaza, and most have Jacuzzis. $$.

Hyatt Regency San Antonio Riverwalk. 123 Losoya St.; (800) 233-1234 or (210) 222-1234; hyatt.com. This beautiful hotel, with its open atrium and glass elevators, is located directly on the River Walk. A stream flows through the hotel outside to the River Walk, where an open-air jazz bar provides nightly entertainment. $$$.

Marriott Plaza San Antonio. 555 S. Alamo St.; (210) 229-1000 or (800) 421-1172; marriott.com. This elegant establishment has the most beautiful grounds of any downtown hotel: 6 acres dotted with gardens, Chinese pheasants, and historic buildings. Most of the 248 rooms and 3 suites have private balconies. The hotel received international attention in 1992 as host of the initializing ceremony of the North American Free Trade Agreement on the grounds. $$$.

Mokara Hotel & Spa. 212 W. Crockett St.; (866) 605-1212; omnihotels.com. Located in a historic building, the Mokara Hotel is aimed at discerning travelers looking for a quiet retreat from the busy River Walk. Along with its luxury rooms and suites, the hotel is also home to the 17,000-square-foot Mokara Spa, the fine-dining restaurant Ostra, and a rooftop cafe. $$$.

Omni La Mansión Del Rio. 112 College St.; (210) 518-1000; omnihotels.com. This Spanish Colonial–style hotel has long been a River Walk favorite with travelers. The structure began as St. Mary's Academy in 1854, later becoming a college, a university, and a law school, until 1966 when it became a hotel. Today the hotel captures the atmosphere of San

> ## hot tamales
>
> *Tamales, both mild and spicy varieties, are found on just about every Tex-Mex menu throughout the state, but they're most popular during the Christmas season. Stores and restaurants sell tamales by the dozen during the holidays, when it's popular to bring them to office parties and home get-togethers.*
>
> *Making tamales at home is a time-consuming job, often tackled by large families as a holiday tradition. Tamales start with the preparation of a hog's head, boiled with garlic, spices, peppers, and cilantro. After cooking, the meat is ground and then simmered with spices.*
>
> *As the filling is prepared, other family members ready the hojas, or corn husks, used to wrap the tamale. Others prepare the masa, a cornmeal worked with lard and seasonings, spread thinly on the shucks before filling with meat. Finally, the tamales are steamed in huge pots.*

Antonio in its architecture, courtyards, and restaurants, and bar, El Colegio, which recalls the building's early days as a school. $$$.

St. Anthony Hotel. 300 E. Travis St.; (210) 227-4392; marriott.com. This historic hotel a few blocks off the River Walk offers 277 rooms, the ReBelle restaurant, a health club, and an outdoor heated swimming pool. $$$.

downtown: market square

Colorful Market Square, bounded by San Saba, Santa Rosa, West Commerce, and Dolorosa Streets, is a busy shopping and dining area from early morning to late evening. It is also the scene of many San Antonio festivals.

To reach Market Square from the River Walk, follow Commerce Street west across the river to just east of I-10. Or leave your car and take an inexpensive ride on the VIA streetcars, the open-air trolleys that stop at many downtown San Antonio attractions. (For information on VIA routes, stop by the Official Visitor Information Center mentioned earlier.)

The history of Market Square goes back to the early 1800s, when Mexico ruled the settlement of San Antonio de Bejar. Fresh produce and meats filled the farmers' market. Originally an open-air market, the structure was built as a WPA project during the Great Depression, a time when farmers sold fresh produce directly from their pickup beds.

Chili con carne, the state dish of Texas, was invented here over a century ago. Back then, young girls known as "chili queens" sold the spicy meat-and-bean concoction from kiosks.

Today Market Square includes the renovated Farmers Market Plaza (rife with Mexican imports and crafts rather than produce), an open-air restaurant and shopping area, and El Mercado, the largest enclosed Mexican-style marketplace in the country. Also located nearby are two historic structures: the Spanish Governor's Palace and Casa Navarro, home of a Texas patriot.

where to go

Casa Navarro State Historic Site. 228 S. Laredo St.; (210) 226-4801; thc.texas.gov/historic-sites/casa-navarro-state-historic-site. This was formerly the residence of José Antonio Navarro (1795–1871), a signer of the Texas Declaration of Independence. The adobe and limestone structure, located just a short walk from Market Square, includes an office used by Navarro, who was a lawyer and legislator. Open Tues through Sun. Fee.

El Mercado. 514 W. Commerce St.; (210) 207 8600; marketsquaresa.com. Styled after a typical Mexican market, El Mercado's shops sell a profusion of goods, from silver jewelry, Mexican dresses, and piñatas to onyx chess sets, leather goods, and much more. Prices are slightly higher than in the Mexican border markets, and you can't bargain with the vendors like you can south of the border. Open daily. Free admission.

Spanish Governor's Palace. 105 Plaza de Armas, (210) 207-7527; spanishgovernorspalace.org. Part of an old Spanish fort that was built at the site in 1722, this structure was converted to a military commander's residence in 1749. San Antonio was once the capital of the Spanish province of Texas, and the Spanish governors occasionally resided here. The walls are 3 feet thick, and the home is filled with Spanish Colonial antiques. Open Tues through Sun. Fee.

where to eat

La Margarita. 120 Produce Row; (210) 227-7140; lamargarita.com. This establishment also is owned by Mi Tierra and is best known for its excellent fajitas, which are brought to your table in cast-iron skillets. Open Mon, Thurs, Fri, Sat, and Sun for lunch and dinner. $–$$.

Mi Tierra. 218 Produce Row; (210) 225-1262; mitierracafe.com. If we have a chance for just one meal in San Antonio, it will be here. This is the place to head for an unbeatable Tex-Mex meal that includes homemade tortillas, enchiladas, and *chiliquiles*, a spicy egg-and-corn tortilla breakfast dish served with refried beans. Decorated year-round with Christmas ornaments, this San Antonio institution is open 24 hours a day, 365 days a year. $–$$.

within the city

Although the downtown area has plenty of attractions, other stops lie on the outskirts of the city, including a zoo, missions, and botanical gardens.

where to go

Buckhorn Saloon and Museums. 318 E. Houston St.; (210) 247-4000; buckhornmuseum .com. There's nothing more Texan than Lone Star beer, and you can sample the product at the Buckhorn Saloon. This historic bar once was frequented by short-story writer William Sydney Porter (O. Henry), whose home has been relocated to the brewery grounds 2 blocks from the Alamo.

The Buckhorn Saloon building also contains the Buckhorn Museum, featuring a huge collection of animal horns and mounted bird and fish specimens, and the Texas Ranger Museum, with a wealth of Texas Ranger weapons, badges, and historic photographs. The museum's *Ranger Town* exhibit includes famed outlaws Bonnie and Clyde's getaway car, a 1934 Ford. Open daily. Fee.

Fort Sam Houston Self-Guided Tour. N. New Braunfels Avenue and Stanley Road; (210) 221-1886; jbsa.mil. This National Historic Landmark, an army base dating back to 1870, has nine times as many historic buildings as Colonial Williamsburg. These include the residence where General John J. Pershing lived in 1917; the Chinese Camp, once occupied by Chinese who fled Mexico to escape Pancho Villa; and the home where Lieutenant and Mrs. Dwight Eisenhower lived in 1916. Visitors can stroll past the structures (they are not open to the public). The fort's historic Quadrangle is listed on the National Register of Historic Places. This is a grassy enclosed park area where tame deer and birds are frequently seen. Call for hours. Free admission.

The post also includes two museums. The **Fort Sam Houston Museum** (210-221-1886; history.army.mil) is filled with exhibits about the site's early days. The FSH Museum is located in the US Army North Quadrangle at 2108 Wilson Way. The **US Army Medical Department Museum** (210-221-6358; ameddmuseum.amedd.army.mil) houses exhibits on military medical practices dating to the Revolutionary War. Open Tues through Sat. Free admission.

Japanese Tea Garden. 3853 N. St. Mary's St. (by the zoo); (210) 212-4814; saparks foundation.org/Japanese-tea-garden. San Antonio's semitropical climate encourages the lush flowers, climbing vines, and tall palms found inside this quiet, serene place. Koi (large goldfish) swim through the ponds, complete with beautiful rock bridges and walkways. Open daily. Free admission.

Marion Koogler McNay Art Museum. 6000 N. New Braunfels Ave.; (210) 824-5368; mcnayart.org. Located in a Spanish Mediterranean mansion that was once the home of art lover Marion Koogler McNay, the museum houses a nationally known collection of modern art as well as medieval and Gothic works. It also holds the largest collection of European and American graphic art in the Southwest. In the Tobin wing, visitors find one of the country's best theater arts research centers. Open Tues through Sun. Fee.

San Antonio Botanical Gardens and Halsell Conservatory. 555 Funston Place, near Fort Sam Houston; (210) 207-3250; sabot.org. Roses, herbs, a garden for the blind, and native plants are found within the lovely setting of these 33-acre gardens. The centerpiece here is the $6.9 million Halsell Conservatory. The futuristic-looking, 90,000-square-foot structure is composed of seven tall glass spires. A self-guided tour of these seven areas takes visitors through the plants and flowers found in different environments, from desert to tropics. The conservatory sits partially underground for a cooling effect in the hot Texas summers. Open daily. Fee.

San Antonio Museum of Art. 200 W. Jones Ave.; (210) 978-8100; samuseum.org. This extensive art museum is housed in the former Lone Star Brewery. The collection ranges from ancient Egyptian artifacts to 19th-century art. The museum boasts the Nelson A. Rockefeller Collection of Mexican Folk Art, one of the best in the nation. Open Tues through Sun. Fee.

San Antonio Missions National Historical Park. This national park stretches for 9 miles along the San Antonio River and is composed of four remaining missions (outside of the Alamo) constructed by the Franciscan friars in the 18th century. The missions are active parish churches today, and all are open to the public. For a map of the mission locations, visit the National Park Service website at nps.gov/saan. Each of the four illustrates a different concept of mission life. Open daily. Free admission.

> **Mission Concepción.** 807 Mission Rd.; (210) 534-1540. Built in 1731, this mission holds the title as the oldest unrestored stone church in the country.

> **Mission San Francisco de la Espada.** 10040 Espada Rd.; (210) 627-2021. Established in 1731, its original chapel was in ruins by 1778 and the building was reconstructed around 1868.

> **Mission San José.** 6701 San José Dr.; (210) 932-1001; nps.gov/saan/planyour visit/sanjose.htm. The most complete structure in the tour, Mission San José was built in 1720. It has beautiful carvings, 84 rooms that once housed Native Americans, a restored mill with waterwheel, and what may be the only complete mission fort in existence. Make this mission your first stop; it is also home to the Visitors Information Center.

> **Mission San Juan Capistrano.** 9101 Graff Rd.; (210) 534-0749. This mission was relocated here from East Texas in 1731 but never completed.

San Antonio Zoological Garden and Aquarium. 3903 N. St. Mary's St.; (210) 734-7184; sazoo.org. This world-class zoo features bar-less "habitat cages" for many of its animals. The cliffs of an abandoned quarry are home to more than 8,500 birds, fish, mammals, and other fauna, making the zoo one of the largest animal collections in North America. There's a children's petting area, a reptile house, and an aquarium. Open daily year-round; call for seasonal hours. Fee.

Witte Museum. 3801 Broadway; (210) 357-1900; wittemuseum.org. This excellent museum focuses on natural history, especially as it relates to the state's Native American, Spanish, and Mexican heritage. The museum is also home to the H–E–B Body Adventure, a four-floor interactive experience that emphasizes physical health. Open daily. Fee.

far northwest

Beyond Loop 410, the city begins to give way to the Hill Country, the rolling, oak-covered land that's still largely rural. This is also the home of San Antonio's two theme parks.

where to go

SeaWorld San Antonio. 10500 SeaWorld Dr. (18 miles northwest of downtown, between Loop 410 and Loop 1604); (800) 700-7786; seaworld.com. This 250-acre, Texas-size park is one of the largest marine-life parks in the world. It's the home of Shamu the killer whale, plus dolphins, penguins, sea otters, and more. Visitors can enjoy fast-moving roller coasters and water rides, live entertainment, and interactive encounters with dolphins, beluga whales, or California sea lions. Other tours include a chance to go behind the scenes to watch the care of SeaWorld's animals and a petting pool with people-friendly dolphins. Open Mar through Dec with changing hours. Fee.

Six Flags Fiesta Texas. 17000 I-10 West (I-10 and Loop 1604, 15 miles northwest of downtown); (800) 473-4378 or (210) 697-5050; sixflags.com/fiestatexas. This extensive theme park located, like SeaWorld, near Loop 1604 on the northwest side of town, offers a staggering array of rides. There are over 50 in all, ranging from the tame to the terrifying. Some of these are "dry" rides, including the Iron Rattler roller coaster and the Crow's Nest Ferris wheel, while others are wet rides designed to cool you down in the Texas heat. The park is divided into eight different sections, each featuring a different style of rides, entertainment, dining, and shopping, and each exploring the cultural diversity of San Antonio and the Southwest. Open Mar through Oct with changing hours. Fee.

where to stay

Hyatt Regency Hill Country Resort and Spa. 9800 Hyatt Resort Dr.; (800) 233-1234 or (210) 647-1234; hyatt.com. This full-service resort offers the area's most luxurious getaway, with 27 holes of golf and a 5-acre water park with a cascading waterfall and man-made Ramblin' River for inner-tube floaters. The 500-room resort nestles on 300 acres of a former cattle ranch, rolling land sprinkled with prickly pear cacti, wildflower meadows, and live oaks. With its limestone architecture and Western decor, the four-story hotel captures the atmosphere of the Hill Country, from windmills to gingerbread trim featuring the Lone Star (which often decorated homes of the German pioneers who settled the area). For meetings, the resort boasts 54,000 square feet of flexible function space, ranging from boardrooms and ballrooms to indoor and outdoor pavilions. $$$.

especially for winter texans

Admiralty RV Resort Park. 1485 N. Ellison Dr., off Loop 1604; (877) 236-4715 or (210) 647-7878; qualityrvresorts.com. This 207-pad RV park is located minutes from SeaWorld and Loop 1604. It includes a heated pool, brick patios at each site, cable TV hookups, and organized get-togethers during the winter (potluck dinners, card games, and dominoes). $.

day trip 02

southwest

old-world fun:
gruene, new braunfels

Fun abounds along the track of this day trip, whether it be splashing in water parks and scenic Hill Country rivers, boot-scooting at famous Greune Hall, or soaking up German heritage at Wurstfest in New Braunfels.

gruene

Once a separate community but now part of New Braunfels, Gruene is a popular destination for shoppers and water recreation lovers. Head south on I-35 for 30 miles to San Marcos (see South Day Trip 04 for attractions in that city). Continue south for 17 miles to exit 191. Turn west and continue to the intersection with Hunter Road, then turn left and continue to this historic area.

Once a ghost town, Gruene has been transformed into a very popular shopping destination. A historic inn, river rafting, lots of good food, and Texas's oldest dance hall draw visitors from around the state. Like Waxahachie and Refugio, the pronunciation of Gruene is one of those things that sets a real Texan apart. To sound like a local, just say "Green."

In the days when cotton was king, Gruene was a roaring town on the banks of the Guadalupe River. Started in the 1870s by H. D. Gruene, the community featured a swinging dance hall and a cotton gin. Prosperity reigned until the boll weevil came to Texas, with the Great Depression right on its heels. Gruene's foreman hanged himself from the water

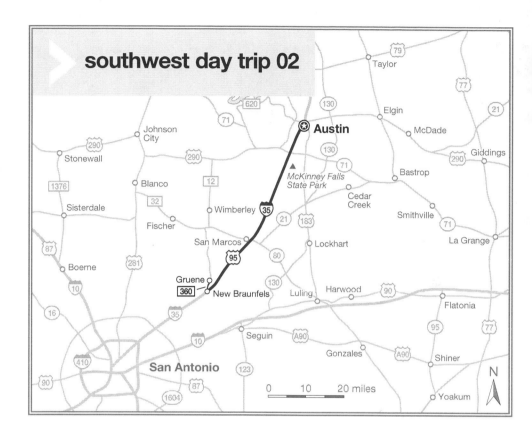

southwest day trip 02

tower, and H. D.'s plans for the town withered like the cotton in the fields. Gruene became a ghost town.

One hundred years after its founding, investors began restoring Gruene's historic buildings, and, little by little, businesses began moving into the once-deserted structures. Now Gruene is favored by antiques shoppers, barbecue and country music lovers, and those looking to step back into a simpler time. On weekdays, you may find Gruene's streets quiet, but expect crowds every weekend.

There's free parking across from the Gruene Mansion Inn, former home of H. D. Gruene. Today the mansion is a private residence owned by the proprietors of an adjacent bed-and-breakfast.

Gruene is compact, with everything within easy walking distance. Plan to just park and enjoy the stroll from shop to shop.

where to go

Gruene Hall. 1281 Gruene Rd.; (830) 606-1281; gruenehall.com. The oldest dance hall in Texas is as lively today as it was a century ago. Dances and concerts are regularly held here (even though the hall has no air-conditioning), and it is also open to tour. Burlap bags draped from the ceiling dampen the sound, and 1930s advertisements decorate the walls. The hall opens at 11 a.m. most days. On weekdays, there's usually no cover charge for evening performances; weekend cover charges vary with the performer. Call for a schedule of events.

Gospel Brunch with a Texas Twist. Gruene Hall hosts this event on the second Sun of Feb through Dec. Put your hands together and enjoy the sounds of gospel in this New Orleans–inspired event that includes brunch and, for an extra charge, libations. Seating is limited, so reservations are a must.

where to shop

Gruene Antique Company. 1607 Hunter Rd.; (830) 629-7781; grueneantiqueco.com. Built in 1903, this was once a mercantile store. Today it's divided into several vendor areas and filled with antiques. Open daily.

Gruene General Store. 1610 Hunter Rd.; (830) 629-6021; gruenegeneralstore.com. This shop brings back memories of small-town life during Gruene's heyday as a cotton center. This was the first mercantile store, built in 1878 to serve the families that worked on the cotton farms. It also served as a stagecoach stop and a post office. Today instead of farm implements and dry goods, this general store sells cookbooks, fudge, and Texas-style clothing. Belly up for a soda at the old-fashioned fountain, and have a taste of homemade fudge. Open daily.

Gruene Haus. 1297 Gruene Rd.; (830) 837-5590. Built in the 1880s, this shop was the former home of H. D. Gruene's suicidal foreman. Apparel, linens, lace runners, silk bluebonnets, gifts for cat lovers, and decorative accessories are for sale. A "mantiques" section sells automobile and motorcycle memorabilia aimed at male shoppers. Open daily.

Old Gruene Market Days. 1724 Hunter Rd.; (830) 832-1721; gruenemarketdays.com. Shoppers flock to this community especially during Old Gruene Market Days. The event includes plenty of arts and crafts, a farmers' market, and lots of live entertainment. More than 125 vendors give you the chance to make purchases including one-of-a-kind quilts, pottery, jewelry, and more. Held the third full weekend of the month from Feb through Nov and the first weekend of Dec.

where to eat

Gristmill River Restaurant and Bar. 1287 Gruene Rd.; (830) 625-0684; gristmillrestaurant.com. Housed in the ruins of a 120-year-old cotton gin, this restaurant serves chicken, chicken-fried steak, catfish, burgers, and other Texas favorites. You can eat inside or outside on the deck overlooking the Guadalupe River. Open daily. $$.

where to stay

Gruene Mansion Inn. 1275 Gruene Rd.; (830) 629-2641; gruenemansioninn.com. Guests at this inn stay in restored 1870s cottages on a bluff overlooking the Guadalupe River as well as in the historic mansion, a converted corn crib, and a former carriage house. Thirty-one lovely rooms are decorated with period antiques and each includes a private entrance, private bath, and porch. A two-night rental is required on most weekends. $$$.

new braunfels

Continue south on Gruene Road into New Braunfels. This city has just about everything to offer travelers, including historic buildings, German food, an enormous water theme park, and enough antiques shops to merit the title "Antique Capital of Texas."

If you're looking for a romantic getaway in a historic inn or a weekend of outdoor fun, New Braunfels is the place. Just a half hour south of Austin on I-35, this town of 79,438 offers something for every interest, from antiques and water sports to German culture.

In the 1840s a group of German businessmen bought some land in Texas, planning to parcel off the acreage to German immigrants. Led by Prince Carl of Germany's Solms-Braunfels region, the group came to Texas to check on their new purchase. They discovered that it was more than 300 miles from the Texas coast, far from supplies in San Antonio, and located in the midst of Comanche territory. Prince Carl sent a letter warning other settlers not to come, but it was too late—almost 400 already had set sail for Texas. The prince saved the day by buying another parcel of land, this in the central part of the state. Called "The Fountains" by the Native Americans, it offered plentiful springs and agricultural opportunities. The Germans soon divided the land into farms, irrigating with spring water. The settlement they founded was named New Braunfels in honor of their homeland.

New Braunfels has never forgotten these ties to the Old Country. Even today German is spoken in many local homes. Every November the town puts on its lederhosen for Wurstfest, one of the largest German celebrations in the country.

The German settlers were a practical lot, and they saved old items of every description. Everything from handmade cradles to used bottles and jars was kept and passed down through generations.

The early settlers of New Braunfels also were attracted by the Comal and Guadalupe Rivers. Today swimmers, rafters, inner-tubers, and campers are drawn to these shady banks. The 2-mile-long Comal holds the distinction as one of the world's shortest rivers. Its crystal-clear waters begin with the springs in downtown Landa Park, eventually merging with the Guadalupe River, home to many local outfitters. Located on the scenic drive called River Road, the outfitters provide equipment and transportation for inner-tubers and rafters of all skill levels who like nothing better on a hot Texas day than to float down the cypress-shaded waters.

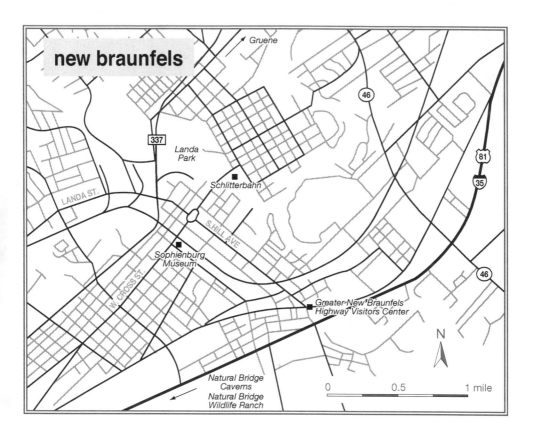

where to go

Greater New Braunfels Highway Visitors Center. I-35, exit 187; (800) 572-2626; playin newbraunfels.com. Drop by for maps, brochures, shopping information, and friendly home-town advice about the area. Open daily.

Canyon Lake. 3934 FM 306 (northwest of town); (800) 528-2104 or (830) 964-2223; canyonlakechamber.com. With 80 miles of protected shoreline, Canyon Lake is very popu-lar with campers, bicyclists, scuba divers, and boaters. Canyon Lake has four parks with camping facilities (Potter's Creek Park, North Park, Cranes Mill Park, Canyon Park) and five day-use parks with picnic facilities and hiking trails. Some also have swimming beaches. Fee for some parks.

Heritage Village–Museum of Texas Handmade Furniture. 1370 Church Hill Dr., in Conservation Plaza; (830) 629-6504; texashandmadefurniture.com. This 19th-century home contains cedar, oak, and cypress furniture handcrafted by early German settlers. Open Wed through Mon or by appointment. Fee.

Landa Park. 164 Landa Park Dr.; (830) 221-4350; nbtexas.org/2595/Lande-Park. Named for Joseph Landa, New Braunfels's first millionaire, this downtown park includes a miniature train, paddleboats, a golf course, and a 1.5-acre spring-fed swimming pool. This is the headwaters of the Comal River, where springs produce eight million gallons of pure water every hour. Picnicking is welcome in the park, but no camping. Free admission.

Lindheimer House. 491 Comal Ave.; (830) 629-2943; newbraunfelsconservation.org. Located on the banks of the Comal River, this home belonged to Ferdinand Lindheimer, a botanist who lent his name to more than 30 Texas plant species. Now restored, it contains early memorabilia from Lindheimer's career as both botanist and newspaper publisher. A backyard garden is filled with examples of his native flora discoveries. Tours are available through the New Braunfels Conservation Society. Fee.

McKenna Children's Museum. 801 W. San Antonio St.; (830) 606-9525; mckennakids .org. Bring the kids to enjoy hands-on fun at this interactive museum that features educational exhibits designed to appeal to a child's curiosity about the world and to stimulate childhood imagination. Open Mon through Sat. Fee.

Natural Bridge Caverns. 26495 Natural Bridge Caverns Rd. (from I-35 south of New Braunfels, take RM 3009 west; from TX 46 west of town, you also can take a left on RM 1863 for a slightly longer but more scenic route); (210) 651-6101; naturalbridgecaverns .com. Named for the rock arch over the entrance, this cave is one of the most spectacular in the area. The guided tour is well lit; the slope of the trail may be taxing for some. Kids can "pan" for small pieces of amethyst, sapphire, obsidian, topaz, and more at the attraction's Natural Bridge Mining Company. And intrepid travelers can make reservations for the Hidden Passages Adventure Tour, rappelling and crawling in spelunking gear to see remote cave regions. Open daily year-round; call or visit website for tour times. Fee.

Natural Bridge Wildlife Ranch. 26515 Natural Bridge Caverns Rd. (next to the caverns); (830) 438-7400; wildliferanchtexas.com. For more than a century, this property has operated as a family ranch, and since 1984 it has showcased exotic species, today holding the title as the oldest and most-visited safari park in the state. More than 40 native, exotic, and endangered species roam the grounds. The ranch offers a drive past zebras, gazelles, antelope, ostriches, and more. You'll be given animal feed when you arrive, so be prepared for the animals to come right up to the car for a treat. (Watch out or the ostrich will put his head inside the car in search of that food!) Another area houses three species of primates, as well as scarlet macaws and other exotic birds. A walking area holds some species that require a little more attention, such as reticulated giraffes, Bennett wallabies, and Patagonian cavies. Children love the petting zoo for the chance to get face to face with pint-size, friendly animals. Open daily. Fee.

River Road. This winding drive stretches northwest of the city for 18 miles from Loop 337 at the city limits to the Canyon Lake Dam. It's lined with river outfitters and beautiful spots where you can pull over and look at the rapids, which delight rafters, canoeists, and inner-tubers.

Schlitterbahn Waterpark & Resort New Braunfels. 400 N. Liberty Ave. (from I-35 take the Boerne exit [Loop 337] to Common Street, then turn left and continue to Liberty Street); (855) 246-0273 or (830) 625-2351; schlitterbahn.com. This water park ranks first in Texas and is tops in the US among seasonal water parks. This is the largest water theme park in the state. Schlitterbahn, which means "slippery road" in German, is also the largest tubing park in the world, with tube chutes, uphill water coasters, water slides, children's playgrounds, and more. The Comal River supplies 24,000 gallons a minute of cool spring water and also provides the only natural river rapids found in a water theme park.

Among the most colorful rides is the Soda Straws, made of huge Plexiglas-enclosed slides that take riders from the top of a 27-foot concrete soda to a pool below. In 1986. the cola glasses were filled with 2,000 gallons of soda and Blue Bell ice cream to create the world's largest Coke float. There's a steep Downhill Racer and the mile-long Raging River tube chute for daredevils, and a 50,000-gallon hot tub with a swim-up bar and the gentle wave pool for the less adventurous.

Two popular attractions here are the Boogie Bahn, a moving mountain of water for surfing, and the Master Blaster, the world's first uphill water coaster. The latter shoots riders on inflatable boats uphill for a roller-coaster-type ride through hills, dips, and curves. Plan to spend a whole day here, and bring a picnic if you like. Open Mar through Sept. Fee.

Sophienburg Museum and Archives. 401 W. Coll St.; (830) 629-1572; sophienburg.com. For a look at the hard-working people who settled this rugged area, spend an hour or two here. Named for the wife of settlement leader Prince Carl, the museum's displays include a reproduction of an early New Braunfels home, a doctor's office (complete with medical tools), a blacksmith's shop, and carriages used by early residents. Open Tues through Sat 10 a.m. to 4 p.m. Fee.

where to shop

New Braunfels Marketplace. 651 N. Business I-35 (exits 187 and 189); (830) 620-7475; nbmarketplace.com. What started out as a single factory store has become a destination for shoppers from Houston and Dallas. Goods from sportswear to books to leather goods are featured in the many shops. There are several restaurants on-site as well. Open daily.

where to eat

Gristmill River Restaurant & Bar. 1287 Gruene Rd.; (830) 625-0684; gristmillrestaurant .com. Located on the banks of the Guadalupe River in an 1878 cotton gin, the Gristmill serves chicken-fried steak, burgers, fresh fish, and popular desserts like Hill County strawberry shortcake and Jack Daniel's pecan pie a la mode. Dine on the shady patio with river views. Open daily. $$.

McAdoo's Seafood Company. 196 N. Castell Ave.; (830) 629-3474; mcadoos.com. Serves Texas Creole and Cajun specialties in the old downtown post office. Menu favorites include redfish pontchartrain, mahi mahi Boudreaux, and shrimp and scallops Baton Rouge. Signature drinks include the Postmaster Hurricane and Sazerac, made with rye whiskey, absinthe, and Peychaud bitters. Enjoy the covered patio with live music. Open daily. $$.

Naegelin's Bakery. 129 S. Seguin Ave.; (877) 788-2895 or (830) 625-5722; naegelins .com. Naegelin's has operated on the same spot since 1868. The original building is gone, replaced by the current structure in 1942. The store's specialty is apple strudel, a 2-foot-long creation that is certain to make any pastry-lover's mouth water. During the holidays, some of Naegelin's biggest sellers are springerle, a licorice cookie, and lebkucken, a frosted gingerbread cookie. Open daily. $.

where to stay

New Braunfels has plenty of accommodations for everyone. Check with the chamber of commerce (800-572-2626).

Faust Hotel. 240 S. Seguin Ave.; (830) 625-7791; fausthotel.com. A New Braunfels tradition, this 1929 four-story, renovated hotel features a bar that's popular with locals and visitors. The lobby is appointed with beautiful antique furnishings. The hotel is also the home of the Faust Brewing Company, a brewpub serving its own beers, including Faust Golden Ale, in the on-site restaurant. $$.

Prince Solms Inn. 295 E. San Antonio St.; (830) 312-5387; princesolmsinn.com. Built in 1898, this quiet bed-and-breakfast has 8 guest rooms, 1 suite, and 3 cottages, plus 3 more rooms in the adjacent Feedstore Building. All rooms are furnished with period antiques. $$$.

especially for winter texans

Heidelberg Lodges. 1020 N. Houston Ave.; (830) 625-9967; heidelberglodges.com. Located near the headwaters of the Comal River, this scenic family resort is popular in the summer with swimmers, snorkelers, and scuba divers. During off-season, Winter Texans are welcomed with potluck dinners and get-togethers. Accommodations include A-frame cottages and motel units. Call for long-term winter rates. $$.

day trip 03

southwest

kodak country:
wimberley, devil's backbone scenic drive,
fischer, blanco

Some of the most scenic highways in the Hill Country await you as you meander west through rugged canyons and wooded valleys. Huge cypress trees line sparkling Hill Country streams, and hilltop pullovers command spectacular views. Here, small towns attract resident artisans who display their wares in galleries and small shops.

wimberley

From Austin follow US 290 west to the small community of Dripping Springs. Turn south on RM 12 and continue 15 miles to Wimberley, a favorite shopping destination from Thursday through Monday. Wimberley's also a great summer destination because of its location on the Blanco River and Cypress Creek.

Wimberley's history goes back to the 1850s, when a resourceful Texas Revolution veteran named William Winters opened a mill here. As was tradition at the time, he named the new community Winters' Mill. When Winters died, John Cade bought the mill, and the town became Cade's Mill. Finally, in 1870 a wealthy Llano man named Pleasant Wimberley rode into town. Tired of Native American raids on his horses in Llano, he moved in, bought the mill, and changed the town's name one last time.

The small town of Wimberley is one of those "shop 'til you drop" kinds of places. Even with only 3,037 residents, the town boasts dozens of specialty stores, art galleries and studios, and accommodations ranging from river resorts to historic bed-and-breakfasts.

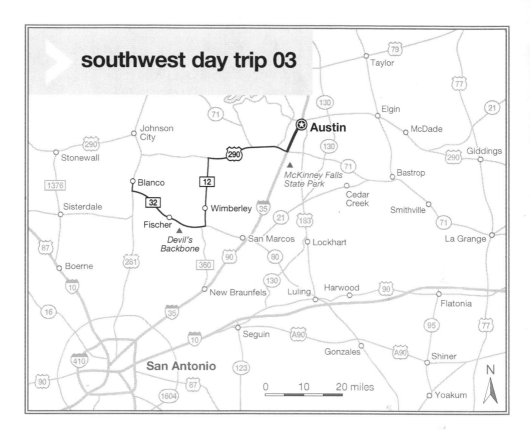

southwest day trip 03

Wimberley is a quiet place except when the shops open their doors on Monday, Thursday, Friday, and on weekends. The busiest time to visit is the first Saturday of the month from March through December. This is Market Day, when more than 475 vendors set up to sell antiques, collectibles, and arts and crafts.

Many visitors come to enjoy the town's two water sources: the Blanco River and clear, chilly Cypress Creek. Both are filled with inner-tubers and swimmers during hot summer months. The waterways provide a temporary home for campers and vacationers who stay in resorts and cabins along the shady water's edge

where to go

Pioneer Town. 7-A Ranch Resort, 1 mile west of RM 12 on CR 178, at the intersection with CR 179; (866) 369 6426 or (512) 847-2517; 7aresort.com/index.php/pioneer-town. See a medicine show, tour a general store museum, or spend some time at the town jail in this Wild West village. There's also a child-size train ride with a mile of tracks, an old log fort, cowboy shows, and a western cafe. Open Thurs through Tues during the summer, Sat only Sept through Nov and Mar through May. Fee.

where to shop

Like the nearby town of Blanco, Wimberley is home to many artists who've relocated to Texas's serene Hill Country. Specialty shops abound, selling everything from imports to sculptures and antiques. Arts and crafts are especially well represented. Plan to shop Thurs through Mon. Some stores are open all week, but some close midweek, especially during cooler months. A good time to shop is during Market Day, held the first Sat of every month from Mar through Dec at the Wimberley Lions Field, 601 RM 2325; (512) 847-2201; wimberleymarketday.com.

Bent Tree Gallery. 101 Henson Rd.; (512) 847-9438; benttreegallery.com. This artist-owned gallery features original works by local artists. The gallery hosts an open house with wine and snacks on the second Sat of each month. Open daily.

Rancho Deluxe. On the square, 14010 RM 12; (512) 847-9570; ranchodeluxe.net. Bring the cowboy look to your home with this shop's Western merchandise. You'll find everything from spurs and Mexican sideboards to horns and handcrafted furniture. Open daily.

Wimberley GlassWorks. 6469 RM 12; (512) 393-3316; wgw.com. Watch demonstrations on the art of glassblowing and shop for one-of-a-kind creations. Open Wed through Sun.

where to stay

Wimberley is filled with bed-and-breakfast accommodations that range from historic homes in town to ranches in the surrounding Hill Country to camps along Cypress Creek. For information on these many accommodations, give one of the reservations services a call: **Texas Hill Country Cabin and Resort Rentals,** (512) 847-3909, texashillcountryreservations.com; **Wimberley Bed and Breakfasts,** (844) 271-6829, vrbo.com. For brochures on Wimberley's other accommodations, call the chamber of commerce at (512) 847-2201.

devil's backbone scenic drive

From Wimberley continue south on RM 12 to RM 32. Turn west and sit back for this slow, scenic drive. There aren't any steep climbs or stomach-churning lookouts; a high ridge of hills provides a gentle drive with excellent views along the way. There's very little traffic, and there's a beautiful picnic spot on the left, just a few miles before Fischer. This stretch of road is often cited as one of the most scenic drives in Texas and is well known for its fall color.

fischer

Continue on RM 32 to the tiny hamlet of Fischer. Retrace your drive south on US 281 for a couple of miles to the intersection with RM 32. Take a left and enjoy a quiet ride through miles of ranch land and rolling hills.

musical chairs with the county seat

*Built in 1888, the former **Blanco County Courthouse** has been one of the most used buildings in the county—for everything except as a courthouse, that is. The year after its construction, an election moved the county seat to Johnson City. The courthouse was used for its original purpose for a total of four years, then it went into a long career of different uses. For two different periods, the building served as a schoolhouse; it also became a bank. Later it served the community as a town hall, library, opera house, and even the office of the local newspaper. From 1937 to 1961 the building served as a hospital but later became a Wild West museum and then a barbecue restaurant. Today the building houses the visitor center and is used for community events.*

Fischer is on the left side of the road. A short drive on Fischer Store Road takes you right into the community and to the store for which the road is named. Through the years, the store has served many purposes, acting as a bank and post office in addition to a mercantile.

While you're at the store, you'll notice some buildings next door. The red building is home to the Fischer Bowling Club, a 9-pin bowling league. Next door you'll see Fischer Hall, an old-fashioned dance hall that's still popular for wedding and reunion rentals.

blanco

After passing through Devil's Backbone, continue on RM 32 to US 281. Turn right and head north to Blanco, the home of a beautiful state park. Formerly a "Wild West" kind of town, the community was originally the seat of Blanco County. Although the county seat eventually moved to nearby Johnson City, where it remains today, local residents have restored Blanco's old limestone courthouse as a visitor center, gift shop, and community center. The former courthouse is located at the intersection of US 281 and FM 165. Stop by for brochures and shopping.

Around the courthouse square are several art galleries and antiques shops aimed at weekend visitors, many of whom stop to camp at the Blanco State Park south of town.

where to go

Blanco Bowling Club. 310 Fourth St.; (830) 833-4416; blancobowlingclub.com. Housed in 1940s buildings, the bowling club and the adjacent cafe have changed little with the passing

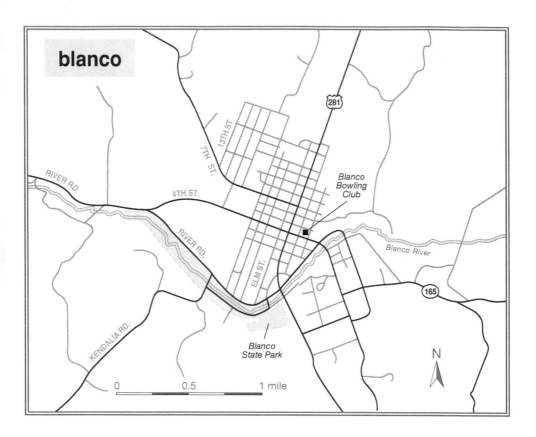

years. The nine-pin game is still set up by hand. The bowling club opens at 7:00 p.m. Mon through Thurs. To bowl you must be a league member. Free admission.

Blanco State Park. 101 Park Road 23 (south of Blanco on US 281); (830) 833-4333; tpwd .texas.gov/state-parks/blanco. During the Depression, the Civilian Conservation Corps built two stone dams, a group pavilion, stone picnic tables, and an arched bridge in this 104-acre riverside park. Today the park is popular with swimmers, anglers, and campers. Fee.

where to eat

Chess Club Café. 1020 Hwy. 281 S; (830) 833-4930; chessclubcafe.com. Serves breakfast and lunch Wed through Sun. House specialties for breakfast include the Breakfast Club Sandwich with fried egg, American cheese, bacon, mayonnaise, lettuce, and tomato served on toasted homemade bread. Lunch house favorites include the chef's own recipe for meatloaf topped with brown gravy, and pork schnitzel (breadcrumb encrusted pork cutlet) topped with brown gravy. $.

Uptown Blanco Restaurant. 317 Main St.; (830) 833-0738; uptownblanco.com. Where the community gathers for lunch, dinner, and Sunday brunch. Favorites are Portobello beet risotto, grilled pork shop, pan-seared duck breast, and shrimp and grits. Food is made from scratch with fresh and local ingredients. Features of the week might include pan-seared ribeye topped with brandy portobella sauce. Sunday brunch popular choice is crab cake benedict and Texas toast sprinkled with powdered sugar, dollop of whipped cream, and syrup. Open daily. $$.

day trip 04

southwest

that's history:
comfort, sisterdale, boerne

This is a cultural journey from Austin, a trip through three small towns that share a strong German heritage. It includes some curving farm-to-market roads that are very susceptible to flooding. If it's raining heavily, save this trip for another day!

comfort

From Austin head west on US 290 to Johnson City and Fredericksburg (see West Day Trips 02 and 03 for attractions in these cities). In Fredericksburg turn south on US 87 and continue for 23 miles to Comfort. This small community is big in history and attractions. The downtown area is a National Historic District, filled with homes and businesses built by early settlers.

Comfort was founded by German pioneers in 1854, who wanted to name the town *Gemütlichkeit*, meaning peace, serenity, comfort, and happiness. After some deliberation, though, they decided on the easier-to-pronounce "Comfort" instead.

Today Comfort offers tourists numerous historic buildings to explore, filled with antiques shops and restaurants. Visitors also find a historic inn. Weekends are the busiest time to visit, but even then the atmosphere is relaxing, unhurried, and, well, comfortable.

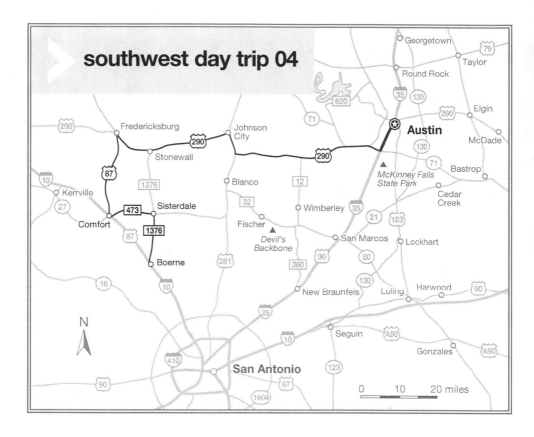

southwest day trip 04

where to go

Bat Roost. FM 473, on private land; (830) 995-3131. As you leave Comfort for Sisterdale, this historic structure sits 1 mile from town on the right side of the road behind private gates. While it's generally known now that bats feed on disease-spreading mosquitoes, the folks here have been aware of the importance of these furry mammals since 1918, when Albert Steves constructed hygieostatic bat roosts in an experimental attempt to control malaria. The roosts were intended to encourage the area's large bat population to remain in the region. Only 16 such roosts were built in the country, and this is the oldest of three known still to exist. Free, but view only from the road.

Old Tunnel State Park. 10619 Old San Antonio Rd. (15 miles northeast of Comfort off FM 473 on old TX 9); (866) 978-2287; tpwd.texas.gov/state-parks/old-tunnel. From May through Oct visitors to this unique park can watch at dusk when up to three million Mexican free-tailed bats emerge from an abandoned railroad tunnel and take to the skies to hunt mosquitoes and other flying insects. The park is open daily year-round for other activities such as hiking. Unlike most Texas state parks, dogs are not allowed. Free admission; fee to view bats during season.

treue der union

"Treue der Union" (True to the Union) Monument. 348 High St., between Third and Fourth Streets; (830) 995-3131. During the Civil War, German residents of Comfort who did not approve of slavery and openly swore their loyalty to the Union were burned out of their farms. The Confederates responsible also lynched locals who refused to pledge their allegiance to the movement. Several German farmers decided to defect to Mexico but were caught by Confederate soldiers and killed on the banks of the Nueces River, their bodies left unburied.

Finally retrieved in 1865, the remains were returned to Comfort and buried in a mass grave. A white obelisk, the oldest monument in Texas, was dedicated here in 1866. The flag that waves here has 36 stars, the same number it had when the marker was dedicated in 1866. Free admission.

where to shop

Comfort Crockery. 402 Seventh St.; (830) 995-5299; comfortcrockery.com. This shop sells unique pottery, jewelry, art objects, and mesquite furniture inside Comfort's historic Faitin Building. Open Wed through Sun.

where to stay

Hotel Giles. 717 High St.; (830) 995-3030; hotelgiles.com. This historic property has been updated and offers a blend of traditional and modern touches. The boutique hotel offers 14 rooms and suites. Guests enjoy a homemade breakfast and use of the hotel's retro bicycles. Because of the historic nature of the hotel, it is not handicap accessible and cannot accommodate pets. Chilren 16 and older are welcomed. $$–$$$.

sisterdale

From Comfort head out on FM 473 to nearby Sisterdale, best known as the home of a small winery. The burg, like nearby Boerne, was settled by a group of intellectuals. Today the population has dwindled to a handful of residents, and you have to look carefully to keep from passing right through town.

where to go

Sister Creek Vineyards. 1142 Sisterdale Rd.; (830) 324-6704; sistercreekvineyards.com. These vineyards thrive in "downtown" Sisterdale, located between the East and West Sister

Creeks. The winery, a restored cotton gin, produces traditional French-style wines. Open daily for self-guided tours. Fee for tastings.

where to eat

Black Board Bar B Q. 1123 Sisterdale Rd.; (830) 324-6858; sisterdalesmokehouse.com. If you're near Sisterdale on a weekend, this is a good place to stop for some tasty barbecue. You can choose from brisket, sausage, ribs, or chicken and enjoy the meal inside or outside on the deck. Open Fri, Sat, and Sun. $.

boerne

From Sisterdale head south on FM 1376 to Boerne (pronounced "Bernie"). Boerne is located on the banks of Cibolo Creek in the rolling Texas Hill Country. The community was founded in 1849 by German immigrants, members of the same group who settled nearby New Braunfels. They named the town for author Ludwig Börne, whose writings inspired many people to leave Germany for the New World.

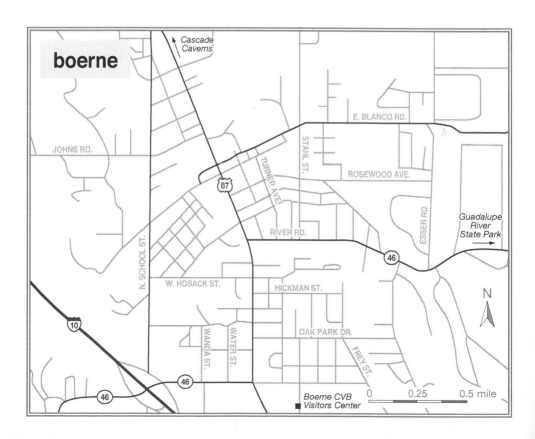

During the 1880s Boerne became known as a health spot, and vacationers came by railroad to soak in mineral-water spas and enjoy the clean country air. Although no mineral spas remain today, Boerne still offers a country atmosphere and dozens of antiques shops in which to browse. Thanks to its proximity to San Antonio and Austin, the town gets pretty busy on weekends.

Summer also brings seasonal fun to Boerne. A favorite activity on Main Plaza is *Abendkonzerte*, summer concerts performed by the Boerne Village Band. Since 1860 this German band (the oldest continuously active German band in the country and the oldest in the world outside of Germany) has entertained residents and visitors with its Old World sound. *Abendkonzerte* takes place on select Tuesday nights throughout the summer.

where to go

Boerne Convention and Visitors Bureau Visitors Center. 282 N. Main St.; (888) 842-8080 or (830) 249-7277; ci.boerne.tx.us. Stop here for brochures and maps to Boerne attractions and shopping areas. Open Mon through Sat.

Agricultural Museum and Art Center. 102 City Park Rd.; (210) 445-1080; theagricultural .org. This museum features farm and ranch tools used by pioneers in the late 19th and early 20th centuries, including a working steam-operated blacksmith shop. Six acres surrounding the museum are covered with hand-drawn plows, wagons, early tractors, and woodworking tools. Check the website for bluegrass jams, antique tractor pulls, Halloween spooktacular, and much more. Open Sat 10 a.m. to 4 p.m. and by appointment. Fee.

Boerne Turn Verein. 221 E. Theissen St.; (830) 249-2271; boerneturnverein.com. This bowling club has been operating in downtown Boerne since 1908. The lanes are open only for league play during the week, but the public is welcome on weekends. Open Tues through Sat. Fee.

Cascade Caverns. 226 Cascade Caverns Rd. (from I-10 take exit 543 and follow signs); (830) 755-8080; cascadecaverns.com. This family-owned cavern, located in a 105-acre park, maintains a year-round temperature of 68°F, so the attraction is popular on both cold winter days and sweltering summer days. The cave has a 100-foot waterfall, an unusual underground sight. Guided tours take an hour. Call before visiting as the cave is periodically closed due to flooding, especially during May, Aug, and Sept. Open daily. Fee.

Cave Without a Name. 325 Kreutzberg Rd.; (830) 537-4212; cavewithoutaname.com. Guided tours take groups through six rooms of this family-owned cavern, now designated a National Natural Landmark. A subterranean river and numerous cave formations fill the tour. Open daily. Fee.

Cibolo Nature Center & Farm. 140 City Park Rd.; (830) 249-4616; cibolo.org. Enjoy grassland, marshland, and woodland in this park that offers a slice of the Hill Country. Visitors can also view dinosaur tracks. The wilderness area includes both reclaimed prairie and reclaimed marsh, with walking trails that range from 0.25 mile to 1 mile in length. Open daily. Free admission.

Guadalupe River State Park. 13 miles east of Boerne off TX 46 at 3350 Park Road 31; (830) 438-2656; tpwd.texas.gov/state-parks/guadalupe-river. The star of this park is the clear, cold Guadalupe River. Camp, swim, hike, or just picnic on its scenic banks, or on Sat mornings, take an interpretive tour of the Honey Creek State Natural Area to learn more about the plants and animals of the region. Open daily. Fee.

Honey Creek State Natural Area. 13 miles east of Boerne off TX 46 on Park Road 31; (830) 438-2656; tpwd.texas.gov/state-parks/honey-creek. Use of this park is limited to those on guided tours. A two-hour guided look at the park's history and ecology is offered every Sat morning at 9 a.m.; reservations aren't necessary, but call to confirm that a tour will be offered. Access into the park is through the Guadalupe River State Park. Fee.

where to eat

Bumdoodlers. 929 N. Main St.; (830) 249-8826; bumdoodlers.com. One of the most popular spots in town for lunch, Bumdoodlers serves up homemade soups, salads, and deli sandwiches. And, they are locally famous for their pies as well. Open Mon through Sat. $.

Creek Restaurant. 119 Staffel St.; (830) 816-2005; thecreekrestaurant.com. Popular for its seafood and steak, the Creek Restaurant offers a rustic, romantic setting with a deck over-looking a creek. Serving crab cakes, calamari, lobster, escargot, tuna, scallops, snapper, halibut, shrimp, and salmon for seafood lovers. Also offering steaks, chops, pasta, lamb, and sides like lobster mac and cheese in a green chili and three-cheese sauce. Open for lunch and dinner Tues through Sat. $$.

Po Po Family Restaurant. 829 FM 289 (6 miles north of Boerne, 0.5 mile off I-10 at exit 533); (830) 537-4194; poporestaurant.com. Once a stagecoach stop, this site now houses a locally popular restaurant. Along with its home-cooked meals, the restaurant is also known for its plates themselves—over 1,300 of them decorate the walls! Open daily for lunch and dinner. $$.

day trip 05

southwest

cowboy country:
bandera, medina, vanderpool

In the far west reaches of the Texas Hill Country the antelope (well, white-tailed deer) play, cowboys (both real and pretend) ride herd, and brilliant maple trees blaze so brightly in the fall, you'll think you're in New England. The ranches are a little bigger here, the towns a little farther apart, and you'll learn the meaning of the longtime Texas slogan "Drive Friendly" as oncoming motorists are quick to greet you with a welcoming wave.

bandera

Take I-35 south from Austin through San Marcos and New Braunfels (see South Day Trip 04 and Southwest Day Trip 02 for information). In New Braunfels, take TX 46 west to Boerne (see Southwest Day Trip 04). Continue on TX 46 for 11 miles until it adjoins TX 16. Continue west for 12 miles to Bandera, "The Cowboy Capital of the World." This town is well known for its plentiful dude ranches, country-and-western music, rodeos, and horse racing.

Once part of the Wild West, Bandera Pass, located 12 miles north of town on TX 173, was the site of many battles between Spanish conquistadors and Apaches and Comanches. Legend has it that, following a battle with the Apaches in 1732, a flag (or *bandera* in Spanish) was hung at the pass to mark the boundary between the two opposing forces.

Bandera has open rodeos weekly during the summer. Typically rodeos are held on Friday night at the Twin Elm Guest Ranch and another at the BR Lightning Ranch. For

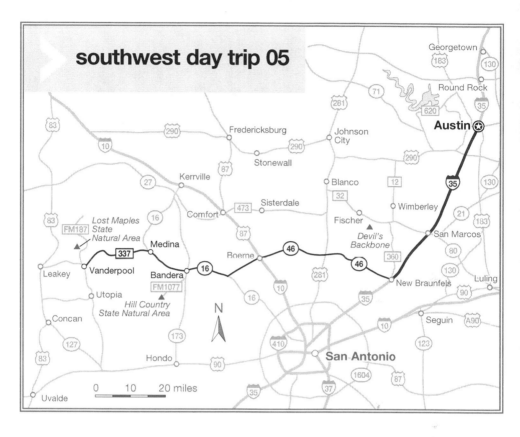

southwest day trip 05

schedules, call the Bandera Convention and Visitors Bureau at (830) 796-3045 or see ban deracowboycapital.com.

Today the wildest action in town occurs in the dance halls every night except Monday and Tuesday. Put on your boots, crease your best jeans, and get ready to two-step with locals and vacationers alike.

where to go

Arkey Blue's Silver Dollar. 308 Main St.; (830) 796-8826. Pick up a longneck, grab a partner, and start boot-scootin' at this Texas honky-tonk. Owner and singer Arkey Blue performs country-and-western hits here as crowds fill the sawdust-covered dance floor. Open daily 10 a.m. to 2 a.m. Free admission; fee for weekend entertainment.

Frontier Times Museum. 510 13th St. (1 block north of the courthouse); (830) 796-3864; frontiertimesmuseum.org. Established in 1927, this museum is a good place to learn more about Bandera's early days. The stone building is filled with cowboy paraphernalia, Native American arrowheads, and prehistoric artifacts. Its most unusual exhibit is a shrunken head

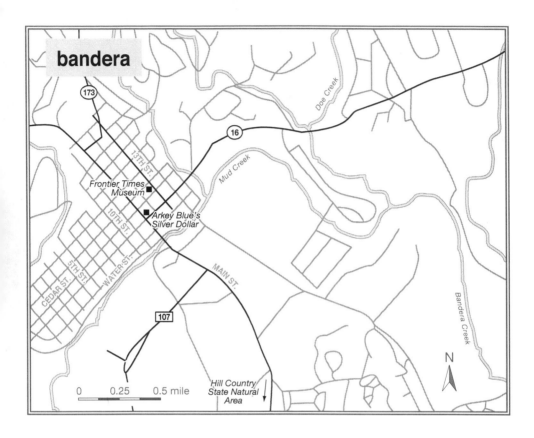

from Ecuador, part of a private collection donated to the museum. Open Mon through Sat. Fee.

Hill Country State Natural Area. 10600 Bandera Creek Rd. (south on TX 173 to FM 1077, then right for 12 miles); (830) 796-4413; tpwd.texas.gov/state-parks/hill-country. This rugged park preserves 5,400 acres of Hill Country land. Only primitive camping is available; you must bring your own water and pick up and remove your own trash. This park was originally open primarily for horseback riding, but today it has become popular with hikers and bicyclists. There are 40 miles of quiet trails and camp areas for backpackers and equestrians. Cool off with a dip in West Verde Creek or fish for catfish, perch, and largemouth bass. Horse rentals are available off-site. Open daily. Fee.

Historical Walking Tours. (830) 796-3045. Have a look at the buildings that witnessed Bandera's evolution from a frontier town to a vacation destination with a self-guided tour. Thirty-two sites along the route lead visitors to the county courthouse, the old jail, Bandera's first theater, and many homes that date back to the community's earliest days. Pick up your walking-tour brochure at the Bandera County visitor center, 126 TX 16 South. Open Mon through Sat. Free admission.

Medina River. TX 16, east of town. The cypress-lined Medina River is a popular spot during the summer months, when swimmers, canoeists, and inner-tubers enjoy the cool water. The Medina can be hazardous during high water, however, with rocky rapids and submerged trees. There is public access to the river from the TX 16 bridge in town. Free admission.

where to shop

Bandera General Store. 306 Main St.; (830) 796-4925; banderageneralstore.com. If you've decided you just need some real cowboy boots or other Western wear, this is a good place to find them. The store is housed in an old dance hall and sells Texas-inspired gift items, and it boasts a real old-time soda fountain (as well as a resident ghost named Henry!).

where to eat

Brick's River Café. 1205 N. Main St.; (830) 796-9900; bricksrivercafe.com. Family-run restaurant in a casual setting offers country dinners, seafood, and sandwiches. Favorites include catfish platter, queso fried pork chop, and jager schnitzel. Open daily. $.

O.S.T. Restaurant. 311 Main St.; (830) 796-3836. Named for the Old Spanish Trail, this restaurant serves a Texas-size breakfast as well as popular lunches and dinners, featuring Lone Star favorites such as chicken-fried steak, burgers, and fried chicken. Don't miss the bar and its unique barstools—each topped with a saddle. Open daily. $.

where to stay

The country around Bandera is dotted with dude ranches. Rates usually include three meals daily as well as family-style entertainment and supervised children's programs. Horseback riding is often part of the weeklong package. A minimum stay of two or three days is required at most ranches during peak summer season.

For a complete listing of Bandera's dude ranches, as well as other accommodations and campgrounds, call the Bandera Convention and Visitors Bureau, (830) 796-3045.

2E Twin Elm Guest Ranch & RV Park. 810 FM 470 (4 miles from Bandera via TX 16); (888) 567-3049 or (830) 796-3628; twinelmranch.com. This 230-acre dude ranch is on the Medina River. All the usual cowboy activities are available, from angling to horseback riding to horseshoe pitching. Rodeos are offered every Fri night throughout the summer. Twin Elm Ranch offers 21 units. $$$.

Bandera Bunkhouse on Main. 406 Main St.; (830) 460-3690; banderabunkhouseonmain .com. Located in the heart of Bandera and within walking distance to local attractions, shopping, dining, and entertainment, Bandera Bunkhouse on Main offers rustic rooms with private baths, free Wi-Fi, flat-screen TVs, and free parking. $$.

Dixie Dude Ranch. 833 Dixie Dude Ranch Rd. (south on TX 173 1.5 miles to FM 1077, then southwest for 9 more miles); (800) 375-9255 or (830) 796-7771; dixieduderanch.com.

Five generations of the Whitley family have welcomed guests to this ranch since 1937. The Dixie Dude Ranch offers potential cowpokes the opportunity to enjoy a taste of ranch life. Start your morning with a leisurely trail ride followed by a genuine cowboy breakfast, then enjoy a day filled with hiking trails, hunting for Native American arrowheads, taking country-and-western dance lessons, fishing, or tossing horseshoes. The ranch includes 20 units made up of individual cottages, duplex cabins, and lodge rooms featuring early Texas architecture. Rates include three home-cooked meals each day (except Sun night dinner), evening entertainment (except Sun night), and two horseback rides daily. Call for rates. $$$.

Flying L Ranch Resort. 675 Flying L Dr. (from TX 16, turn south on TX 173 for 1.5 miles, then left on Wharton Dock Road); (800) 292-5134; flyingl.com. This 542-acre ranch has a variety of room styles and sizes, including suites and villas to accommodate families or larger groups. You can choose from a variety of packages offering horseback riding, hayrides, and even golf at the ranch's 18-hole course. During the summer, there's a supervised children's program. Western music Tues through Sat nights. $$$.

Mayan Ranch. 350 Mayan Ranch Dr. (TX 16, 2 miles west of Bandera); (830) 796-3312 or (830) 460-3036; mayanranch.com. For more than 50 years, this 68-room ranch has entertained vacationers with cowboy breakfasts, cookouts, horseback riding, angling, and hayrides. Summer also brings organized children's programs. Rooms are appointed with Western-style furniture. Call for rates. $$$.

especially for winter texans

Besides the dude ranches, Bandera has excellent RV parks. Many weekly activities are of special interest to the Winter Texans who call Bandera home. Country-and-western dances are held Wed through Sat, and there's bingo on Fri and Sun. For a complete listing, contact the Bandera Convention and Visitors Bureau, (830) 796-3045.

medina

From Bandera continue west on TX 16 to the tiny community of Medina, best known for its dwarf apple trees that produce full-size fruit in varieties from Crispin to Jonagold.

where to go

Love Creek Orchards. 13495 TX 16; (830) 200-0302; lovecreekorchards.com. From May through Oct these beautiful orchards are open to the public by guided tour only; call to set up a tour time. Fee.

taking a shine to medina

If there's any truth to the saying "An apple a day keeps the doctor away," then the physicians of Medina, Texas, better just close up shop. This Hill Country community is the core of the booming Texas apple industry.

Today Medina is recognized as the capital of the Texas apple industry, a business that took root in 1981 when Baxter Adams and wife Carol moved to Love Creek Ranch outside of Medina. Baxter spent 30 years as an exploration geologist in the oil industry before moving to this region. It's a land of rocky, rugged hills, with fertile valleys irrigated by the cool waters of Love Creek, a spring-fed creek that originates on the ranch.

These valleys gave Adams the idea for an orchard—one that would not require a great deal of land. "I don't have much tillable land," Adams once explained to us, pointing to the steep hills where goats once grazed. "I've got to really make it count. It's a matter of trying to squeeze the most possible dollars out of the smallest possible area."

And that's just what Baxter Adams did, launching a Texas apple business that continues today.

This Texas version of Johnny Appleseed specialized in dwarf apple trees, plants that reach a height of only 5 or 6 feet. The Lilliputians boast full-size apples, however, up to 50 pounds per tree, in varieties from the common Red Delicious to the more unusual Gala and Crispin.

Baxter and Carol started with just 1,000 trees in 1981, and they were soon in the apple business. Unlike the full-size trees that take seven years to produce a crop, the dwarfs yield fruit in just a year and a half. Another advantage Texas apples have over the northern producers is the growing season: Texas apples ripen weeks before their northern cousins.

where to shop

The Apple Store. 14024 TX 16; (830) 200-0302; lovecreekorchards.com. This shop sells Love Creek apples from June through Nov. Butter, sauces, vinegars, jellies, syrups, pies, breads, and even apple ice cream are sold here year-round. Open daily.

where to stay

Escondida Resort. 23670 TX 16 North; (888) 589-7507 or (830) 589-7507; escondida resort.com. Founded by *Texas Country Reporter* star Bob Phillips, the 10-room Escondida (Spanish for "hidden") Resort is filled with elegant hardwood and iron furniture and subtle

continuing to concan

*Want to extend your day trip with a more in-depth look at this portion of the Hill Country? From Utopia head west on RM 1050 to **Garner State Park** (234 RM 1050; 830-232-6132; tpwd.texas.gov/state-parks/garner), near the community of Concan. One of the most loved parks in the state system, the focal point of this getaway is the Frio River. This beautiful park, named for former US vice president John Nance Garner, is located on the chilly, spring-fed waters of the river (frio means "cold" in Spanish), promising a cool dip even on the hottest summer day. You'll also find camping and over 12 miles of trails built by the Civilian Conservation Corps during the 1930s. The park is one of the state's busiest, so plan your trip accordingly; we try to visit midweek whenever possible.*

*If you don't want to camp, Concan is also home to **Neals Lodges** (20970 TX 127; 830-232-6118; nealslodges.com). Since 1926 this riverside resort has been a family favorite, growing to now include cabins, condominiums, lodges, and RV sites.*

Mexican tile accents. Explore the 125-acre property for a day of birding, following Roberston Creek; relax in the pool or hot tub; or head inside to pamper yourself at the spa. $$$.

vanderpool

Vanderpool is a quiet getaway in all but the fall months. Tucked into the hills surrounding the Sabinal River, this small town is a center for sheep and goat ranching.

where to go

Lost Maples State Natural Area. 37221 FM 187 (west on RM 337 to the intersection with FM 187; turn north and continue 5 miles); (800) 792-1112 or (830) 966-3413; tpwd.texas .gov/state-parks/lost-maples. This state park is one of the most heavily visited sites in Texas during Oct and Nov, when the bigtooth maples provide some of the best color in the state. Weekend visits at this time can be very crowded, so note that parking is limited to 250 cars. The least crowded time to visit is midweek.

There are 10 miles of hiking trails to enjoy all year along the Sabinal River Canyon. In the summer visitors can swim and fish in the river. Camping includes primitive areas on the hiking trails and a 30-site campground with restrooms and showers as well as a trailer dump station. Open daily. Fee.

> ## leaf peeping

Are you starting to dream about the feel of a cool autumn breeze? Hearing the crackle of leaves beneath your feet? Smelling the smoke of an evening campfire?

Central Texas may not have the blazing colors of New England, but with a little looking, you will find a brilliant quilt of fall colors. The brilliant colors require cold night temperatures, an occurrence that can reach the Hill Country valleys long before the warmer city locations.

*The top destination for many leaf peepers is **Lost Maples State Natural Area** in Vanderpool. The maples, located so far from other specimens of the beautiful tree, may seem lost, but there's no doubt that the park itself has been found. This state park is one of the most heavily visited sites in Texas during October and November when the bigtooth maples provide some of the best color in Texas. Weekend visits during this time can be very crowded, and note that the parking here is limited to only 250 cars. The best time to visit is during midweek, when you can enjoy a walk into the park without crowds. To find the status of fall colors, visit the weekly fall foliage report on the park's website, tpwd.texas.gov/state-parks/lost-maples/foliage-reports.*

Fall colors generated by blazing sumacs, sycamores, chinaberries, and cottonwoods can be seen on the scenic drive along RM 1050 from Utopia to US 83. RM 337 from Camp Wood to Leakey is another favorite of ours, as is the Devil's Backbone Scenic Drive, a stretch of RM 32 from Wimberley to Blanco.

Scenic Drive. Utopia to US 83. West of Utopia, RM 1050 winds its way through the Hill Country, crossing the Frio River before eventually intersecting with US 83 north of Concan. During late fall the drive is dotted with blazing sumacs, sycamores, chinaberries, and cottonwoods. Free admission.

Scenic Drive. RM 337. This drive from Camp Wood to Leakey (pronounced "LA-key") is often termed the most scenic in Texas and is an excellent spot for fall color. The road climbs to some of the highest elevations in the Hill Country at more than 2,300 feet, and roadside lookouts offer great vistas of reds, greens, and golds. Free admission.

where to stay

Foxfire Log Cabins. 117 Olsen Ranch Rd.; (830) 966-2200 or (877) 966-8200; foxfire cabins.com. Located along the Sabinal River, these cabins are just a mile from Lost Maples

State Natural Area, making a convenient home base for your trip, although, with a look at the beautiful swimming hole on this property, it might be tough to pull yourself away! Each cabin has two bedrooms, one bath, and a furnished kitchen (no microwave). You'll also find a wood-burning fireplace as well as a fire ring outdoors. $$–$$$.

west

day trip 01

west

willie nelson's backyard:
bee cave, spicewood and south lake travis

Yes, the "red headed stranger" himself, Willie Nelson, one of Austin's most famous residents, owns an 800-acre spread near Spicewood. Willie's place is far more than just a place to kick off his boots, though; the private complex includes a recording studio, golf course, and even a miniature Western "town" named Luck that's used for movie shoots. Spicewood and the surrounding communities make an easy getaway from Austin when you're short on time.

bee cave

This small community is quickly growing as Austin expands westward toward the Hill Country.

where to go

Austin Zoo and Animal Sanctuary. 10807 Rawhide Trail, Austin; (512) 288-1490; austin zoo.org. The Austin Zoo is a rescue and rehabilitation zoo, home to many animals that have been removed or surrendered by owners because of their inability to care for exotic species. Some have been rescued from circuses, others given up by owners who just didn't realize an exotic animal wasn't the same as a dog or cat. There's nothing fancy about this zoo, but look for a wide variety of animals here: lions, tigers, cougars, Galapagos tortoises, monkeys, and more. There's an extensive petting zoo featuring potbellied pigs, Barbados sheep,

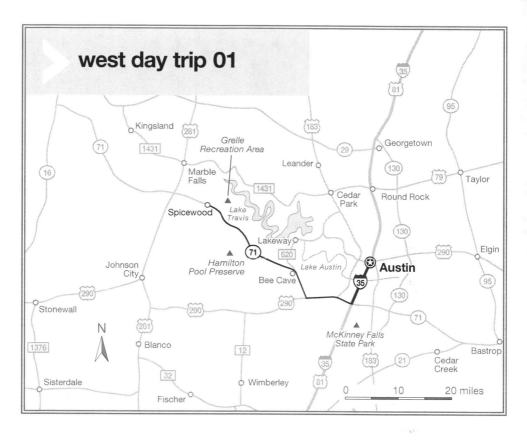

west day trip 01

pygmy goats, llama, and deer. A miniature train offers rides through nearby fields, home to longhorn cattle, a Sicilian donkey, emus, zebras, and others. Fee.

Hamilton Pool Preserve. 24300 Hamilton Pool Rd. (TX 71 west then turn left onto FM 3238, which is Hamilton Pool Road; travel 13 miles to preserve entrance on right); (512) 264-2740; parks.traviscountytx.gov. This beautiful swimming hole is a grotto fed by a 50-foot waterfall. After a dip, enjoy a picnic or hike along the canyon, which is home to several rare plant species. Guided tours are available Oct through Apr. Call before a swimming trip to this site, as elevated bacteria levels occasionally cause temporary closing of the pool. Fee.

where to eat

County Line on the Hill. 6500 W. Bee Caves Rd.; (512) 327-1742; countyline.com. Like its sister restaurant, County Line on the Lake, this eatery serves traditional Texas barbecue ranging from brisket to ribs. Diners enjoy a 20-mile view of the Hill Country scenery from the dining room. Open daily for lunch and dinner. $$–$$$.

where to stay

Omni Barton Creek Resort and Spa. 8212 Barton Club Dr.; (800) 336-6158 or (512) 329-4000; omnihotels.com. This expansive resort is known for its four golf courses; guests can also sign up for the golf school. The spa features a variety of treatments incorporating local elements, such as the lavender and honey sugar scrub, which uses local lavender and honey made at the resort's own apiary. $$$.

spicewood and south lake travis

This day trip takes anglers, swimmers, and boaters to the numerous parks found on the southern reaches of Lake Travis.

where to go

Grelle Recreation Area. 640 CR 412 (from Spicewood take CR 404 east approximately 1 mile to intersection with CR 412, a gravel road; turn left and travel just over 0.5 mile to entrance); (512) 473-3366; lcra.org. This county park on the south side of Lake Travis is near the community of Spicewood. Grelle is often visited for its 2-mile hiking trail, which leads visitors along a steep path to a plateau with views of Lake Travis. The site is also popular for its shoreline. Visitors here will find only primitive facilities: a portable toilet, metal fire rings, and a small parking area. Fee.

Krause Springs. 404 Krause Springs Rd. (from Spicewood take CR 404 east, then turn left on Krause Springs Road); (401) 236-7554; krausesprings.net. Krause Springs is one of Central Texas's hidden wonders. As its name suggests, the highlight of this private park is the natural springs. Clear, cool waters and waterfalls draw swimmers and snorkelers during warm-weather months. Camping also is available. Fee.

Muleshoe Bend Recreation Area. 2820 CR 414 (from Spicewood take CR 404 east to CR 414; turn right and travel about 1.5 miles, then turn right before entrance to Ridge Harbor and continue for about 0.25 mile on gravel road to entrance); (800) 776-5272 or (512) 473-3366; lcra.org. Muleshoe Bend is appropriately named: A 2-mile looped trail is a favorite with those looking to take a four-legged ride through undeveloped Hill Country. Horseback riders, bike riders, and hikers enjoy the trail located on the upper area of the park. With its 1,000 acres on the upper south side of Lake Travis near the Ridge Harbor subdivision, this is the largest property in the Lower Colorado River Authority (LCRA) system, but it offers only primitive facilities: restrooms, metal fire rings, and a parking area. Fee.

Narrows Recreation Area. 2550 CR 411 (from Spicewood take CR 410 north to intersection with CR 411, which is a gravel road; once on CR 411, travel approximately 1.5 miles north to entrance); (800) 776-5272 or (512) 473-3366; lcra.org. This free recreation area is used by boaters looking for a launching site onto the upper south side of Lake Travis. The ramp, however, should be used with caution during low water periods. Only minimal facilities are available here, with a restroom, a few camping sites, and metal fire rings. This recreation area should be avoided during heavy rains; the access road traverses a low water crossing that may become impassable. Fee.

Spicewood Vineyards. 1419 CR 409 (from TX 71 turn onto CR 408 south for about 1 mile, then right onto CR 409 for 1.5 miles); (830) 693-5328; spicewoodvineyards.com. This vineyard offers tours and tastings. Check for dates and times. Fee.

where to eat

Poodie's Hilltop Roadhouse. 22308 TX 71 West; (512) 264-0318; poodies.net. Willie Nelson is almost an unofficial symbol of Austin, but the musician is all too often on the road again, playing Austin fewer days than he did in his early days. But, Willie does make an appearance at Poodie's from time to time. You might not see him during your visit, but keep an eye out for other stars. Serving up burgers and Texas food, the roadhouse is really known for its live music, enjoyed almost every night. Open daily. $–$$.

day trip 02

west

lbj country:
pedernales falls state park, johnson city, hye, stonewall

The memory of one of Texas's most famous politicians, President Lyndon Baines Johnson, still looms here over hills and valleys and in local lore. While the larger-than-life Johnson was president in the 1960s, the Hill Country became the focus of attention as world leaders gathered at the Johnson Ranch, dubbed the "Texas White House," for discussion, politicking, and debate.

pedernales falls state park

For the stair-stepped **Pedernales Falls** (2585 Park Road 6026; 830-868-7304; tpwd.texas .gov/state-parks/pedernales-falls), head 32 miles west of Austin on US 290 then north on FM 3232 for 6 miles. A favorite summer getaway, this 4,800-acre state park is highlighted by gently cascading waterfalls. Although the falls themselves are closed to swimming, they make a great photo opportunity and other portions of the river are open for swimming, wading, and angling for catfish. The falls are spectacular, but visitors should note that this park can experience dangerous flash floods. With even a slight rise in the river, visitors should get to higher ground immediately. Activities such as tubing, angling, hiking, and camping are available. Open daily. Fee.

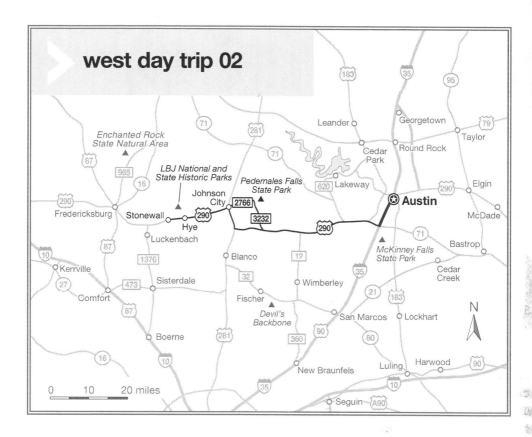

> ## west day trip 02

johnson city

From Pedernales Falls State Park, turn southwest on Park Road 6026 to CR 201 (Pederna-les Falls Road) and turn right. Continue to the intersection of RM 2766 (Robinson Road) and head west for 9 miles to Johnson City and LBJ country. President Johnson's boyhood home is open to visitors, along with the Johnson Settlement where LBJ's grandfather organized cattle drives over a century ago. The Lyndon B. Johnson National Historic Park takes in two areas: Johnson City and the LBJ Ranch, located in Stonewall.

LBJ brought the attention of the world to his hometown, located 14 miles north from Blanco on US 281. The most popular stop here is the LBJ Boyhood Home, managed by the National Park Service. LBJ was five years old in 1913 when his family moved from a coun-try home near the Pedernales River to this simple frame house. The visitor center provides information on this location, nearby Johnson Settlement, and other LBJ attractions. Park admission is free, a stipulation of the late president.

Johnson City hosts Market Days on the fourth full weekend of every month from Febru-ary through November, with antiques, crafts, collectibles, and food booths.

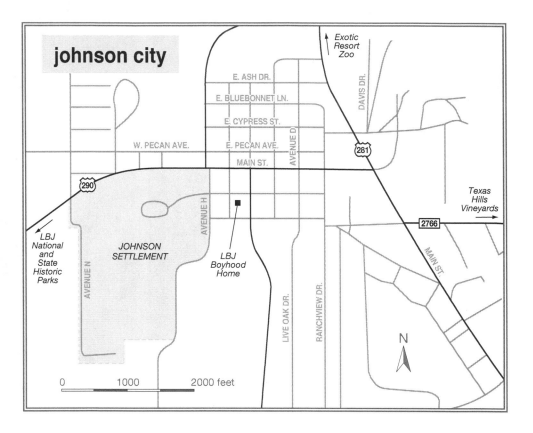

johnson city

E. ASH DR.

E. BLUEBONNET LN.

E. CYPRESS ST.

W. PECAN AVE.   E. PECAN AVE.

MAIN ST.

Exotic Resort Zoo

DAVIS DR.

AVENUE D

281

290

Texas Hills Vineyards

2766

AVENUE H

LBJ National and State Historic Parks

JOHNSON SETTLEMENT

LBJ Boyhood Home

AVENUE N

LIVE OAK DR.

RANCHVIEW DR.

MAIN ST.

N

0   1000   2000 feet

where to go

The Exotic Resort Zoo. 235 Zoo Trail (4 miles north of Johnson City on US 281); (830) 868-4357; zooexotics.com. Unusual species (including many endangered animals) roam the 137 acres of wooded Hill Country. In this park, leave the driving to someone else and enjoy a guided ride aboard a safari truck. Professional guides conduct tours of the ranch and provide visitors with information such as animal behavior as you feed the friendly park residents. After the tour, you can see some wildlife up close at the petting zoo. Kids enjoy petting child-size miniature donkeys, baby deer, llama, baby elk, and even a kangaroo at this special area. Open daily 9 a.m. to 5 p.m. Fee.

Hill Country Science Mill. 101 S. Ladybird Ln.; (844) 263-6405; sciencemill.org. For the young and young-at-heart travelers in your group, this nonprofit science museum offers over 25 exhibits, a 3-D theater, and interactive maker stations, all on the theme of the wonders of science. The museum itself is a wonder, housed in the historic 1880s mill that has long been a landmark in the community. You'll also find a small farm-to-table cafe featuring organic and all-natural dishes. Open Wed through Sun. Fee.

LBJ National Historic Park. South of US 290 at Ninth Street; nps.gov. Park at the visitor center and go inside for brochures and a look at exhibits. From the center, you can walk to Johnson Settlement and the LBJ Boyhood Home.

> **Johnson Settlement.** The settlement, located just down the street from the LBJ Boyhood Home, gives visitors a look at the beginnings of the Johnson legacy. These rustic cabins and outbuildings once belonged to LBJ's grandfather, Sam Ealy Johnson, and his brother Tom. The two cattle drivers lived a rugged life in the Hill Country during the 1860s and 1870s. An exhibit center tells their story in pictures and artifacts. You also can tour the brothers' cabins and see costumed docents carrying out 19th-century chores. Open daily. Free admission.

> **LBJ Boyhood Home.** LBJ was a schoolboy when his family moved here in 1913. The home is still furnished with the Johnsons' belongings. Guided tours run every half hour. Open daily. Free admission.

Texas Hills Vineyard. 878 RM 2766 (1 mile east of Johnson City); (830) 868-2321; texas hillsvineyard.com. Texas wines produced with an Italian influence are the specialty of this vineyard. Open daily for tastings. Fee.

where to shop

Echo. 100 N. Nugent Ave.; (830) 321-0080; echoinjohnsoncity.com. Gallery contains art work from more than 30 artists plus jewelry, wearable art, home furnishings, antiques, and more. Open Thurs through Mon.

Whittington's Jerky. 602 US 281 South; (877) 868-5501 or (830) 868-5500; whittingtons jerky.com. This factory produces true Texas jerky; stop by for free samples or to shop for jerky and other food items. Open daily.

where to stay

The Exotic Resort Zoo Safari Cabins. 235 Zoo Trail (4 miles north of Johnson City on US 281); (830) 868-4357; zooexotics.com. The Exotic Zoo, known for its guided safari tours and petting zoo, now operates an eight-cabin bed-and-breakfast on the property. Three cabins include kitchenettes; they all include access to two swimming pools, a hot tub, a barbecue area, playscape, community patio, and a fire pit for evening bonfires. The cabins overlook the animal areas, and all cabin stays include a zoo tour. $$–$$$.

hye

For years Hye had just one highlight: the Hye General Store and Post Office, on whose front porch President Johnson swore in Lawrence F. O'Brien as US Postmaster General in 1965. Johnson is said to have mailed his first letter at the age of four from this historic post office.

Today that general store and post office are still a focal point in town, but Hye has grown into its own day-trip destination. Attracting wineries and even a distillery, the small unincorporated community has become a popular stop on the way to Fredericksburg.

where to go

Garrison Brothers Distillery. 1827 Hye Albert Rd.; (830) 392-0246; garrisonbros.com. The first and oldest legal whiskey distillery in Texas, this operation makes Texas Straight Bourbon Whiskey. Located on a cattle ranch, the distillery is located 1.7 miles south of the Hye Market. (Can't make it to the distillery? Hye Market also carries the award-winning product.) Tours Wed through Sat; tour reservations are required on Sat. Fee.

Hye Market Restaurant and Tasting Room. 10261 W. US 290; (830) 868-2300; hyemarket.com. The Hye Post Office still operates in the back of this store (and adjacent restaurant). Looking up at the pressed-tin ceilings, it's easy to imagine the many years of history that this building has witnessed since Hiram G. (Hye) Brown founded the post office in 1886. Today those ceilings look down on the many visitors who come here to sample local wines in the tasting room. Store open Tues through Sun; tasting room open Wed through Sat. Fee for tastings.

Hye Meadow Winery. 10257 W. US 290; (830) 308-8551; hyemeadow.com. Pull up a chair on the covered patio, gaze out at the 42 oak-shaded acres, and enjoy a taste of these whites and Mediterranean-based reds. Closed Tues. Fee for tastings.

William Chris Vineyards. 10352 US 290; (830) 998-7654; williamchriswines.com. This family-owned-and-operated winery focuses on handcrafted Texas wine, growing Malbec, Merlot, Cabernet Sauvignon, Petit Verdot, Tannat, MourvËdre, and Trebbiano Toscano. Open daily. Fee for tastings.

where to eat

Hye Market Restaurant and Tasting Room. 10261 W. US 290; (830) 868-2300; hyemarket.com. Located in the historic Hye Post Office, this casual restaurant has a small-town feel but with "Hye end," sophisticated tastes. Look for locally sourced produce, cheeses, and meats including bison and quail in dishes ranging from salads to naan bread pizzas to sandwiches. Open for lunch Tues through Sun. $–$$.

stonewall

Continue west on US 290 to the tiny community of Stonewall, the capital of the Texas peach industry. The road passes through miles of peach orchards, and during early summer, farm-fresh fruit is sold at roadside stands throughout the area. Stonewall is also the home

peach fun

Stonewall is called "The Peach Capital of Texas," and every June Stonewall is ripe with fun and festivities. The third weekend of June is set aside for a celebration of the Hill Country's sweetest product at the annual Peach JAMboree. The festivities are genuine Texas fun, from a rodeo with bareback riding, calf roping, team roping, and bull riding to a parade and a baking contest at the Stonewall Chamber of Commerce. Other activities include a domino tournament (open to competitors), a washer pitching tournament, and, of course, the Gillespie County Peach Queen Pageant. The sweetest event is the Peach Show and Auction, with plenty of prize-winning examples of Stonewall's fuzzy treasure.

Gillespie County, including Stonewall and nearby Fredericksburg, is filled with orchards where you can pick your own peaches. These shady groves yield their fruit until late July and offer a dozen varieties. The earliest to ripen are the cling peaches, varieties whose fruit clings to the pit. As the summer progresses, varieties such as Red Skin, Loring, and Harvest Gold begin to mature.

of the LBJ National and State Historic Parks, encompassing the LBJ Ranch. This is a great opportunity to visit a working cattle ranch.

where to go

Becker Vineyards. 464 Becker Farms Rd.; (830) 644-2681; beckervineyards.com. With 46 acres of French vinifera vines, Becker Vineyards boasts Texas's largest underground wine cellar. It has also boasted such specialties as the 2002 Viognier, an elegant wine with a hint of violets and peach, served at a dinner for Australia's prime minister at President Bush's Prairie Chapel Ranch, and the 2002 Cabernet Sauvignon Reserve, poured at a White House dinner. Along with the tasting room and gift store, you'll also find that this vineyard is known for its lavender farm, even hosting a lavender festival the first weekend of May. Open daily. Fee for tasting.

Grape Creek Vineyards. 10587 US 290 East (4 miles west of Stonewall); (830) 644-2710; grapecreek.com. The fertile land of the Pedernales Valley is a natural for vineyards, and you'll find acres of beautiful grapevines at this winery that produces cabernet sauvignon and chardonnay varieties. The winery is open daily. Call for tour times. Free admission; fee for tours and tastings.

LBJ National and State Historic Parks. (830) 644-2252; nps.gov or tpwd.texas.gov. Located 14 miles west of Johnson City on US 290, these two combined parks together span approximately 700 acres. The area is composed of three main sections: the visitor center, the LBJ Ranch and tour, and the Sauer-Beckmann Farm. The most scenic route to the LBJ park falls along RR 1, paralleling the wide, shallow Pedernales River (exit US 290 a few miles east of Stonewall).

During Johnson's lifetime, the ranch was closed to all but official visitors. In hopes of catching a glimpse of the president, travelers often stopped along RR 1, located across the river from the Texas White House, the nickname of the Johnsons' home. Today the parks draw visitors from around the world.

Make your first stop the visitor center for a look at displays on LBJ's life, which include mementos of President Johnson's boyhood years. Attached to the visitor center is the Behrens Cabin, a dogtrot-style structure built by a German immigrant in the 1870s. Inside, the home is furnished with household items from more than a century ago.

While you're in the visitor center, get a free permit for a self-guided drive through the LBJ Ranch. You'll drive across the president's spacious ranch, making a stop at the one-room Junction School where Johnson began his education and the small family cemetery along the Pedernales River where LBJ and Lady Bird are buried. Next you'll stop at the president's airstrip. Here you'll park and join a guided tour of the Texas White House, which opened to the public after Lady Bird's death. Presently, the Texas White House is closed due to health and safety concerns arising from structural issues. Contact the Texas White House for updated information about tours.

Other stops on your self-guided drive include LBJ's cattle barns, the reconstructed birthplace home, and the Sauer-Beckmann Living Historical Farm. Here, two 1918 farm homes are furnished in period style. Children can have a great time petting the farm animals. From here it's just a short walk back to the visitor center. Although the park does not have overnight facilities, there are two picnic areas and hiking trails for day use. Open daily. Free admission.

where to shop

Burg's Corner. 15194 US 290 East; (830) 644-2604; burgscorner.com. You can't come to Stonewall without trying some Hill Country peaches. During season, Burg's Corner is a great place to buy straight-off-the-tree peaches (as well as other local fruits and vegetables). You'll also find plenty of other peach products here: ice cream, salsa, preserves, cider, and even peach-scented candles. Open daily early May through Sept, then Thurs through Mon until Christmas.

where to eat

Cowboy Catina. 6435 Ranch Rd. 1623; (512) 779-5401; ccalbert.com. A new food truck concept offering good food and music. Favorites are the "Albert Freakin' Texas" with southern fried chicken breast, avocado slaw on a toasted brioche bun; and "Cowboy Fries," mound of crispy fries loaded with carnitas cheddar cheese, pickled onion, and jalapenos, plus a side of sour cream. Open Wed through Sun. $.

day trip 03

west

wine country:
luckenbach, fredericksburg,
enchanted rock state natural area

One of the most popular getaways in the Austin area, the Fredericksburg region is known for not only its German heritage, seen in the restaurants and biergartens, but also its booming wine industry. Dozens of wineries provide a Napa-type getaway, Texas style, with tasting rooms, restaurants, and special events. This region is also the bed-and-breakfast capital of Texas, known for its stand-alone guesthouses that give day-trippers the ability to extend their stay and call this activity-filled region home for a few days.

To reach this day trip, follow the directions from Austin through West Day Trip 02, traveling through LBJ Country and the historic town of Johnson City, passing through the LBJ Ranch on the way west.

luckenbach

Waylon Jennings's popular country-and-western song made this community a Texas institution. The town consists of a shop or two and a small general store serving as a post office, dance hall, beer joint, and general gathering place.

To reach Luckenbach (888-311-8990 or 830-997-3224; luckenbachtexas.com), leave Stonewall on US 290. Turn left on FM 1376 and continue for about 4.25 miles. Don't expect to see signs pointing to the turnoff for Luckenbach Road; they are often stolen as fast as the highway department can get them in the ground. After the turn for Grapetown, take the next right down a narrow country road. Luckenbach is just around the bend.

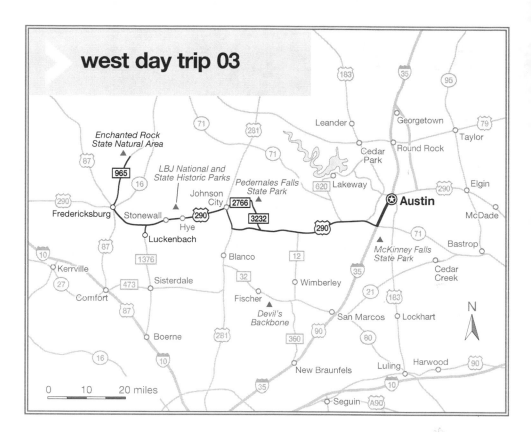

west day trip 03

This town was founded in 1852 by Jacob, William, and August Luckenbach. The brothers opened a post office at the site and called it South Grape Creek. In 1886, a man named August Engel reopened the post office and renamed it Luckenbach in honor of the early founders.

The most happening place in town is the dance hall, an expansive traditional Texas dance hall. Dances are held most weeks, usually on Saturday night. Other nights feature live music concerts and free open-mic "Picker's Circles."

The old post office is still there in the general store, the walls covered with scrawled names penned by Luckenbach fans. The store sells souvenirs of the town. Open daily. Free admission; fee for concerts and dances.

fredericksburg

Retrace your steps from Luckenbach and continue west on US 290 to Fredericksburg, once the edge of the frontier and home to brave German pioneers. These first inhabitants faced many hardships, including hostile Comanches. Now the town is a favorite with antiques shoppers, history buffs, and fans of good German food.

US 290 runs through the heart of the downtown district, becoming Main Street within the city limits. Originally the street was designed to be large enough to allow a wagon and a team of mules to turn around in the center of town. Today, Main Street is filled with shoppers who come to explore the stores and restaurants of downtown Fredericksburg.

Fredericksburg welcomes all visitors—just look at the street signs for proof. Starting at the Adams Street intersection, head east on Main Street and take the first letter of every intersecting street name: They spell "all welcome." Drive west on Main Street starting after the Adams Street intersection. The first letter of the intersecting streets spell "come back."

where to go

Fredericksburg Convention and Visitors Bureau. 302 E. Austin St.; (888) 997-3600 or (830) 997-6523; visitfredericksburgtx.com. Stop by the visitor center for brochures, maps, and information on a self-guided walking tour of historic downtown buildings, many of which now house shops and restaurants. The staff here also can direct you to bed-and-breakfast facilities in the area. Open daily. Free admission.

290 Wine Tours. (210) 724-7217; 290wineshuttle.com. Want to sample multiple wineries without worrying about driving yourself from location to location? The 290 Wine Tours shuttle picks up at the Inn on Barons Creek, located at 308 S. Washington St., one block south of Main Street every 10 minutes starting at 11 a.m. each Sat and 10 a.m. Sun. The tours stop at 12 wineries in the region; they can also offer hotel pickup. Fee.

Arrowhead Creek Vineyard. 13502 E. US 290, Stonewall; (830) 307-7200; arrowhead vineyard.com. Started as a small vineyard for the family, Chris and Tia Aspra grew 2.5 acres of grapes into a destination winery on the Texas Wine Trail. The winery offers a rich variety of wines composed of Estate, Texas, and other regions both national and international. The winery has several areas on site to taste wines and enjoy a charcuterie board or snack. Open daily.

Augusta Vin Winery and Vineyards. 140 Augusta Vin Ln.; (830) 307-1007; augustavin .com. Augusta Vin offers a beautiful two-story, timber-framed tasting room, plus winery tours, wine and food pairings, yoga in the vineyard, live music, and more. Open daily.

Chisholm Trail Winery. 2367 Usener Rd.; (830) 990-2675; chisholmtrailwinery.com. This winery prides itself on being one of the area's most dog-friendly, but it's also a great place to unwind thanks to its quiet location. Located 9 miles west of Fredericksburg and known for its Western saloon style, the winery's covered patio overlooks Spring Creek Vineyards. Open Wed through Mon. Fee for tastings.

Fort Martin Scott Frontier Army Post. 1606 E. Main St.; (830) 997-7521; fbgtx.org/416/ ft-martin-scott. Established in 1848, this was the first frontier military fort in Texas. Today the original stockade, a guardhouse, and visitor center with displays on local Native Americans are open to tour, and monthly historic reenactments keep the history lesson lively. Ongoing archaeological research conducted here offers a glimpse into the fort's past. Open Thurs through Mon for self-guided tours. Free admission.

Fredericksburg Herb Farm. 405 Whitney St.; (800) 259-HERB or (830) 997-8615; fredericksburgherbfarm.com. These gardens produce the herbs for everything from teas to potpourri. Tour the grounds, then visit the shop for a look at the final product. A bed-and-breakfast, spa, and the Farm Haus Bistro are also located on-site. Open daily. Free admission.

Fredericksburg Trolley Tours. (830) 998-8986; fbgtours.com. A great way to get an entertaining and informative overview of Fredericksburg aboard vintage-style trolleys. Several tours are offered including the Historic Fredericksburg Tour, Boutique Winery Tour, LBJ Ranch Presidential Tour, Haunted History Tour, and more. Public and private tours are available. Fee.

Fredericksburg Winery. 247 W. Main St.; (830) 990-8747; fbgwinery.com. Like many local wineries, this is a family-run operation, headed by no-nonsense Cord Switzer (look for the man in the gimme cap), along with his wife, Sandy, brothers Jene and Burt, and their families. Its signature labels, like its Texas white Der Keller (named for the winery's cellar room, which dates from 1923), feature artwork and a little history. Open daily. Free admission.

Kalasi Cellars. 414 Goehmann Ln.; (830) 992-3037; kalasicellars.com. A boutique winery, Kalasi opened its tasting room in 2020 and production winery in 2021. Five generations ago, the family began farming in India, cultivating crops of cocoa, coconuts, rice, and turmeric. Today, the family calls Texas home and has reincarnated its farming roots by growing wine grapes. Dalai the llama and six Olde English Babydoll Southdown sheep also call Kalasi home. Open Thurs through Mon. Open Tues and Wed for wine tasting reservations only.

National Museum of the Pacific War. 311 E. Austin St.; (830) 997-8600; pacificwar museum.org. This historic park (formerly Admiral Nimitz State Historical Park) is composed of numerous sections: the former Nimitz Steamboat Hotel, the Japanese Garden of Peace, the George H. W. Bush Gallery, the Pacific Combat Zone, the Plaza of the Presidents, and the Memorial Courtyard.

The complex was first named for Admiral Chester Nimitz, World War II Commander in Chief of the Pacific (CinCPac), Fredericksburg's most famous resident. He commanded 2.5 million troops from the time he assumed command 18 days after the attack on Pearl Harbor until the Japanese surrendered. The Nimitz name was well known here even years earlier. Having spent time in the merchant marine, Captain Charles H. Nimitz, the admiral's grandfather, decided to build a hotel here, adding a structure much like a ship's bridge to the front of his establishment. Built in 1852, the Nimitz Steamboat Hotel catered to guests who enjoyed a room, a meal, and the use of an outdoor bathhouse.

The heart of the museum is the **George H. W. Bush Gallery,** an extensive collection devoted to World War II Pacific campaigns. The exhibits include media-based interactive displays that illustrate the history, the scope, and the cost of the war in the Pacific. Behind the museum lies the **Garden of Peace,** a gift from the people of Japan. This classic Japanese garden includes a flowing stream, a raked bed of pebbles and stones representing the sea and the Pacific islands, and a replica of the study used by Admiral Togo, Nimitz's counterpart in the Japanese forces. Follow the signs from the Garden of Peace for 1 block to the **Pacific Combat Zone.** This takes you past a collection of military artifacts, including a "fat man" Nagasaki-type atomic bomb case, a Japanese tank, and a restored barge like the one used by Nimitz. Open Wed through Mon. Fee.

Old Tunnel State Park. 10619 Old San Antonio Rd. (10.5 miles south of US 290 on the Old San Antonio Road); (866) 978-2287; tpwd.texas.gov/state-parks/old-tunnel. This abandoned rail tunnel became the perfect home for three million Mexican free-tailed bats who chose the location as their summer home. Every May through Oct the tunnel fills with the annual visitors who provide the important service of mosquito control for the region. You can view the emerging bats every night (or their return during the early morning) from the free upper viewing platform. Thurs through Sun evenings during peak season, you can view the bats from the tunnel level on ranger-guided tours for a fee. Unlike most state parks, this park is not open for canine visitors. To make sure you visit during the proper time, call (866) 978-2287 to learn the current bat schedule. Free admission; fee to view bats during season.

Peach Groves. Almost half the peaches in the state of Texas come from this region, and a drive through the peach groves is a fun way to look at this important crop, whether you visit during the spring bloom or the summer harvest. The numerous varieties of peaches grown here mature on a staggered schedule, so look for fresh fruit at local stands (and even pick your own offerings at some farms) from mid-May into early Aug. Visit the Fredericksburg visitor center for a brochure about the peach growers or visit texaspeaches.com for more information.

Pioneer Museum. 325 W. Main St.; (830) 990-8441; pioneermuseum.net. This collection of historic old homes includes an 1849 pioneer log home and store, the old First Methodist Church, and a smokehouse and log cabin. You'll also see a typical 19th-century Sunday house. Built in Fredericksburg, Sunday houses catered to farmers who would travel long distances to do business in town, often staying the weekend. With the advent of the automobile, such accommodations became obsolete. Today the old Sunday houses scattered throughout the town are used as bed-and-breakfasts, shops, and even private residences. They are easy to identify by their small size and the fact that most have half-story outside staircases. Open Mon through Sat. Fee.

Southold Farm + Cellar. 330 Minor Threat Lane; (512) 829-1650; southoldfarmandcellar .com. Southold's mission is to make wines that speak of time and place. The Wine Study offers a wine tasting with accompanying food by reservation only. The Kitchen is a 36-seat dining experience with an ever-changing menu paired with wine. The Parlour is a space created to explore the adventurous side of wine with a delicious plate of bites. In addition,

Southold offers a beautiful view from atop a ridge in Texas Hill Country. Open Thurs through Mon.

Texas Rangers Heritage Center. 1618 E. Main St.; (830) 997-2698; trhc.org. This new addition to Fredericksburg's museum scene will be of special interest to anyone looking to learn more about the long history of the Texas Rangers. Showcasing a collection previously housed in San Antonio's Buckhorn Museum, this facility features authentic Texas Ranger artifacts, from guns to badges. The expansive museum includes the Ranger Ring of Honor, an open-air pavilion, amphitheater, campanile bell tower, theater, and more. Open Thurs through Mon 9 a.m. to 5 p.m. Fee.

Vereins Kirche Museum. 117 W. Main St.; (830) 990-8441; pioneermuseum.net. You can't miss this attraction: It's housed in an exact replica of an octagonal structure erected in 1847. Back then the edifice was used as a church, as well as a school, a fort, a meeting hall, and a storehouse. The museum is sometimes called the Coffee Mill (or Die Kaffe-Muehle) Church because of its unusual shape. Exhibits here display Fredericksburg's German heritage, plus Native American artifacts from archaeological digs. Open Mon, Tues, Thurs, Fri, Sat 10 a.m. to 5 p.m. Fee.

Wildseed Farms. 100 Legacy Dr.; (830) 990-1393; wildseedfarms.com. The nation's largest working wildflower farm with more than 200 acres in Fredericksburg, Wildseed Farms offers walking trails, flower beds, wildflower and culinary seeds for sale, and a vineyard and tasting room. Fields of wildflowers bloom from March through Oct. Beer and other refreshments are available. Open daily.

where to shop

Fredericksburg's many specialty shops offer antiques, linens, Texana, art, and collectibles. Most stores are in historic buildings along Main Street.

Antique Mall of Fredericksburg. 116 B N Crockett St.; (830) 997-6329; antiquemall fredericksburg.com. Great selection of antiques with new arrivals almost daily. Open Tues through Sun.

Blackchalk Home and Laundry. 306 S. Lincoln St.; (830) 998-1556; blackchalkhome .com. Built in the 1920s as a laundry, this historic building now houses a fascinating mix of items for the home "discovered by chance or unexpectedly." The clothing boutique offers eclectic and fun merchandise. Open Mon through Sat.

Carol Hicks Bolton Antiques. 301 S. Lincoln St.; (830) 997-5551; carolhicksbolton.com. Shop offers one-of-a-kind beds, huge farm tables, ulholstery, romantic bed linens, illuminations, curiosities, and much more. Open Mon through Sat.

Das Peach Haus. 1406 S. US Hwy. 87; (830) 997-7194; jelly.com. In 1969, Mark Wieser opened Das Peach Haus as a roadside fruit stand built from the logs of an 1870 German log cabin. The shop became famous for its locally harvested peaches and preserves made from local ripe fruit. In 1979, 15-year-old Case Fischer went to work harvesting peaches. By 1986, Case had officially teamed up with Mark to become Fischer & Wieser Specialty Foods. Das Peach Haus now offers public and private cooking classes plus award-winning favorites like roasted raspberry chipotle sauce, peach preserves, Mom's spaghetti sauce, mesquite horseradish mustard, wine, and much more. Check the website for hours.

Der Kuchen Laden. 258 E. Main St.; (830) 997-8969; derkuchenladen.com. Located in the historic Keidel Hospital Building, this store highlights all things kitchen. From cookie cutters to small appliances, each room of the store is packed with gadgets you didn't know you needed but now you can't live without. (You really do need that pineapple corer, right?!) Check out the selection of Yeti Coolers, too, to see the Texas product that's quickly becoming a favorite with Lone Star tailgaters. Open Mon through Sat.

Dietz Distillery. 1406 S. US Hwy. 87; jelly.com. Opened in 2021, Dietz Distillery is the brainchild of Dietz Fischer who developed a passion for crafting fruit-based spirits while earning a distilling degree in Scotland. The popular Five Judges Gin uses a Juniper-forward recipe combined with fruit-based ingredients fresh from the farm for a gin with a less floral and uniquely Texas flavor. Five Judges Gin honors the five judges who called the property home during the past century. Check the website for hours.

Dogologie. 148 E. Main St.; (830) 997-5855; dogologie.com. Fredericksburg is definitely one of the most dog-friendly destinations in the Hill Country, but, if you're feeling guilty for day-tripping without your doggie, you can pick up a present at this downtown shop. (Or, if you've got a doggie day-tripper, bring him in the store for shopping!) Located in the heart of the town's shopping district, this fun boutique sells goodies for dogs and dog lovers ranging from apparel and bedding to toys and treats (as well as fun baked goods). Open daily.

Dooley's 5–10 & 25c Store. 131-33 E. Main St.; (830) 997-3458. Dooley's preserves the tradition of old-fashioned five-and-dime stores, offering sundry items in a nostalgic building with pressed-tin ceilings. You'll find gifts, toys, toiletries, craft supplies, and souvenirs. Open Mon through Sat.

Gathered & Good. 401 E. Augusta St.; (830) 307-3032; gatheredandgood.com. Located in the historic Easter Haus, the shop features home decor, holiday decor, vintage items, and constantly changing gathered goods. Open Wed through Sun.

San Saba Soap Company. 102 W. Austin St.; (830) 992-3624; sansabasoap.com. Skincare and colognes are all natural, made fresh, and formulated with every skin type in mind. Small family-owned business offers cold processed, fragrant goat milk soaps, body oils, and other high-end bath and skin care products. Company became the first pecan oil bath brand using premium pecans from the Pecan Capital of the World. Open Fri through Sun.

Smitten. 307 S. Washington St.; (830) 990-1222. Shop carries vintage and new home goods, local treats, gifts, and other delights. Open Mon through Sat.

where to eat

Altdorf German Biergarten and Restaurant. 301 W. Main St.; (830) 997-7865; altdorfs .com. This is our go-to restaurant in Fredericksburg, especially when we're traveling with our dogs and looking for some relaxed patio dining. Take a break from shopping and enjoy some good German food in a pleasant outdoor setting. Sandwiches, steaks, burgers, and Mexican food are served here as well. There's also dining in an adjacent stone building erected by the city's pioneers. Live music on weekends. Open Wed through Sun. $–$$.

August E's. 203 E. San Antonio St.; (830) 997-1585; august-es-fbg.com. One of Fredericksburg's most sophisticated dining options, August E's features nouveau Texas cuisine in a tasteful main dining room often displaying fine art by local artists. The restaurant is especially known for its dry-aged prime Angus steaks as well as its fresh, never frozen, seafood that is shipped in daily. Hours of operation change. Check the website or call. $$$.

Ausländer Restaurant and Biergarten. 323 E. Main St.; (830) 997-7714; theauslander fredericksburg.com. This popular German eatery has served up schnitzel, sausage, and suds for over two decades. Opt for indoor or outdoor dining with a selection that includes traditional bratwurst, wiener schnitzel, jager schnitzel, and even Texas schnitzel, topped with a spicy ranchero sauce. The beer garden features an extensive selection of beverages accompanied by live music. Open for lunch and dinner Thurs through Tues. $$.

Caliche Coffee Bar. 338 W. Main St.; (830) 992-3536; calichecoffee.com. Located under the roof of what was once a local beer shack, Caliche serves small batch coffee roasted in house by Hill County coffee pioneers Ranch Road Roasters. Caliche offers delicious food items including avocado toast, scones, muffins, and breakfast burritos.

Eaker Barbecue. 607 W. Main St.; (830) 992-3650; eakerbarbecue.com. Lance Eaker and his wife, Boo, use primarily mesquite with post oak to slow smoke prime meats for their South Texas style barbecue. Boo's Korean heritage inspires menu items like Japchae (sweet potato noodles with veggies) or a side of kimchi with your pulled pork and ribs. Open Wed through Sat from 11 a.m. to 3 p.m. or until sold out.

Fredericksburg Brewing Company. 245 E. Main St.; (844) 596-2303; yourbrewery.com. This downtown brewery is known for its ales and lagers but is equally notable for its casual restaurant, housed in an 1890 building, which also includes a biergarten. Next door, a "bed-and-brew" offers 12 accommodations. Open daily for lunch and dinner. $–$$.

Frisch Juicerie. 334 W. Main St.; (830) 534-1476; Frisch-juicerie.business.site. Menu offers delicious and nutritious house-made beverages from wholesome and organic ingredients.

Features made-to-order juices, smoothies, and nut milks, plus specialty drip coffee and nitro cold brew. $.

Hill & Vine. 210 S. Adams St.; (830) 307-3401; hillandvinetx.com. Opened June 2021, Hill & Vine already has a devoted following. No wonder. This fine dining establishment was inspired by a love for Texas food and wine. The menu incorporates southern staples with Hill County flavors like black-eyed pea hummus, grilled redfish, chicken schnitzel, watermelon and green tomato salad, and bi-color corn caviar. For dessert, try roadside fried pies with local peaches, spiced pecans, crisp puff pastry, Texas rum hard sauce, powdered sugar, and Clear River ice cream. Beer, wine, and creative cocktails. Open Tues through Sun. $$.

Hondo's on Main. 312 W. Main St.; (830) 997-1633; hondosonmain.com. Named for Hondo Crouch, the late owner and "mayor" of Luckenbach, this popular eatery and live music venue offers indoor dining as well as a large (dog-friendly) patio and shaded garden. Choose from enchiladas, Frito pie, tortilla soup, or "donut burgers," with Angus beef shaped like a doughnut. (Feeling adventurous? Try the chili cheese burger with the doughnut hole filled with Terlingua beef chili!) Open for lunch and dinner Wed through Sun. $–$$.

Nury's on Main. 319 E. Main St.; (830) 307-3404; nuryscuisine.com. Located in the heart of Fredericksburg, Nury's on Main serves fresh seafood such as the popular Seafood Stack, a layered stack of lump crab, ceviche, shrimp, avocado, cucumber, and sprouts with house-made corn chips. Restaurant also offers a sit-down bar with local beer and local wine. Open Tues through Sun. $$.

Otto's German Bistro. 316 E. Austin St.; (830) 307-3336; ottsfbg.com. Opened in July 2013, Otto's offers farm-to-table German cuisine, as well as German and Austrian wines, craft beers, and creative cocktails. The seasonally focused menu serves dinner and Sunday brunch. Entrees include beef, veal, trout, deep sea prawns, salmon, and duck. Try the favorite Wurst Platte with smoked paprika gruyere sausage, German potato salad, senfgurken (pickles), house-made sauerkraut, and house-made spicy mustard. Open daily for dinner and on Sun for brunch. $$–$$$.

Tubby's Ice House. 318 E. Austin St.; (830) 307-3026; tubbysfbg.com. A neighborhood burger and taco joint with indoor and outdoor seating plus a full bar. Try the fried cheese curds, pork loaded fries, grilled fish tacos, or chipotle pulled pork on a brioche bun. A kids' menu features a small hamburger, chicken fingers, grilled cheese, and more. A playground is a good place for kids to run off some energy. Open daily. $.

Twisted Sisters Bake Shop. 111 S. Washington St.; (830) 990-7999. Sweet and savory baked goods plus a full service espresso bar and a modern family atmosphere invite guests to relax. The changing menu offers a hint of German flair with a nice selection of sandwiches, pretzels, hot dogs, muffins, cookies, and much more. Open Tues through Sun. $.

West End Pizza Co. 207 E. San Antonio St.; (830) 990-6646; westendpizzacompany.com. Dining room offers booth and table seating for small and large parties, plus a roof-covered patio and outdoor seating area for four-legged furry friends. Patrons enjoy hot, brick oven-inspired goodness like build-your-own pizza as well as pasta, soup, sandwiches, salads, and desserts. Also offers wine, beer, and cocktails. Open daily for lunch and dinner. $.

Woerner Warehouse Cafe. 305 S. Lincoln St.; (830) 997-2246; woernerwarehouse.com. Located in the iconic Woerner Feed Store, the cafe serves breakfast and lunch with delicious daily specials created from fresh local produce. For lunch, the popular Don Juan features ham, bacon, house slaw, tomato, onion, dill Havarti, and Dijon mayo on grilled sourdough. Bottled beer, local wine, and an espresso bar are available. Before or after dining, browse the renovated warehouse filled with antiques and nifty gifts. Open Mon through Sat from 9 a.m. to 3 p.m. $.

where to stay

Fredericksburg is the capital city of Texas bed-and-breakfast inns, with accommodations in everything from Sunday houses to local farmhouses to residences just off Main Street. Several reservation services provide information on properties throughout the area.

Albert Hotel. 242 E. Main St.; alberthotel.com. Slated to open in late summer 2022 in downtown Fredericksburg, Albert Hotel is a historic preservation effort with four late 19th century buildings and a newly constructed hotel with 110 guest rooms and event space. The hotel is named for architect and historic preservationist Albert Keidel. The hotel is located on the site where the Keidel family pharmacy and homestead remain and will be integrated into the new two-acre site plan. The hotel also will have three restaurants, two bars, a private dining room, outdoor pool, fitness center, spa, and two-level 160-space parking garage.

Blacksmith Quarters on Barrons Creek. 417 E. Main St.; (830) 998-1981; vacasa.com. Lovely compound of cottages with gorgeous stone-and-water landscaping in the heart of Fredericksburg is a walker's paradise. Located on the original Ransleben Blacksmith property, the eight new one-bedroom cottages are named after the family's children. The original Ransleben-Moellering home built in the 1800s also has been restored. Amenities include gas fireplaces, personal hot tubs, flat-screen TVs, fridge, microwave, and continental breakfast in the rooms. $$$.

Gastehaus Schmidt. 231 W. Main St.; (866) 427-8374 or (830) 997-5612; fbglodging.com. This service represents 100 bed-and-breakfast accommodations, including cottages, log cabins, and a 125-year-old rock barn. All price ranges.

Grae's Casita. 621 S. Washington St.; (830) 998-1660. Fredericksburg's first shipping container vacation rental is cozy and fun with one bedroom and one bathroom. The custom-designed tiny home has a full kitchen, coffee station, two large windows on either side, living room, fireplace, TV, hot tub, and is within easy walking distance to Main Street. $$.

Hangar Hotel. 155 Airport Rd. (south of town); (830) 997-9990; hangarhotel.com. This stylish hotel is perfect for airplane or history buffs. Built to look like a 1940s aircraft hangar, the hotel is located right at the Fredericksburg airport; you can sit out on the balcony and watch private planes come and go. The stylish touches continue in the rooms, down to chairs covered in bomber-jacket leather. The hotel includes an "officer's club" bar and an adjacent '40s-style diner. $$–$$$.

Hoffman Haus. 608 E. Creek St.; (830) 997-6739; hoffmanhaus.com. Five rooms, a flagstone terrace, wraparound side porch, and spa are offered at Hoffman Haus. A complimentary seasonal gourmet breakfast is delivered to each guest room in a picnic basket at 9 a.m. Hoffman Haus also offers private cooking classes and private chef dinners. $$–$$$.

Inn on Barons Creek Spa & Conference Center. 308 S. Washington St.; (830) 990-9202; innonbaronscreek.com. This full-service 90-room hotel also features seven creekside rooms separate from the main hotel. $$$.

Peach Tree Inn & Suites. 401 S. Washington St.; (830) 997-2117; thepeachtreeinn.com. Walk to the historic downtown from this charming country-style hotel. All rooms feature minifridges, microwaves, and high-speed wireless Internet; pets are also welcome at this casual inn with parklike grounds that feature grills and picnic areas. $–$$.

Trueheart Hotel. 201 N. Llano St., (830) 992-3489; thetruehearthotel.com. A boutique 13-room hotel just a block off Main Street, The Trueheart offers a beautifully restored historic house plus seven cottages, each uniquely decorated. The adults-only hotel offers king-size beds, gas fireplaces, private baths, flat-screen TVs, mini-fridges, and microwaves. Some rooms have whirlpool tubs or claw-foot tubs. The outdoor limestone fireplace is a popular gathering place for guests. $$.

Vine on Middle Creek. 1027 Middle Creek Rd.; (830) 321-0328; thevineonmiddlecreek .com. A creekside retreat with a Tesla charging station, The Vine is eight minutes to downtown Fredericksburg. The six farmhouse-style cottages have walk-in showers and Jacuzzistyle tubs, fireplaces, porch swings, and breakfast each morning. The property also includes a vineyard, outside eating area, bocce ball, horseshoes, fire pit, and secluded cigar smoking area. $$$.

especially for winter texans

If you're traveling by RV or trailer, spend some time at the 113-site **Lady Bird Johnson Municipal Park** (830-997-4202; fbgtx.org/343/Lady-Bird-Johnson RV-Park), just southwest of Fredericksburg on TX 16 at 432 Lady Bird Dr. Campsites have electrical, water, sewer, and cable TV hookups. There's a 14-day limit on camping from Apr through Sept. The park includes a self-guided nature trail and also sports an 18-hole golf course, 6 tennis courts, badminton and volleyball courts, and a 17-acre lake for fishing. Pick up a checklist of birds or insects found in the region. Primitive tent camping is also available for $10 per night on a five-acre primitive tent camping field. Tent camping is limited to 14 consecutive nights within a 6-month period. Sleeping in vehicles is prohibited.

enchanted rock state natural area

Whether you're a climber or just looking for a good picnic spot, drive out to **Enchanted Rock State Natural Area;** (830) 685-3636; tpwd.texas.gov/state-parks/enchanted-rock. Located 18 miles north of Fredericksburg on RM 965 at 16710 Ranch Rd. 965, this state park features the largest stone formation in the West. Nationally, this 640-acre granite out-cropping takes second only to Georgia's Stone Mountain. According to Native American legend, the rock is haunted. Sometimes as the rock cools at night, it makes a creaking sound, which probably accounts for the story.

People of all ages in reasonably good physical condition can enjoy a climb up Enchanted Rock. The walk takes about an hour, and hikers are rewarded with a magnificent view of the Hill Country. In warm weather (from Apr through Oct), start your ascent early in the morning before the relentless sun turns the rock into a griddle.

Experienced climbers can scale the smaller formations adjacent to the main dome. These bare rocks are steep and dotted with boulders and crevices, and ascending them requires special equipment.

Picnic facilities and a 55-site primitive campground at the base of the rocks round out the offerings. No vehicular camping is permitted. Park visitors are advised to bring their own drinking water. To prevent overcrowding, a limited number of visitors are allowed in the park during peak periods. Arrive early or plan your trips as we do, during midweek when you can enjoy the park in relative quiet. Open daily. Fee.

where to stay

The Trois Estate at Enchanted Rock. 300 Trois Ln. (16 miles north of Fredericksburg on RM 965); (830) 685-3415; troisestate.net. Fredericksburg may be known for its unique lodging options, but the Trois Estate takes it a step further—not only will you not find another property like this in the Hill Country, you'd be hard-pressed to spot a similar accommodation anywhere in the world. This sprawling estate, complete with a view of Enchanted Rock, is the home and handiwork of designer (and former '60s musician) Charles Trois. With a style termed "modern Maya," the facility features not only rooms and suites, but also a chapel that's popular for weddings (it adjoins an underground swimming pool), an elegant Italian restaurant filled with Trois's collections, and even a toy-gun museum. $$$.

day trip 04

west

hill country escape:
kerrville, ingram, hunt, y. o. ranch

Whether you're looking for cowboys or for culture, you'll find it in the Kerrville area. Many consider this the capital of the Hill Country. Kerrville offers visitors plenty of fun, with attractions ranging from fine art to outdoor activities to some of the top festivals in the state.

kerrville

To reach Kerrville from Austin, follow US 290 west through Johnson City and Fredericksburg (see West Day Trips 02 and 03 for attractions in those cities). Turn south on TX 16 to Kerrville.

Kerrville is popular with retirees, hunters, Winter Texans, and campers. The town of 23,370 residents is home to a 500-acre park and many privately owned camps catering to youth and church groups. Started in the 1840s, the town was named for James Kerr, a supporter of Texas independence. With its unpolluted environment and low humidity, Kerrville later became known as a health center, attracting tuberculosis patients from around the country. The town is still considered one of the most healthful places to live in the nation because of its clean air and moderate climate.

Throughout Kerrville the Schreiner name appears on everything, from Schreiner University (formerly College) to Schreiner's Department Store. Charles Schreiner, who became a Texas Ranger at the tender age of 15, came to Kerrville as a young man in the 1850s. Following the Civil War, he began a dry goods store and started acquiring land and raising

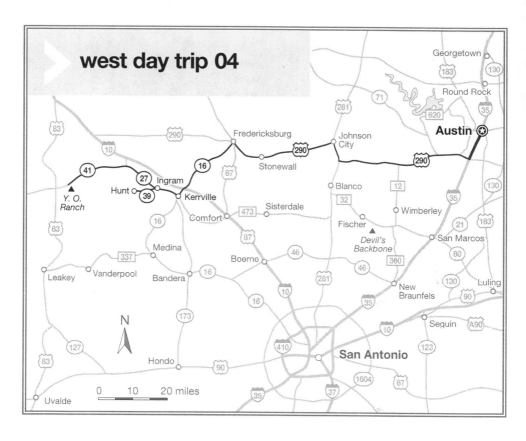

> # west day trip 04

sheep and goats. The Charles Schreiner Company soon expanded to include banking, ranching, and marketing wool and mohair. This was the first business in America to recognize the value of mohair, the product of Angora goats. Before long, Schreiner made Kerrville the mohair capital of the world.

In 1880 Schreiner acquired the Y. O. Ranch, which grew over the next 20 years to more than 600,000 acres, covering a distance of 80 miles. Today the Schreiner family still owns this well-known ranch, located in nearby Mountain Home.

Start your visit with a look at Kerrville's revitalized downtown, where antiques shops and art galleries offer excellent shopping. Under the Texas Main Street program, the city underwent $9.5 million in renovations. Today travelers can "shop 'til they drop" in one-of-a-kind boutiques and galleries and enjoy the special atmosphere of this revitalized 37-block area.

The high quality of the artwork available in Kerrville attests to the community's status as a magnet for artists from across the Southwest. For a look at more Western art, make a visit to the Museum of Western Art. This hilltop museum features Western-themed paintings and sculpture.

Both fine art and performance art headline Kerrville's well-known festivals. Memorial Day weekend brings artists from around the nation to Kerrville to participate in the Kerrville

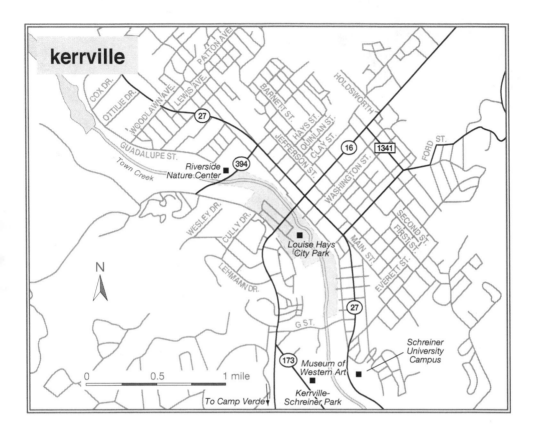

Festival of the Arts. Tap your feet to the tunes of the Kerrville Folk Festival in October. One of Texas's best-loved music gatherings, this extravaganza of song features more than 100 singer-songwriters. The 10-day festival is held 9 miles south of Kerrville at the Quiet Valley Ranch. On the first Saturday of spring and fall months, Kerr Market Days (kerrmarketdays .org) features the work of over 80 Hill Country vendors selling handcrafted art, furniture, woodwork items, toys, jewelry, native plants, and produce.

where to go

The Cailloux Theater. 910 Main St.; (830) 896-9393; caillouxperformingarts.com. The theater features varied performances including the Kerrville Performing Arts Society, Playhouse 2000 (community theater), and the Symphony of the Hills.

The Kerr Arts & Cultural Center. 228 Earl Garrett St.; (830) 895-2911; kacckerrville.com. Features varying exhibits from several local arts groups. Special events include the Texas Furniture Makers Show and the Southwest Gourd Fine Arts Show. Open Tues through Sun 10 a.m. to 4 p.m. Free admission.

Kerrville-Schreiner Park. 2385 Bandera Hwy. (TX 173); (830) 257-7300; kerrvilletx.gov. This park offers 7 miles of hiking trails, as well as fishing and swimming in the Guadalupe River. During summer months, tubes and canoes are for rent for an afternoon excursion on the river. Mountain bikers will find 6 miles of beginner/intermediate trails across the road from the more popular riverside portion of the park. Campsites include water, electricity, and sewage hookups, and mini-cabins are available to rent. Fee.

Louise Hays City Park. 202 Thompson Dr.; (830) 792-8386; kerrvilletx.gov. Bring your picnic lunch to this beautiful spot on the Guadalupe River. Ducks and cypress trees abound, and kids will enjoy a playscape. Open daily. Free admission.

The Museum of Western Art. 1550 Bandera Hwy. (TX 173); (830) 896-2553; museum ofwesternart.com. This museum features work by top Western artists. The building is constructed of 18 boveda brick domes, an old construction method used in Mexico. Western-themed paintings and sculptures fill the museum. The museum also boasts an extensive Western research library. Visitors can take in special programs on the folklore, music, and history of the Old West. Open Tues through Sat. Fee.

Riverside Nature Center. 150 Francisco Lemos; (830) 25RIVER; riversidenaturecenter .org. Features nature trails that focus on native plants of the Hill Country. Facilities include an arboretum, visitor center, and gift shop. Open Mon through Sat. Free admission.

The Schreiner Mansion. 226 Earl Garrett St.; (830) 896-8633. This local history museum traces the development of Kerrville. Housed in the Schreiner Mansion, built in 1879, the building has granite porch columns, wooden parquet floors, and a bronze fountain imported from France. Open Tues through Sat. Fee.

where to shop

Blue Oak Trading Company. 1834 Junction Hwy.; (830) 315-2583; botc.shop. Texas clothing, Hill Country boots, pottery, jewelry, art, locally produced items, and gifts. Open Tues through Sat 10 a.m. to 7 p.m.

Camp Verde General Store. 285 Camp Verde Rd. East, Camp Verde; (830) 634-7722. A working store and post office for over 150 years, this store is adjacent to the site of Camp Verde Army Post, renowned as the location for the army camel experiment in the 1800s. Located 10 miles south of Kerrville on TX 173, the store also has a restaurant that serves lunch. Open daily.

James Avery Visitor Center and Store. 145 Avery Rd. North (3.5 miles north of Kerrville off Harper Road); (830) 353-4001; jamesavery.com. Since 1954 James Avery has been one of Texas's premier silversmiths. He began crafting silver crosses and religious symbols, but today his work includes gold and silver renditions of many subjects, from prickly pears to dolphins. Shop open daily; visitor center open weekdays.

Sunrise Antique Mall. 820 Water St.; (830) 895-2414; sunriseantiquemall.webs.com. Kerrville's largest antiques shop is housed in a century-old building that once served as a furniture store. Open Mon through Sat.

where to eat

1011 Bistro. 1011 Guadalupe St.; (830) 896-1169; 1011bistro.com. Located along the Guadalupe River, this upscale spot offers continental and American dining with a great view of the river from the deck or inside dining room. Live music is featured Fri and Sat during the spring and summer months. Open daily for dinner. $$$.

Bill's Barbecue. 1909 Junction Hwy.; (830) 895-5733; billsbbq.net. This barbecue eatery serves up Texas favorites, such as brisket, sausage, and chicken, with the usual side dishes. Open Tues through Sat 11 a.m. to 7 p.m. $$.

Cowboy Steak House. 416 Main St.; (830) 896-5688; cowboysteakhouse.com. With Kerrville being in the heart of cowboy country, it's not surprising that this restaurant has become a local favorite for its mesquite-broiled steaks. The menu also offers seafood, pork, and chicken entrees, all served inside rustic dining rooms decorated with arts and crafts from around the world. Open for dinner Mon through Sat. $$–$$$.

Francisco's. 201 Earl Garrett St.; (830) 257-2995; franciscoskerrville.com. Located downtown in the historic Weston Building, this restaurant features steak, seafood, and Mexican dishes. Patrons can choose to dine indoors or alfresco at sidewalk tables. Open Mon through Sat 11 a.m. to 2:30 p.m. and Thurs through Sat 5:30 to 8:30 p.m. $$–$$$.

Hill Country Cafe. 806 Main St.; (830) 257-6665; hill-country-cafe.com. This diner is a favorite with local citizens as well as travelers looking for a small-town atmosphere. The day starts out with traditional American breakfast as well as specialties such as huevos rancheros; for lunch look for burgers as well as chicken-fried steak. Open for breakfast and lunch Tues through Fri; breakfast only Sat. $$.

Lakehouse Restaurant. 1655 Junction Hwy.; (830) 895-3188; hillcountrycookin.com. Opened in 1989, Lakehouse offers great views of Guadalupe River, plus a decor with fishing tackle from days gone by and Coca-Cola memorabilia. Southern-style seafood menu features fried catfish, shrimp, clams, fried crawfish tails, grilled salmon, steaks, and fried chicken, plus bottled beer and Texas wine. Open daily at 11 a.m., serving lunch and dinner Mon through Sat, lunch only on Sun. $–$$.

Rio Ranch Café. 2590 Junction Hwy.; (830) 367-1850; therioranchcafe.com. Hill Country down-home cooking features favorites such as barbecue, cowboy ribeye, fried chicken, grilled pork chops, fried catfish, and brisket chili. Known for its hearty breakfasts, the menu features such taste treats as "The Boss Lady's Breakfast" with two of Martha's homemade pork tamales topped with two eggs any style, salsa ranchera, and cheddar jack cheese, served with refried beans, hashbrowns, a chile torreado, and homemade blue corn or flour tortillas. Open Mon for breakfast and lunch, Tues through Fri for breakfast, lunch, and dinner, Sat and Sun for breakfast and lunch. $–$$.

where to stay

Carlton Club Inn. 126 Plaza Dr.; (830) 353-2799; carltoninnhotel.com. Nine separate accommodations are set around a lovely landscaped courtyard in this boutique-style inn. Guests can choose between one- or two-bedroom suites or studios, each with private entrance and distinctive theme. Rooms are decorated with antiques and original artwork. Rooms have fully equipped kitchens plus washers and dryers. $$$.

Y. O. Ranch Hotel and Conference Center. 2033 Sidney Baker, at TX 16 and I-10; (877) 967-3767 or (830) 257-4440; yoranchhotel.com. This 190-room hotel salutes the famous Y. O. Ranch in Mountain Home, located 30 miles from Kerrville. The lobby is filled with reminders of the area's major industries—cattle and hunting. Twelve hotel suites include amenities such as fireplaces, furniture covered in longhorn hide, and wet bars. In keeping with the Wild West spirit, the hotel has a bar called the Elm Waterhole Saloon and the restaurant is dubbed The Branding Iron. $$.

especially for winter texans

Kerrville is home to over a dozen RV parks, some of which are designated "adults only." For a listing, contact the **Kerrville Convention and Visitors Center,** (800) 221-7958, kerrvilletexascvb.com. The chamber can also provide a listing of condominium and apartment properties with short-term leases. A welcoming committee greets Winter Texans as well as the many retirees who relocate to the area.

ingram

To reach Ingram, leave Kerrville on TX 27 and continue northwest for 7 miles. This small community on the banks of the Guadalupe River was started in 1879 by Reverend J. C. W. Ingram, who built a general store and post office in what is now called Old Ingram.

Old Ingram, located off TX 27 on Old Ingram Loop, is home to many art galleries and antiques shops. Ingram proper lies along TX 27; it features stores and outfitters catering to hunters of white-tailed deer, turkey, and quail. The town is particularly busy during deer season, from November to early January. Hunting licenses are required and are sold at local sporting-goods stores. For more information call the Texas Parks and Wildlife Department at (512) 389-4800 in Texas or (800) 792-1112 elsewhere, or visit tpwd.texas.gov.

> ## son of stonehenge

*Unsuspecting drivers might do a double take when driving past the Hill Country Arts Foundation campus as they spy **Stonehenge II,** a nearly life-size replica of the famous standing stones near Salisbury, England. The idea for Stonehenge II came from a rancher who commissioned the replica to be built by sculptor Doug Hill on his ranch near Hunt. The rancher, the late Al Shepperd, later put his ranch up for sale and chose the Hill Country Arts Foundation as a suitable location for his creation. The installation's stones, constructed mainly of plaster over a wire mesh framework, were moved to Ingram in 2010. Stonehenge II is 90 percent as high and 60 percent as wide as the original. Two replicas of Easter Island statues stand nearby as well. It has become one of the most photographed sites in the state, both in its original location in Hunt and at its current home in Ingram. The roadside statues are open-air and available for viewing without charge.*

A gallery exhibits the work of many artists and is open Tues through Sat. The Gazebo Gift Shop is a sales outlet for local artists, open Mon through Fri afternoons. The HCAF campus is also the current home of the Stonehenge II replica. Call for a schedule of play times or special events. Free admission.

where to go

Hill Country Arts Foundation. Located west of the Ingram Loop at 120 Point Theatre Rd., South Ingram (off TX 39); (800) 459-HCAF or (830) 367-5121; hcaf.com. The foundation, located 6 miles west of Kerrville in Ingram, is one of the oldest multidiscipline arts centers in the nation. For more than 50 years, this 15-acre center on the banks of the Guadalupe River has encouraged students in the fields of art, theater, photography, printmaking, and even quilt making. American musicals and plays are performed during the summer months at the open-air Point Theatre; indoor shows entertain audiences at other times throughout the year.

Kerr County Historical Murals. At TX 27 and TX 39. Sixteen murals decorate the T. J. Moore Lumber Company building, the work of local artist Jack Feagan. The scenes portray historical events in Kerr County, starting with the establishment of shingle camps (where wooden roofing shingles were produced in 1846). Other paintings highlight cattle drives, the birth of the mohair industry, and the last Native American raid. Free admission.

where to shop

Clint Orms Engravers and Silversmiths. 229-B Old Ingram Loop; (830) 367-7949; clintorms.com. Mr. Orms's works have been purchased for presidents, top musicians, and other well-known personalities. His silver belt buckle sets are of heirloom quality, using the finest materials. Open Mon through Sat.

Southwestern Elegance. 206 Old Ingram Loop; (830) 367-4749; southwesternelegance .com. This unique store specializes in Mexican collectibles and antiques (especially primitives), Mennonite furniture, and Tarahumara collectibles. Another section of the store sells women's boutique apparel and jewelry. Open Tues through Sat.

hunt

Continue west on TX 39 for 7 miles to Hunt, a small community best known for its year-round outdoor recreational camps catering to Scouts as well as youth and church groups.

where to go

Ingram Lake and Dam. 610 TX 39. Located just west of town, this dam on the Guadalupe River is a popular spot where swimmers can slide down the dam on mats for a cooling dip in the river. Above the dam, the small lake is a favorite place to swim or float on tubes. Free admission; fee for parking.

Kerr Wildlife Management Area. 2625 RM 1340 (12 miles northwest of Hunt); (830) 238-4483; tpwd.texas.gov. Enjoy a driving tour over this 6,493-acre research ranch owned by the Texas Parks and Wildlife Department. Purchased to study the relationship between wildlife and livestock, the ranch is home to white-tailed deer, javelinas, wild turkeys, bobcats, gray foxes, and ringtails. Open daily, but call during hunting season, when the area may be closed for a hunt. Free admission.

y. o. ranch

From Hunt, head west on FM 1340 to TX 41. Turn left and the Y. O. Ranch will soon appear on your right. This ranch dates back to 1880, a part of the 550,000 acres purchased by Captain Charles Schreiner, former Texas Ranger and longhorn-cattle owner.

The Y. O. spans 50 square miles and supports one of the largest herds of registered Texas longhorns in the nation. Charlie Schreiner III, the original owner's grandson, brought the breed back from near extinction in the late 1950s, founding the Texas Longhorn Breeders Association. After the devastating Texas drought in the 1950s, the Schreiners began to diversify the use of their ranch, stocking the land with the largest collection of natural roaming exotics in the country, including many rare and endangered species. More than 10,000 animals range the hills, including zebra, ostrich, giraffe, emu, and ibex.

You may visit the Y. O. Ranch only by reservation. Both day and overnight programs are offered. Day-trippers can enjoy the spread on a lunch tour or photo safari. The ranch also hosts several outdoor camp events that teach horseback riding, rappelling, gun handling, and wildlife study. Overnight accommodations are available in the 1800s-era cabins; meals are included. For general information, call (800) YO-RANCH or (830) 640-3222.

where to stay

River Inn Resort and Conference Center. 2960 TX 39; (800) 841-0501 or (830) 238-4226; riverinnresort.com. This property is a good choice for relaxing on the Guadalupe River, as it sits right on the water. The 60 condominium units are independently owned and all have separate living rooms, bedrooms, and fully equipped kitchens. The resort offers swimming, fishing, tennis courts, and kayaks for exploring the river. $$–$$$.

northwest

day trip 01

northwest

lakeside luxury:
lake austin, lake travis, lakeway

This is a popular hot weather day trip. Bring your swimsuit from April through October, along with an old pair of sneakers to navigate the rocky Lake Travis beaches.

lake austin

Within the city limits of Austin you'll find this picturesque man-made "lake." Technically speaking, it's a reservoir and was formed by the construction of the Tom Miller Dam in 1939, which also assists with generating electricity for the city of Austin. Aside from the practicality of Lake Austin and its dam, it offers water-related activities and camping opportunities.

where to go

Fritz Hughes Park. 3100 Fritz Hughes Park Rd.; (512) 854-7275; parks.traviscountytx.gov. From the intersection of RM 620 and RM 2222, take RM 620 south 3.7 miles to Low Water Crossing Road (just before Mansfield Dam). Turn left on Low Water Crossing Road and travel 0.2 mile to Fritz Hughes Park Road, then turn left to park entrance. Along with Mary Quinlan and Selma Hughes Parks, this is one of only three access points along the north side of Lake Austin. The small Lower Colorado River Authority (LCRA) park is usually frequented by local residents. The park offers picnicking, swimming, and fishing. Open daily. Free admission.

Loop 360 Boat Ramp. 5019 Capital of Texas Hwy. North; (512) 854-7275; parks.travis countytx.gov. From the intersection of Loop 360 (Capital of Texas Highway) and RM 2222,

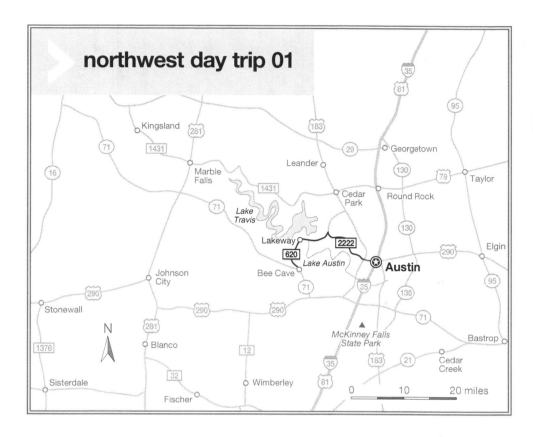

northwest day trip 01

travel south on Loop 360 across the Pennybacker Bridge over Lake Austin. The entrance to the boat ramp is on the east side of Loop 360, directly below the bridge. As its name suggests, this park is primarily used by boaters as a launch onto Lake Austin. You'll also find areas for fishing and picnicking. Open daily. Free admission.

Mary Quinlan Park. 1601 Quinlan Park Rd. South; (512) 854-7275; parks.traviscountytx .gov. From the intersection of RM 620 and RM 2222, take RM 620 south 2.1 miles to Quinlan Park Road. Turn left onto Quinlan Park Road and travel 5.5 miles to the park entrance. This quiet park has the only public boat ramp for miles along Lake Austin. It is a beautiful place to enjoy the quiet of one of Lake Austin's narrow passages and to view the bluffs against the water's emerald depths. Open daily. Free admission.

Mount Bonnell. 3800 Mount Bonnell Rd.; mountbonnell.com. A beautiful lookout is located within the Austin city limits. Turn left off RM 2222 onto Mount Bonnell Road, which will take you to the highest point in town, with a panoramic view of the city and the surrounding hills. Visitors must park and walk up some steep steps to the lookout, but the view is well worth the climb. Free admission.

Selma Hughes Park. 11921 Selma Hughes Park Rd.; (512) 854-7275; parks.traviscounty tx.gov. From the intersection of RM 620 and RM 2222, take RM 620 south 2.1 miles to Quinlan Park Road. Turn right on Quinlan Park Road and travel 4.6 miles to Selma Hughes Road. Turn left on Selma Hughes Road and proceed to park entrance. Along with Fritz Hughes and Mary Quinlan Parks, Selma Hughes Park is one of the few public-access sites along this part of Lake Austin. Here the lake is narrow and quiet; and in the park, visitors are usually local residents. Visitors will find picnicking, swimming, and fishing areas. Free admission.

where to eat

County Line on the Lake. 5204 RM 2222; (512) 346-3664; countyline.com. This is one of the few barbecue restaurants in Texas where you could wear a coat and tie and not look like a city slicker. Enjoy full table service at this excellent restaurant on Lake Austin, ordering from a menu that features brisket, sausage, and ribs. Located right on the shores of Lake Austin with an excellent view, this is a popular summer stop. Open for lunch and dinner daily. $$–$$$.

where to stay

Lake Austin Spa Resort. 1705 S. Quinlan Park Rd.; (800) 847-5637 or (512) 372-7300; lakeaustin.com/spa-resort. This well-known resort caters to guests, with special menus, dietary consultations, and European spa services. The 40-room resort lies on the shores of Lake Austin, a narrow swath of water that begins at the foot of the Hill Country and flows through the western part of the city. The resort, a longtime favorite in the Lone Star State, became a world-class destination spa thanks to the opening of the 25,000-square-foot LakeHouse Spa (available to day visitors as well as to guests). The two-story, Texas-size structure, resembling traditional Hill Country farmhouses with its limestone exterior and screened upstairs porch, houses 20 treatment areas. $$$.

lake travis

Continue northwest on RM 2222. This winding road is filled with treacherous curves, so take it slow. At the intersection with RM 620, you have two choices: turn west onto RM 620 and continue to Mansfield Dam and the remainder of this trip, or turn east to some county parks and Austin's best-known outdoor dining spot. This side excursion affords a beautiful drive past some of Austin's most expensive homes.

where to go

Bob Wentz at Windy Point. 7144 Comanche Trail (1 mile past Hippie Hollow); (512) 854-7275; parks.traviscountytx.gov. Mention Windy Point and Austinites think of windsurfing, sailing, or scuba diving. A top spot on Lake Travis for water sports, this LCRA park offers a hiking and biking trail, sand volleyball courts, and a boat ramp for sailboats. Open daily. Fee.

Cypress Creek Park. 13601 Bullick Hollow Rd.; (512) 854-7275; parks.traviscountytx.gov. From the intersection of RM 620 and RM 2222, take Bullick Hollow Road west 2 miles. The park entrance is on your left, just before the intersection of Bullick Hollow Road and FM 2769 (Old Anderson Mill Road). A favorite for lake lovers, this day-use LCRA park includes a boat ramp. It is frequented by many campers, boaters, picnickers, and anglers. Open daily and offers unimproved camp sites. Fee.

Hippie Hollow Park. 7000 Comanche Trail (from RM 620, turn right onto Comanche Trail); (512) 854-7275; parks.traviscountytx.gov. This is a clothing-optional park, the only one in the Austin area. On summer weekends, it is packed with nudists, curious onlookers, and swimmers who want to enjoy a beautiful swimming hole. The parking area is located away from the bathing area. (Nudity is not permitted in the parking lot.) Onlookers outnumber nudists many weekends, but to see the beach (and the swimmers), you must leave your car and walk down the trail to the water's edge. The swimming area is protected from curious boaters by patrolling Parks Department boats. No children allowed. Day use only. Fee.

Mansfield Dam Park. 4370 Mansfield Dam Park Rd.; (512) 854-7275; parks.traviscountytx .gov. From the intersection of RM 620 and RM 2222, travel south 4.9 miles. Turn right onto Mansfield Dam Road, just south of Mansfield Dam; the park entrance is on the left. One of the most visited LCRA parks along Lake Travis, Mansfield Dam Park is among the top boat-launching sites on the lake. The park also appeals to campers and picnickers; a primitive area is located nearby. Open daily. Fee.

Pace Bend Park. 2011 N. Pace Bend Rd.; (512) 264-1482; parks.traviscountytx.gov. From the intersection of RM 620 and TX 71, take TX 71 west 11 miles to RM 2322 (Pace Bend Park Road). Turn right on RM 2322 and travel 4.6 miles to the park entrance. Pace Bend is one of the top parks, not only of the LCRA sites, but also in the entire region. Nine miles of shoreline appeal to swimmers and boaters; horseback riders and hikers also find diversions with a large natural area. Part of the park is managed as a wildlife preserve and can be reached by rugged trails—an excellent destination for wildlife-viewing and bird-watching. Offers 20 improved camp sites. Open daily. Fee.

Sandy Creek Park. 9500 Lime Creek Rd.; (512) 854-7275; parks.traviscountytx.gov. From the intersection of RM 620 and RM 2222, take Bullick Hollow Road west 2.5 miles to FM 2769. Turn left onto FM 2769 and travel 4 miles to Lime Creek Road, through the town of Volente. Entrance is on the left. This quiet park is far less visited than many other north Lake Travis sites and is popular with swimmers and nature lovers. Offers unimproved camp sites. Open daily. Fee.

Tom Hughes Park. 12714 Hughes Park Rd.; (512) 854-7275; parks.traviscountytx.gov. From the intersection of RM 620 and RM 2222, take RM 620 south 2.3 miles to Marshall Ford Drive. Turn right onto Marshall Ford Drive and travel 0.2 mile to Park Drive. Turn right and travel 2.8 miles to park entrance. Scuba divers call this park a favorite. The walk to the water's edge is steep and brushy. Fee.

Volente Beach Waterpark. 16107 FM 2769 in Volente; (512) 258-5110; beachsidebillys .com. This favorite summer hangout offers a pool, giant water slides, a sand beach, motorized water sports, volleyball, and more. There's also a casual restaurant on-site, and visitors may bring coolers with prepared food and drink (no glass containers or alcohol). Hours vary with season. Fee.

where to eat

The Oasis. 6550 Comanche Trail; (512) 266-2442; oasis-austin.com. Known as "The Sunset Capital of Texas," this restaurant is famous for its open decks overlooking Lake Travis. On weekends, it becomes a popular stop after a day of boating or swimming. The lake views and the surrounding hills provide a lovely backdrop for a sunset meal at this unusual restaurant. Open daily for lunch and dinner. $–$$.

lakeway

At the intersection of RM 2222 and RM 620, turn right and continue west on RM 620 across Mansfield Dam to the village of Lakeway and the Lakeway Resort and Conference Center. This 8,000-person resort community boasts recreational facilities and accommodations for golf and tennis buffs. You can't miss it; just look for the water tower shaped and painted like a golf ball.

where to go

The Hills of Lakeway. 26 Club Estates Pkwy.; (512) 261-7200; clubcorp.com/Clubs/The -Hills-of-Lakeway. The Live Oak and the Yaupon 18-hole courses are open to members. Golf packages in conjunction with the Lakeway Resort and Spa also are available. Fee.

where to stay

Lakeway Resort and Spa. 101 Lakeway Dr.; (800) LAKEWAY or (512) 261-6600; lakeway resortandspa.com. Adjacent to the marina on Lake Travis, this large resort has rooms featuring elegant decor and a lake view. Some accommodations include fireplaces. A lobby bar serves evening cocktails, and Masterson's Steakhouse offers breakfast, lunch, and dinner. An adjacent marble-topped bar features views of the lake. $$$.

day trip 02

northwest

>>> **lake love:**
jonestown, lago vista, marble falls, kingsland

The Highland Lakes region is made up of a series of seven lakes that form back-to-back "stair steps" along the Colorado River. Built in the 1930s by the Lower Colorado River Authority (LCRA) to bring electricity to rural Texas and to control flooding along the river, the lakes now provide 150 miles of water recreation.

To start this day trip and reach the north shores of Lake Travis, head to Cedar Park on US 183 (see Northeast Day Trip 03 for Cedar Park details), then turn west on FM 1431.

jonestown

Head west from Cedar Park, and the road soon begins twisting and turning, dipping into what many describe as the first wave of the Texas Hill Country. Just after Cedar Park gives way to cedar breaks and untamed countryside, you'll pass through a small pocket of homes and a few businesses, the remains of the community of Nameless.

From Nameless continue west to the community of Jonestown. Named for founders Emmet and Warren Jones, this town was first envisioned as a retirement community on the shores of Lake Travis. Today the town has grown somewhat, though, and serves as a home base for many commuters into Austin.

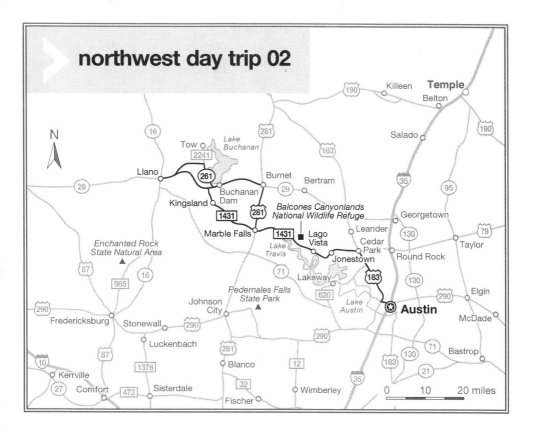

northwest day trip 02

where to go

Jones Brothers Park. 10301 Lakeside Dr.; (512) 267-3243. This 32-acre public-use park includes 3 boat ramps, walking paths, picnic areas, a children's playscape, and more. Fee.

lago vista

With a name that translates as "Lake View," it's no surprise that much of Lago Vista boasts a view of Lake Travis. This sprawling lake offers anglers, boaters, and swimmers innumerable coves and quiet stretches. The LCRA operates many public parks in this region. Lago Vista is called the gateway to the Balcones Canyonlands National Wildlife Refuge, a preserve that protects two endangered species. Along with hikes and birding at the refuge, nature buffs also find many opportunities at LCRA parks in the region.

where to go

Balcones Canyonlands National Wildlife Refuge. 5 miles west of Lago Vista on FM 1431 at 24518 Ranch Rd. 1431; (512) 339-9432; fws.gov/refuge/balcones_canyonlands.

This preserve protects the juniper habitat of the tiny golden-cheeked warbler and black-capped vireo. The 22-square-mile preserve schedules its public hours around the breeding schedule of the birds, so you may find the park closed at certain periods. The best place to view the vireos is at the Shin Oak Observation Deck (it closes when the vireos arrive in the spring). Several hiking trails are open most of the year. The preserve also hosts several special events every year, most notably the Balcones Songbird Festival in the spring. The event includes guided nature walks focusing on birding, wildlife, and butterflies. Free admission.

Flat Creek Estate Winery & Vineyard. 24912 Singleton Bend East; (512) 267-6310; flat creekestate.com. Go 6 miles west of Lago Vista on FM 1431, then turn south on Singleton Bend Road. Continue 2.5 miles to Singleton Bend East, then turn left and continue to gate. Tucked in a quiet valley, this winery's 20 acres of vineyards produce Italian, Rhône, and port varietal grapes that Flat Creek transforms into wines that have won competitions across Texas and beyond. The winery offers guided tours followed by a tasting. Check website for various wine tastings offered as well as dates and times. Fee for tastings.

Lago Vista Airpower Museum and Library. 314 Flightline Rd. (at Rusty Allen Airport); (512) 267-7403; aviationmuseum.eu. Continue west of Lago Vista on FM 1431, then turn north on Bar-K Ranch Road and follow signs to the airport. The Lago Vista private airport is home to a museum showcasing military aircraft through model plane displays, many photos, and various other displays. Open Sat and Sun 1 to 5 p.m. or by appointment. Free admission.

where to eat

The Bistro at Flat Creek Estate. 24912 Singleton Bend East; (512) 267-6310; flatcreek estate.com. Enjoy a multicourse wine-paired menu prepared by Executive Chef Sean Fulford at this casual restaurant with indoor and outside options. Rustic lunch specials include wood-fired pizzas, the Flat Creek Angus burger, roasted chicken, and more. Weekend brunch is offered 11 a.m. to 1 p.m. and ranges from eggs Benedict to barbacoa tacos. Reservations required. Open Thurs through Mon. $$–$$$.

marble falls

Continue west on FM 1431 to Marble Falls. Drive south on US 281 to the overlook at the edge of town for a terrific view of the 780-acre Lake Marble Falls. It's said that this sight inspired local songwriter Oscar J. Fox (who penned "The Cowboy's Lament" and "Get Along Little Dogie") to write his popular tune "Hills of Home." Today a marker commemorates this local hero.

Normally the falls that gave this town its name are beneath the lake, but occasionally they are visible when the LCRA does repair work on the dam.

While the town may be named for marble, granite is king here. Granite Mountain at the western edge of town is the home of a huge quarry that sells pink granite to places around the country. This quarry supplied the granite used in building the State Capitol and also many of the jetties along the Texas coast. Visitors are not allowed in the quarry but can observe the operation from the rest stop on the side of FM 1431.

where to go

Marble Falls Chamber of Commerce & CVB Visitor Center. 916 Second St.; (830) 693-2815; marblefalls.org. Stop by for brochures and maps on area shopping, dining, and parks recreation. Open Mon through Fri 9 a.m. to 5 p.m. Free admission.

lake parks

Arkansas Bend Park. FM 1431 south to Lohmans Ford Road at 16900 Cherry Ln.; (512) 854-PARK; parks.traviscountytx.gov. Turn left on Lohmans Crossing Road and travel 4.5 miles to Sylvester Ford Road. Turn left on Sylvester Ford Road and travel 1.5 miles to the park entrance. This is one of the quieter parks along Lake Travis, thanks to its remote location and "Quiet Hours" enforced between 10 p.m. and 7 a.m. All radios and generators must be turned off at this time. The park offers camping, picnicking, fishing, trails, RV dump stations, restrooms, and two boat ramps. Open daily. Fee.

Camp Creek Recreation Area. (512) 473-3366; lcra.org. North side of Lake Travis, about 18 miles west of Lago Vista or 8 miles east of Marble Falls near the Smithwick community at 3408 1221 CR 343. Take FM 1431 to CR 343 and continue about a half mile to the site entrance. Camp Creek Area offers a loop hiking trail, and, in early mornings and late evenings, visitors can see local wildlife. The park is shaded by large pecan trees and is especially good for those looking for a quiet, undeveloped site. This area should, however, be avoided during heavy rains. The access to Camp Creek is a steep gravel road with two low-water crossings that are often covered after rainstorms. Open daily. Fee.

Gloster Bend Recreation Area. (512) 473-3366; lcra.org. North side of Lake Travis, approximately 6 miles west of Lago Vista near the Travis Peak community. Take FM 1431 to Singleton Road and continue 3.3 miles to the site entrance at 3533 Hollingsworth Rd. This large day-use park, divided into woodlands on the south and grasslands on the north, boasts the highest visitation of all the Lake Travis recreation areas. The site has only minimal facilities, including a boat ramp,

The Falls on the Colorado Museum. 2001 Broadway St.; (830) 798-2157; fallsmuseum .org. Located on the campus of the Marble Falls Elementary School, this local history museum is housed in a historic school building that dates from 1891. Exhibits include a photograph collection of the town and the Colorado River before the construction of the Max Starcke Dam created Lake Marble Falls. Hours are seasonal. Check the website. Free admission.

Highland Arts Guild Gallery. 318 Main St.; (830) 693-7324; highlandartsguild.org. Have a look here at the work of numerous local artists who call the Highland Lakes their home. The gallery sells original arts and crafts, including many bluebonnet paintings. In addition to the gallery, the guild sponsors a series of classes and workshops on the arts. Open Mon through Sat 10 a.m. to 5 p.m. Free admission.

a flushing restroom at park entrance, composting toilets, fire rings, and trash cans. More than 1 mile of shoreline can be easily accessed. Open daily. Fee.

Shaffer Bend Recreation Area. *(512) 473-3366; lcra.org. 17 miles west of Lago Vista or 9 miles east of Marble Falls near the Smithwick Community. Take FM 1431 to CR 343A and continue about 1 mile to 706 CR 343A. This park is one of the largest on Lake Travis, with 523 acres, and one of the top LCRA parks. Shaffer is a favorite with day-trippers and campers looking for an undeveloped site that offers good lake views, plenty of wildlife, and various kinds of vegetation. The recreation area, located between Marble Falls and Lago Vista on the lake's north shore, is dotted with hills of dense cedar. From these peaks, you can enjoy good lake views at several points along the park road.*

The hills gradually give way to savanna shaded by oaks and pecan trees. Here you can also see the guayacan, a plant not usually seen east of Del Rio. A mile long swimming area offers a chance to cool off after hiking. Open daily. Fee.

Turkey Bend Recreation Area. *(512) 473-3366; lcra.org. North side of Lake Travis, approximately 9.5 miles west of Lago Vista. Take FM 1431 to Shaw Drive and continue 1.8 miles to the site entrance at 4000 Shaw Dr. This 400-acre park winds along 2 miles of Lake Travis's northern shoreline. The recreation area is popular with those looking for a real back-to-nature getaway. The site has been left mostly undeveloped, with only one portable toilet, no drinking water, and no trash collection. Some primitive campsites are marked with fire rings.*

Horseback riders and hikers frequent the park for its loop trail with good views of the lake. One warning: During hunting season, there is hunting on adjacent private land, so be wary when approaching fence lines. Open daily. Fee.

Hills of Home Memorial. US 281, south of the Colorado River. The memorial remembers Oscar J. Fox, the composer of "The Cowboy's Lament," "Get Along Little Dogie," and "Hills of Home," said to be inspired by the view from this spot. Free admission.

where to eat

Blue Bonnet Cafe. 211 US 281 (near the bridge); (830) 693-2344; bluebonnetcafe.net. This is an example of a good old-fashioned Texas diner at its best. For more than 80 years, the Blue Bonnet Cafe has served locals and visitors plenty of country cooking, including chicken-fried steak, fried chicken, burgers, and breakfast all day. $–$$.

Inman's Ranch House Bar-B-Que. 707 Sixth St.; (830) 693-2711. This little restaurant uses Texas's favorite cooking method—barbecue—on turkey to produce a spicy sausage that's mighty tasty and not as greasy as its pork cousin. Beef brisket and sides of coleslaw and beans also appear on the menu. Open Tues through Sun. $.

where to stay

Horseshoe Bay Resort. 200 Hi Circle North (west of Marble Falls off FM 2147); (877) 611-0112 or (830) 598-2511; hsbresort.com. Horseshoe Bay, located on Lake LBJ, is one of the premier resorts in Central Texas. Golfers have their choice of four courses, including Robert Trent Jones's Apple Rock. Other features include the Bayside Spa and Fitness Center, a yacht club, and tennis courts. Accommodations range from rooms and suites in the hotel tower to fully equipped apartments and condos. $$$.

The McKenzie Guest House. 910 Third St.; (830) 299-3530. Named for the owners, Matt and Lindsay McCormack 's daughter McKenzie, this downtown bed-and-breakfast property features six suites in a century-old house. Each suite is furnished with period-correct antique furniture, private bath, and full kitchen area. $$.

kingsland

Continue west on FM 1431 from Marble Falls to the community of Kingsland on Lake LBJ. Originally named Granite Shoals, Lake LBJ was renamed for President Lyndon Baines Johnson, who, as a young US representative, brought the Highland Lakes project to Central Texas. Today the narrow, winding lake is popular with both anglers and water-skiers. Edged by steep hills, its clear and calm waters are protected from the winds that often buffet the larger lakes.

Kingsland is a sleepy community catering to those who come to enjoy a few days of bass fishing. Several lodges lie near the junction of the Llano and Colorado Rivers, where quiet coves afford a catch of black bass, white bass, crappie, catfish, and perch. Be sure to stop at the scenic overlook on FM 1431 just past the edge of town for a grand view of the lake and its shoreline homes.

where to go

Nightengale Archaeological Center. From Kingsland travel south on FM 1431 for 3 miles, then turn right on CR 126 and proceed 0.2 mile, turning left on Circle Drive for 300 feet to the entrance at 1010 Circle Dr; (830) 598-5261; texasluas.org. Since its discovery in 1988, this site has proven to be rich in archaeological finds, some of which date back to the Paleo-Indian period, over 10,000 years ago. The site is managed by the LCRA and the Llano Uplift Archeological Society, which conducts guided tours on the second and fourth Sat of each month, Feb through Nov. A visitor center and museum display artifacts found at the site. Free admission.

"The Slab." West of Kingsland where FM 3404 crosses the Llano River. This informal swimming hole is a favorite summertime hangout. In fact, this section of 3404 is known as "Slab Road." The river here is shallow and wide, with numerous channels of clear water creating pools just perfect for wading and splashing. There is limited parking on the roadside but no facilities. For more information, check out visitmarblefalls.org/discover/the-slab. Free admission.

day trip 03

northwest

>>> **ranch road rambling:**
cedar park, leander, bertram, burnet,
buchanan dam, tow

Leaving bustling US 183 in your rearview mirror, this getaway travels on a winding road that snakes into the northern Hill Country, ending on the shores of massive Lake Buchanan.

cedar park

Cedar Park is north from Austin via US 183. Now primarily a suburb, once this was called "cedar chopper" country. Cedar choppers were independent people who worked the hilly land to the west, cutting juniper trees to provide fence posts for area ranchers. This generations-old trade is still plied by some Hill Country families.

where to go

Austin Steam Train. 401 E. Whitestone Blvd. (US 183 and FM 1431); (512) 402-3830; austinsteamtrain.org. Take a ride on the Hill Country Flyer, running from Cedar Park to Burnet (where visitors stop to have lunch and shop). Each of the 1930s-era cars is restored to original splendor. Other rides include the Bertram Flyer for a ride from Cedar Park to Bertram (with a chance to get out and see the old depot) and a host of themed excursions such as the Spring Break Flyer, Murder Mystery Excursions, and the holiday-themed North Pole Flyer. Reservations required. Fee.

Brushy Creek Regional Trail. 204 E. Little Elm Trail; (512) 943-1920; wilco.org. This trail, with a total length of nearly 7 miles, is a favorite with outdoor enthusiasts thanks to its water

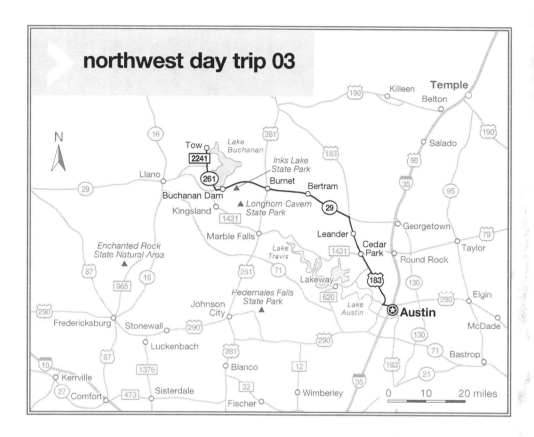

northwest day trip 03

fun and wide gravel paths. Although the park may get busy in the areas of the splash pads and playgrounds, much of the trail is quiet. It winds along the water with multiple entry points and facilities for fishing and picnicking, and photo sessions in wildflower fields. The trail is wide and easily shared by hikers and bikers. Free admission.

Cedar Bark. 2525 W. New Hope Dr.; (512) 401-5500; cedarparktexas.gov. If you are making a day trip with your dog, this park is definitely a must-see for dogs who enjoy the company of fellow canines. The large, fenced dog park features separate sections for small and large dogs as well as a canine swimming area. The swimming pond features a fountain as well as a platform for dock-diving dogs. Along with benches and fountains for both four- and two-legged visitors, the park also includes a separate fenced dog shower area for rinsing off Rover before you continue on your travels. Free admission.

Cedar Park Sculpture Garden. 1435 Main St.; (512) 401-5000; cedarparktexas.gov. Located adjacent to the Cedar Park Recreation Center, this large outdoor area features a rotating collection of sculptures created by local artists. Meandering gravel pathways wind through the displays, and if you happen to fall in love with one of the pieces, you're in luck, as most are for sale. Free admission.

H-E-B Center at Cedar Park. 2100 Avenue of the Stars; (512) 600-5000; hebcenter.com. This multipurpose arena, seating 8,000, is the home ice of the Texas Stars professional hockey team, which competes in the American Hockey League as a top-level affiliate of the NHL Dallas Stars and home to the Austin Spurs of the NBA G League. When the Stars and Spurs aren't in town, the facility hosts other special events. Performances have ranged from country music artist George Strait to the Cirque du Soleil. Open daily. Fee for events.

Veterans Memorial. 2525 New Hope Dr.; (512) 401-5000; cedarparktexas.gov. This site honors US military personnel and their families with brick pavers, each engraved with an individual soldier's name, rank, and date of service. A tall granite obelisk towers over the scene as well as a bronze statue honoring a Cedar Park soldier killed during Operation Iraqi Freedom. Free admission.

where to eat

Cajun Skillet Restaurant. 251 N. Bell Blvd., #101; (512) 243-5290; cajunskillet.com. Authentic New Orleans cuisine in a simple family-owned restaurant. Menu favorites are crawfish etouffee, catfish Olivia, beignets, and oyster po'boy. Open Wed through Sun. $.

J&J BBQ & Burgers. 300 W. Whitestone Blvd.; (512) 918-0314; jj-bbq.com. This former home has been transformed into a casa of 'que with a delightful mix of barbecue and Tex-Mex specialties. Brisket and sausage are tops, but breakfast (including tacos, huevos rancheros, and chorizo) is extremely popular, especially on weekends. Open daily. $.

leander

Continue north on US 183 to neighboring Leander, a town of 53,716 that boasts many historic markers. To the right as you approach town, you'll see a marker for the Blockhouse Creek subdivision, named for a blockhouse used as an interim prison by the Texas Rangers a century ago.

Another historic marker stands just east of US 183 on FM 2243. The Davis Cemetery, as the marker recounts, is the site of a mass grave, a reminder of an attack by Native Americans that ended with the deaths of many pioneers. For all its long history, however, the Davis Cemetery is overshadowed by the city's Bagdad Cemetery on CR 279 at the corner of FM 2243, best known for its appearance in the opening scenes from *Texas Chainsaw Massacre*.

However, the most historic Leander site is actually found closer to Cedar Park. This marker recalls the discovery of "Leanderthal Lady" in January 1983. Dating back between 10,000 and 13,000 years, the skeleton and the site are considered one of the country's most important Early Man locations. The historic marker is located east of US 183 on FM 1431,southeast of the intersection with Parmer Lane.

where to go

Dinosaur Tracks. South San Gabriel River, just north of town; (512) 259-1907. Park your car at the bridge and walk upstream for a half mile to see these three-toed dinosaur tracks. Free admission.

where to eat

Mouton's Southern Bistro. 309 US 183 North; (512) 260-6300; moutonsbistro.com. If you're in the mood for an alligator po'boy, you've found your spot at this restaurant that deems its menu as "Cajun with a Texas flair." The large menu includes other Cajun favorites as well, such as jambalaya and boudin. Burgers and pastas are also well represented. Open daily. $$.

bertram

From Leander continue north on US 183 to the intersection with TX 29. Drive west on TX 29 for 12 miles to Bertram. This was once a thriving community, with four cotton gins and a busy railroad constructed to haul granite from Marble Falls to Austin for the construction of the Texas State Capitol. Today, however, this is a sleepy little town most of the year, but on Labor Day weekend the streets throng with travelers from around the state who come for the annual Oatmeal Festival. Visitors attend the celebration to witness an oatmeal cook-off, take part in a fun run, or see a parade. The festival is named for the hamlet of Oatmeal, located 6 miles south of Bertram on RM 243.

where to shop

Texas Mesquite Company Gallery. 244 E. TX 29; (512) 355-3710; texmcs.com. Furniture builder Craig Lagerstrom operates a workshop in Bertram and displays and sells his unique

feeling your oats

If you have some extra time in your day trip and you're looking for a fun photo op, head south to the tiny community of Oatmeal. Located 5.6 miles south of Bertram on RM 243, this unincorporated town was founded by German settlers and named for its gristmill. You'll find a small historic schoolhouse here, but our favorite stop is the famous oatmeal box. While Texas may be home to some uniquely painted water towers, including Luling's watermelon, this site features a water standpipe painted as a 3 Minute Brand Oatmeal box, an homage to the annual Oatmeal Festival.

handmade furniture in this gallery. His tables, desks, chairs, and other items are crafted from Texas mesquite and reclaimed vintage longleaf pine. Custom furniture can be made to order. Open Mon through Sat.

burnet

From Bertram continue west on TX 29 to Burnet. This is the closest town of any size to Lake Buchanan (pronounced "BUCK-an-an"). It's a good place to stop for picnic supplies and sunscreen products during summer visits (there are few facilities once you leave the city limits). Popular outdoor activities include fishing and bird-watching throughout the year as well as hunting during white-tailed deer season.

where to go

Canyon of the Eagles Resort. 16942 RM 2341; (800) 977-0081 or (512) 334-2070; canyon oftheeagles.com. This unique resort, reached by a scenic drive past Lake Buchanan, boasts a 940-acre nature park that serves as an ecotourism destination. Activities include hiking on marked nature trails, birding, butterfly watching, fishing, kayaking, or even enjoying the stars at an observatory. Fee for day use.

Fort Croghan Museum & Grounds. 703 Buchanan Dr. (on the western edge of town); (512) 756-8281; fortcroghan.com. Fort Croghan was constructed here in the 1840s, one of eight forts built from the Rio Grande to the Trinity River to protect the region from attacks by Native Americans. The museum and the adjacent fort sit on the left side of the road. Exhibits include household items used by residents over 100 years ago. You can take a walking tour of the fort, the blacksmith shop, the powder house, and a two-room cabin where one family raised 10 children. Open Thurs through Sat 10 a.m. to 4 p.m. or by appointment and for special events only during winter months. Free admission.

Highland Lakes Squadron Commemorative Air Force. 2402 S. Water St. (at Burnet Municipal Kate Craddock Field, 1.5 miles south of Burnet); (512) 756-2226; highland lakessquadron.com. Here you can have a look at World War II airplanes and memorabilia from the men who fought the battles. Operated by the Highland Lakes Squadron of the Commemorative Air Force. Open weekends, Wed afternoon, and by appointment. Fee.

Inks Lake State Park. 3630 Park Road 4 West (from TX 29 turn left onto Park Road 4); (512) 793-2223 for park information; (512) 389-8900 for reservations; tpwd.texas.gov/state -parks/inks-lake. This 1,200-acre park offers camping, lakeside picnicking, swimming, and even a golf course on constant-level Inks Lake. White-tailed deer are a common sight during evening hours. Open daily. Fee.

Longhorn Cavern State Park. From TX 29, turn left onto Park Road 4 to 6211 Park Rd. 4 S; (877) 441-CAVE or (830) 598-2283; visitlonghorncavern.com. This cavern has relatively few formations but a long and interesting history. In one story, Comanches raided San Antonio, kidnapped a young woman named Mariel King, and brought her back to the cavern, unknowingly followed by three Texas Rangers. A hand-to-hand battle ensued, and Mariel King was rescued. Ending the story with a fairy-tale flourish, Miss King later married one of her rescuers, and the couple lived on in Burnet. The guided tour is easy, with wide, well-lit trails through the huge limestone rooms. For the more adventurous, the Wild Cave Tour visits undeveloped portions of the cave system on Sat and Sun (requires reservation). Open daily. Fee.

Vanishing Texas River Cruise. 443 Waterway Ln. (from Burnet, 3 miles west on TX 29, turn right on FM 2341 and follow the signs 14 miles to the cruise entrance); (800) 4RIVER4 or

burnet treasure

Longhorn Cavern, outside Burnet, is said to be the home of more than one treasure trove. One tale involves who else but Sam Bass, who allegedly used the cavern as a hideout following nearby robberies. Today the main opening of the cave is called the Sam Bass Entrance. No Bass treasure has been found, but parts of the 11-mile cavern are still being explored.

Another Longhorn Cavern tale involves the search for a treasure supposedly buried on Woods Ranch near Burnet. After years of searching, one of the treasure hunters went to seek the advice of a palmist, whose cryptic recommendation was to dig "under the footprint." There was speculation that this "footprint" might be a foot-shaped impression on the ceiling of one of the Longhorn Cavern rooms. The crew dug below this formation—only to find a container-shaped hole below the surface. Where there had once been a metal container—and possibly a treasure— there was only a rust-lined hole.

The Sam Bass legends are not the only treasure-filled stories flying around the region. One treasure story dates back to an ancient Spanish document regarding an old Spanish mine, located somewhere near Burnet. According to an Austin American newspaper story in the early 1920s, a "pack train of burros carrying forty jackloads of silver was pursued by a band of Comanche Indians and . . . the men in charge of the pack train buried the silver near where the town of Leander is now located."

No one's found the Spanish silver cache, but some treasure seekers in this area have struck gold—or gemstones, as the case may be. In 1925, W. E. Snavely of Taylor, who had hunted treasure for 60 years, found a ruby arrowhead weighing 15 karats, along with many other gemstones.

(512) 756-6986; vtrc.com. This excellent bird-watching cruise is popular with travelers who come to see American bald eagles from Nov through Mar. The rest of the year, you might see javelinas, wild goats, and white-tailed deer. The route takes in 50-foot Fall Creek Falls and a narrow, cliff-lined passage on the Colorado River. Cruises also travel past Fall Creek Vineyards on the lake's shore. Open daily. Fee.

where to eat

Trailblazer Grille. 216 S. Main St.; (512) 756-7636; trailblazergrille.com. Rustic restaurant serving American standards, plus beer and wine. Live music and poker scheduled as well. Open Mon through Sat. $.

where to stay

Canyon of the Eagles – A Calibre Resort. 16942 RM 2341; (800) 977-0081 or (512) 334-2070; canyonoftheeagles.com. Day-trippers who would like to extend their stay at this nature park on the shores of Lake Buchanan find 61 lodge rooms, including some located in Hill Country–style cottages with stone accents and metal roofs. All rooms include one or two queen-size beds, a coffeemaker, and hair dryer; the cottage rooms offer two queen beds, a mini-fridge, and a microwave. The lodge complex includes a pool and restaurant. $$–$$$.

Canyon of the Eagles RV Park and Campsites. 16942 RM 2341; (800) 977-0081 or (512) 334-2070; canyonoftheeagles.com. Along with the beautiful resort, the Canyon of the Eagles Park also offers an RV park with 25 sites (back-in sites only) as well as 3 camping areas. Dogs are welcome on a leash no longer than 6 feet. $.

buchanan dam

Continue driving west on TX 29 to the village of Buchanan Dam, a fishing and retirement community. Lake Buchanan, the jewel of the Highland Lakes with more than 23,000 surface acres of water, is formed by Buchanan Dam, the largest multiarch dam in the nation.

Lake Buchanan's own gem is the freshwater pearl. Created by freshwater mussels in the Colorado River, some pearls found here have been valued at several thousand dollars.

Many anglers are familiar with one of the most popular sites along Lake Buchanan: Black Rock Park. This park boasts improvements such as new campsites and restrooms. Anglers can try their luck with either bank or boat fishing. Boats can launch without charge from the ramp at neighboring Llano County Park.

Birders also find this park a favorite destination. The northeast side of the lake offers one of the best opportunities to spot the American bald eagle from November through March. Other species often sighted include great blue herons, kingfishers, double-crested cormorants, roadrunners, ospreys, red-breasted mergansers, common loons, horned grebes, and Bonaparte's gulls.

If you'd like to extend your stay at Black Rock, spend the night at one of the park's campsites, each with a table, grill, and fire ring.

where to go

Black Rock Park on Lake Buchanan. 3400 RM 261 (from Burnet travel west on TX 29, then turn right on TX 261 and drive about 4 miles to the park); (800) 776-5272 or (512) 369-4774; lcra.org/parks/black-rock-park. This park offers something for everyone. The northeast side of the lake offers some of the area's best birding; the park has also been a longtime favorite with anglers. If you'd like to extend your visit to Black Rock, stay at one of the park's numerous campsites. There are 15 sites with full electrical hookups and 17 others without electricity, plus 18 cabins with electricity, heat, air conditioning, outside water spigot, and grill. Sites can fill up on busy weekends, and they are offered on a first-come, first-served basis. Fee.

Buchanan Arts and Crafts. 17534 TX 29; (512) 793-2858; buchanan-inks.com/buchanan -arts--crafts.html. The Buchanan Arts and Crafts Guild, the oldest continuously operating artists' cooperative in the country, hosts this gallery featuring the work of local artists. You'll find paintings, sculptures, pottery, and jewelry as well as textile items. It's a great place to buy a bluebonnet painting at a reasonable price. Open Wed through Sun. Free admission.

where to shop

Fain's Honey. 14817 E. TX 29; (512) 793-2491; fainshoney.com. Fain's Honey has been a family-owned business since 1926, when it was founded by farmer H. E. Fain. The third generation of Fains now offers natural honey produced in the area as well as molasses, sugar cane syrup, and a variety of honey spreads (try the jalapeño honey spread!). Open Mon through Fri.

where to eat

Reverend Jim's Dam Pub. 19605 TX 29; (512) 793-3333; reverendjimsdampub.com. Great views and live music on Sat, plus burgers, beer, and wine. Indoor and outdoor seating. Open daily. $.

tow

If you're interested in wine, take a drive up to the community of Tow (rhymes with "cow") on the edge of Lake Buchanan. From TX 29 head north 8 miles on TX 261, then 6 miles on FM 2241.

where to go

Fall Creek Vineyards. 1820 CR 222 (2.2 miles northeast of the Tow Post Office on FM 2241); (512) 476-4477 (Austin sales office) or (325) 379-5361 (winery); fcv.com. Since opening in 1975, Fall Creek has been known as one of the top wineries in Central Texas, winning numerous awards. Located right on the shores of Lake Buchanan, the vineyards here span 400 acres. You can take a tour of the entire operation and sample the wine made on the premises. Private tastings by appointment Tues through Thurs. Open Mon through Sat noon to 5 p.m., Sun 11 a.m. to 5 p.m. Free admission; fee for tastings.

day trip 04

northwest

>>> **rock hound's delight:**
llano, mason

This day trip is filled with winding roads, historic attractions, and natural wonders. Visitors to this Hill Country vicinity must travel over some dirt and gravel roads, especially in rock-hunting areas. Near Mason are numerous low-water crossings, and on some back roads you must drive across dry creek beds. Flash flooding is a very real hazard in the Hill Country, especially during the spring and fall months. Be aware of weather conditions when you make these trips, and never cross swiftly flowing water. To reach Llano, travel US 183 north from Austin through Cedar Park and Leander. Take TX 29 West to Burnet and continue through Buchanan Dam (see Northwest Day Trip 03 for local attractions).

llano

Continuing west on TX 29 from Buchanan Dam, you'll see an increasing number of granite outcroppings—huge boulders protruding from the rugged land. This entire region is called the Llano Uplift, a geological formation caused by igneous rocks from 40 miles below ground being pushed up to the surface.

As a result of the formation, the rich minerals found here turned Llano into a boomtown in the 1880s. Huge deposits of iron ore were found in the area, and some industrialists had dreams of making Llano the "Pittsburgh of the West." Tent cities were erected, mining went full swing, and downtown Llano was spruced up with the money that came pouring into town. All too soon, though, one hard fact came to light: To make steel you have to have

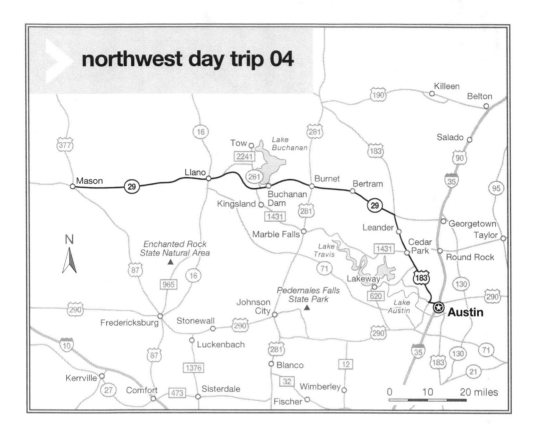

northwest day trip 04

coal as well as iron, and there was no coal in the area. To bring coal in was far too costly. As quickly as it began, the iron ore business came to a halt.

But Llano was by then well known for another mineral: granite. During its heyday, the city boasted 10 granite quarries and 5 finishing plants and shipped several varieties of granite around the country. When rail prices increased, Llano's granite business also came to a stop, although vast quantities of granite still remain.

Granite brought many prominent people to the area. Sculptor Frank Teich, a nationally famous German artist, owned a monument company (as well as the town of Teichville). His World War I monument stands on the courthouse lawn here. Teich came to Llano for its healthy climate when doctors told him that he had only six months to live. Either the doctors were wrong in their diagnosis or Llano's healthy atmosphere really worked, because Teich lived in the town for another 38 years! Even today, Llano is listed by the US Census as one of the healthiest places to live in the country.

Another prominent Llano citizen was Professor N. J. Badu, a mineralogist who came to town to operate a manganese mine and tried to focus the attention of the mineralogy world on Llano's many minerals. Today his home is an elegant restaurant.

The Llano area is still a collector's paradise, with more than 240 different rocks and minerals discovered in the region. The area's granite, feldspar, graphite, and talc have commercial value, while the more precious yields, such as garnet, amethyst, tourmaline, and quartz—even gold and silver—are sought by visiting rock hounds.

Public rock hunting is allowed on the Llano River in town. Stop by the park on the south bank of the river just across from the public library and try your luck. The riverbanks are dotted with rocks of all varieties and offer some pretty picnic spots as well.

where to go

Llano County Historical Museum. 310 Bessemer Ave. (TX 16); (325) 247-3026; llano museum.org. This museum, housed in the old Bruhl Drugstore, has displays on the area's early Native American history and Llano's boomtown days. An exhibit contains samples of Llano's many rocks and minerals. Open Wed through Sat 10 a.m. to 4 p.m. Free admission.

Llano Historic Railyard District. 100 Train Station Dr.; (866) 539-5535 or (325) 247-5354; cityofllano.com/155/Historic-Llano. The extension of the Austin and Northwestern Railroad to Llano in 1892 was a major event in the city's history. For a time, Llano was the last train stop for settlers heading west. The railroad also benefited the granite mining industry, which persists today. Llano also became a shipping out point for cattle. Llano's railroad history is explored in the Railroad Museum and adjacent visitor center. Free admission.

Robinson City Park. FM 152 west of downtown on the Llano River; (325) 248-3685; city ofllano.com/facility/details/Robinson-City-Park-2. This 21-acre park includes RV camping, golf, hiking trails, a swimming pool, fishing, picnicking, and a playground. Open daily. Free admission; fee for camping.

where to shop

Llano Fine Arts Guild and Gallery. 503 Bessemer Ave.; (325) 247-4839; llanofineartsguild .com. Located across from the Llano County Historical Museum, this art gallery features the works of many local residents. Works range from fine arts to ceramics, photographs, and stained glass. Open Fri, Sat, and Sun.

Texana Outfitters. 110 E. Main St.; (325) 423-4096; texasshirts.com. Family-run business offers creative T-shirts, clothing, caps, accessories, jewelry, and lovely home goods. Open Mon through Sat.

where to eat

Badu 1891. 601 Bessemer Ave. (TX 16); (325) 247-2238; badu1891.com. This two-story stone and brick structure (formerly an inn) was built in 1891 as the home of mineralogist N. J. Badu, who put Llano on the map by discovering the mineral llanite here. The building has been elegantly renovated and is home to a fine restaurant and a special events venue.

buried treasure

Following the robber from Round Rock to Burnet and finally to Llano, we're once again on the trail of Sam Bass. Allegedly the robber hid canvas sacks marked "U.S." and filled with gold in a cave on Packsaddle Mountain. Some say the treasure was found by a Mexican laborer, hired by a local rancher to cut fence posts on Packsaddle Mountain. According to one version of the story, the rancher went to look for the laborer when he failed to return to the ranch. All the rancher found was a cave and a piece of canvas sack with "U.S." imprinted on it. Another version of the story says the gold still lies hidden somewhere in the mountain.

Packsaddle Mountain is also the home of the Blanco Mine, named for a Spaniard who found the location long ago. According to J. Frank Dobie's book Coronado's Children, the mine was rediscovered in the 1800s by a Llano settler named Larimore. While hunting, Larimore discovered the old mine—with its contents of lead and a high percentage of silver.

In 1860 Larimore took a last trip to the mine with a man named Jim Rowland. The two men hauled out several hundred pounds of the metal, shaping it into bullets. Larimore, who was leaving the country, declared that he would hide the mine so well no other person would ever find it. Supposedly he diverted a gully directly into the mine, filling it with silt. Rowland carved his initials on a large stone marking the entrance to the mine, then covered it with earth . . . where it remains today.

Llano County is home to other buried treasure sites, including $60,000 in gold and silver coins buried by Sam Bass near the community of Castell in the western part of the county. Bass buried the loot on a creek bed, marking the spot with a rock in a fork of a tree.

Check the website for live music. The restaurant offers everything from filet mignon to grilled quail. $$$.

Cooper's Old Time Pit Barbecue and Catering. 604 W. Young St. (TX 29 West); (325) 247-5713; coopersbbqllano.com. Step up to the smoker and pick out your meat—brisket, sausage, pork ribs, beef ribs, chicken, sirloin steak, pork chops, and even goat. The pit master slices off the amount you want, then you go inside and help yourself to white bread, beans, and sauce in the cinder block dining room. Open daily. $.

Inman's Kitchen Bar-B-Q. 809 W. Young St. (TX 29 West); (325) 247-5257; inmanskitchen .com. Barbecue is king here, including beef brisket, chicken, pork, and the restaurant's specialty: turkey sausage. This spot is more elegant than many barbecue restaurants, with a carpeted, air-conditioned dining area. Open Wed through Sat. $.

Miller's Meat Market & Smokehouse. 705 W. Young St. (TX 29 West); (866) 570-0315 or (325) 247-4450; millers.com. Stop by to take home a fragrant reminder of your Llano visit or to stock up for your day-trip picnic. Miller's sells all manner of smoked meats including ribs, hams, beef and pork tenderloin, and a large variety of smoked sausage as well as venison sausage and meat cuts. If you are a hunter, Miller's can process your deer for you. They also sell mail order. Open Mon through Sat. $–$$.

where to stay

Dabbs Railroad Hotel. 112 E. Burnet St. (behind the Llano Museum); (325) 247-2200; thedabbs.com. At the turn of the 20th century, this railroad hotel was the last outpost of civilization for frontiersmen heading west. Today's guests stay in one of 7 quiet rooms with period furnishings, double beds, a breezy screened porch, and a peaceful atmosphere over-looking the Llano River. An additional large enclosed sleeping porch sleeps 4. $$.

mason

From Llano continue west on TX 29 for 34 miles to Mason, once the home of the late Fred Gipson, author of *Old Yeller.* Like neighboring Llano, the land around Mason is rocky and dotted with granite.

Mason was settled by cattle ranchers and German families who came from nearby Fredericksburg. In 1851 Fort Mason was built on a hilltop to afford a better look at oncoming Comanches. (The post's best-known soldier was Lieutenant Colonel Robert E. Lee.) Con-structed of sandstone, in 1869 the fort was dismantled and the salvaged stone was used to build local businesses and homes.

Even after the fort was no longer necessary, frontier justice was still a part of Mason. In 1875 the Mason County War, also known as the Hoodoo War, broke out. It all started when the sheriff arrested a group of men who were taking cattle to Llano, allegedly without the owner's permission. The men were set free on bond and ordered to remain in town, an order they promptly forgot. The sheriff re-arrested as many of the rustlers as he could find. A few nights later, a group freed the prisoners, sparking a round of shootings and lynchings that left a dozen men dead. The feud continued until January 1877, when the Mason County Courthouse was set on fire, destroying any evidence against the cattle rustlers.

Rock hounds come to Mason County today in search of topaz, the Texas state gem, which develops in colors ranging from clear to sky blue. Most local topaz turns up near the small communities of Streeter, Grit, and Katemcy, all north and northeast of Mason. Search-ers usually find the stones in streambeds and ravines by using picks and shovels to loosen rocks and a wire screen to sift the debris. More information on Mason is available on the Mason Chamber of Commerce website: masontxcoc.com.

where to go

Eckert James River Bat Cave Preserve. Write or call the Mason Chamber of Commerce (PO Box 156, Mason, TX 76856; 325-347-5758; masontxcoc.com) for directions and a map to this bat cave, located about 13 miles south of Mason. The cavern is home to about six million Mexican free-tail bats. This is a "maternity cave," used during the spring and summer months by female bats to bear and rear their young. You can view the evening flight out of the cave, a sight heralded by high-pitched sounds. Open Thurs through Sun 6 to 9 p.m., mid-May through mid-Oct. In-season tour information call (325) 347-5970, offseason call (512) 263-8878. Free admission.

Fort Mason. Follow Post Hill Street south from the courthouse to Post Hill to 314 Spruce St.; (325) 347-5758; texasfortstrail.com/plan-your-adventure/historic-sites-and-cities/sites/fort-mason. These reconstructed officers' quarters are furnished with typical 1850s belongings and feature photographs from Mason's early days. The back porch has an unbeatable view of the town below and miles of Hill Country beyond. Open daily. Free admission.

Gene Zesch Woodcarving Display at the Commercial Bank. 100 Moody St., on the square; (325) 347-6324; tcbmason.com. Gene Zesch is one of Mason's most famous citizens, known for his humorous woodcarvings of modern cowboys. His work was collected by President Lyndon B. Johnson and is sold in galleries nationally. This exhibit features woodcarvings and bronzes made by the artist. Open Mon through Fri 9 a.m. to 3 p.m. Free admission.

Mason County Museum. 210 Bryan St.; (325) 347-6583; masonchc.org/museums.html. Housed in a historic rock building, this museum traces the evolution of the Mason County area from prehistoric times. Exhibits include geological artifacts, a mastodon tusk, and remnants of military life in old Fort Mason. Open 11 a.m. to 4 p.m. Thurs through Sat (closed Dec through Feb). Free admission.

Mason Square Museum. 130 Fort McKavitt St.; (325) 347-0507; masonsquaremuseum .org. The centerpiece at this local history museum is the largest blue topaz ever discovered in the US. Other exhibits focus on historic events in the town and at Fort Mason. An on-site gift shop sells books, gifts, and works of art. Open 11 a.m. to 4 p.m. Thurs through Sat (closed Dec through Feb). Free admission.

Old Yeller Statue. At the Mason County Library at 410 Post Hill St. In 1956 Mason resident Fred Gipson penned a dog story destined to become a beloved American classic: *Old Yeller*. A bronze statue of Old Yeller stands in front of the Mason County Library. Inside the library, you'll find an exhibit on the town's most famous author. Free admission.

Topaz Hunting. Several private ranches charge a daily fee of $15 to $20 per person for topaz hunting. Visitors must bring their own equipment (including water during warm summer months) and may keep whatever they find. Ranches offer topaz hunting from mid-Jan through Sept, closing during deer-hunting season. For current information on topaz hunting, check with the Mason Chamber of Commerce (325-347-5758; masontxcoc.com).

White-tailed Deer Hunting. For information on hunting licenses, contact the Mason Chamber of Commerce (325-347-5758; masontxcoc.com) well before deer season begins. Mason County claims to have more white-tailed deer per acre than any other county in Texas. Hunters flock here from around the Southwest to stalk deer during the winter months.

where to shop

Mason Country Collectibles. 424 Fort McKavitt St.; (325) 347-5249; masoncountrycol lectibles.com. If your search for topaz is futile, stop by this antiques store, which sells topaz and other stones indigenous to the area, along with arrowheads, willow furniture, and collectibles of every description. While you are here, take a look at the "Grand Azure" topaz on display. This 587-carat stone is the biggest Mason County faceted topaz known to exist. Open daily.

where to stay

Mason County is filled with bed-and-breakfast accommodations, RV campsites, and guest ranches located outside of town. For a list, see the Mason County Chamber of Commerce website, masontxcoc.com. Also, **1st Choice B&B Reservations** (325-347-7829; stayin masontx.com) handles a number of properties in and around Mason.

day trip 05

northwest

wild, wild west:
andice, lampasas, bend

This northern Hill Country area is full of the wide-open spaces that characterize much of Texas. This day trip follows US 183 from Austin past Cedar Park and Leander (covered in Northwest Day Trip 03) and continues on to the northwest. As you drive, you'll notice that the jumbled landscape and intimate valleys of the Llano Uplift and the central Hill Country transition to expansive views of large ranches and open skies, punctuated by tiny ranching communities.

The major town in the area, Lampasas, is the county seat of Lampasas County. Once a health destination because of its sulphur springs, Lampasas is now a commercial center for the ranching and hunting industries. It is also the jumping-off point for Colorado Bend State Park, one of the more remote and primitive parks in the state parks system.

andice

Your day trip will take a slight detour if you'd like to head to Andice, a small community just east of US 183. To reach Andice, turn east on FM 970 and continue east for 1.6 miles. Andice lies at the intersection of FM 970 and FM 2338. With just 25 residents (yes, you read that correctly), little Andice is known for one thing: its general store.

And just how do you pronounce Andice? That depends on who you ask. The most common pronunciation is "Ann-Dice," although older residents often say "Ann-Diss." Don't feel badly if you aren't certain about the correct pronunciation: The actual name came about

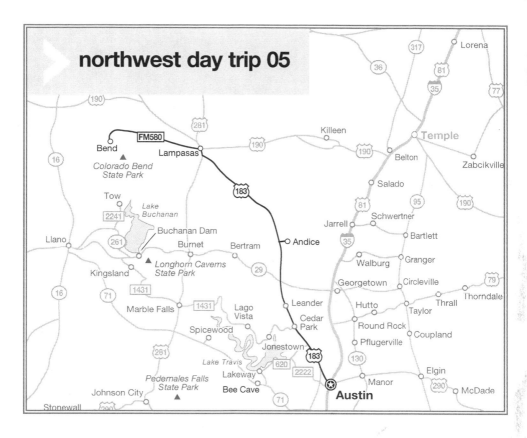

> ## northwest day trip 05

as a big misunderstanding. Andice was originally to be named Audice for the postmaster's young son. Well, the postal officials misread the handwriting on the application, and the rest is history.

where to eat

Andice General Store. 6500 FM 970. Home to what they proclaim are the "world's best burgers," this casual eatery is a true general store. Shelves of staples line the small dining room, filled with communal tables (you'll also find numerous shaded picnic tables outdoors). The Texas-size burgers are worth the trip. Open daily 11 a.m. to 6:45 p.m. $.

lampasas

The town of Lampasas was first known for its mineral springs that many believed had healing properties. Today the health spas are gone, but travelers come to this town as a jumping-off point to the large, wild state park nearby and to enjoy a taste of small-town Texas. The courthouse square, highlighted by a classic courthouse with a red mansard roof, is a National

Historic District. Drive around the square to check out the eight historic murals that depict Lampasas's early days.

where to go

Cooper Spring Nature Park. Hackberry Street between Avenue A and Second Street; (512) 556-6831; lampasas.org/366/Cooper-Spring-Nature-Park. Located near the Hanna Springs Sculpture Garden, this 16-acre park is a piece of wild Texas right in the middle of downtown. Native plants grow freely to encourage local birds, butterflies, and wildlife. Free admission.

Hancock Springs Park. 501 E. North Ave.; (512) 556-6831; lampassas.org/facilities/facility/Details/Hancock-Springs-Park. Dating back to the early 1900s, this pool, fed by natural spring waters, once served as a baptismal font. Today the public pool is still natural, operated without chemicals, all thanks to the powerful springs that continue to feed this expansive pool and keep it a constant 69°F year-around. Even if you don't want to take a dip, take a drive by this beautiful park just to see the spectacular color of the spring water. Open daily through Sun during pool season (June through Aug and weekends only in Sept). The park is open daily to the public year round. Free admission to the park. Fee for swimming.

Hanna Springs Sculpture Garden. 501 E. North Ave.; (512) 525-9173; lafta.org/sculpture-garden/html. This peaceful sculpture garden is one of our favorite stops in Lampasas; when traveling through town, we've often stopped here with our dogs to enjoy a walk along the sculpture path. The garden features both permanent and changing sculptures that range from thought-provoking to just plain whimsical. Our favorites may be Terry Jones's *Music to My Ears*, a red guitar created entirely from historic found objects, and Joe Barrington's *Been Fish'en*, an antique pickup topped with a catfish that's truly Texas-size. Nearby, you can see Hanna Springs, a round pool of sulphur water. The springs are now fenced off, but don't worry, you'll still be able to get a whiff of the powerful spring water! Open daily. Free admission.

Pillar Bluff Vineyards. 300 CR 111; (512) 556-4078; pillarbluff.com. Take FM 1478 (Naruna Road) west of Lampasas for 3 miles to the Burnet County line, then turn left onto CR 111. Located southwest of Lampasas, this winery is one of the region's oldest. Known for its estate-bottled chardonnay and cabernet sauvignon, the winery features vintages produced from Texas-grown grapes. Visit the tasting room and walk through the vineyards on Thurs, Fri, Sat, and Sun year-round. Free admission.

where to eat

Storm's. 201 N. Key Ave.; (512) 556-6269; stormsrestaurants.com. Family owned and operated since 1950, this drive-in was a favorite stop of Elvis Presley when he was stationed at nearby Fort Hood. Enjoy breakfast, lunch, and dinner; the eatery serves everything from breakfast tacos to chicken sandwiches but the tried-and-true remains most popular: the Storm's Special, a 100 percent Texas beef burger with three patties served with french fries. (Our favorites are the old-fashioned malts!) Along with dining in your car, you'll also find an adjacent shaded picnic area for Storm's customers. On the first Sat evening of every month, you can also enjoy an evening of classic cars on display. Open daily, 6:30 a.m. to 10 p.m. $.

bend

The drive from Lampasas to Bend winds through scenic hills and shady pecan bottoms, quickly leaving the bustling county seat for the slower pace of the ranch and farm land to the west. From Lampasas take FM 580 (Nix Road) west to CR 442 for 23.7 miles. When FM 580 turns south and crosses the Colorado River, you'll know that you've arrived in Bend, named for its position on a bend of the river.

Those lush pecan groves that you saw on the drive in are more than ornamental; they are also Bend's biggest cash crop. These aren't any ordinary pecans, either. The trees surrounding Bend are a variety known as the Jumbo Hollis, named for owner Thomas I. Hollis. The product of these trees is true to its name, with larger pecans than other Texas varieties—so large, in fact, that they were award winners at the 1904 World's Fair.

where to go

Colorado Bend State Park. From Bend, take FM 580 to CR 442, turn right on CR 442 then turn right on the unpaved CR 446 (Colorado Park Rd.) and follow the signs to park entrance at 2236 Park Hill Dr.; (325) 628-3240; tpwd.texas.gov/state-parks/Colorado.bend. Are you looking for a real getaway—as in composting toilets and truly an end-of-the-road experience? You just might find it in Colorado Bend State Park. This largely undeveloped park above the Highland Lakes chain is located along a canyon of the Colorado River and features 32 miles of trails. The trails offer great places to spot some of the 155 species of birds found in the park, including golden-cheeked warblers, black-capped vireos, and bald eagles, or just enjoy a lazy day wading the river bed then camping out beneath the stars at night. Check-in at this park is equally basic: Instead of a manned ranger station, you'll find a self-serve check-in at the gate, reached after miles of driving through cattle pastures, open ranch land, and cattle guards. Bring what you need; there's a basic store near the campgrounds but supplies are limited. Fee.

where to eat

Bend General Store. 438 County Rd. 442; (325) 628-3523; bend-generalstore.business .site. Unpretentious store offers groceries, camping supplies, burgers, pizza, beer, and sometimes live music. Popular spot for travelers and campers. Open daily.

regional information

north

day trip 01

Greater Pflugerville Chamber of Commerce
101 S. Third St.
Pflugerville, TX 78660
(512) 251-7799
pfchamber.com

Round Rock Convention and Visitors
Bureau
231 E. Main St., Ste. 150
Round Rock, TX 78664
(512) 218-7023
goroundrock.com

Georgetown Convention and Visitors
Information Center
103 W. Seventh St.
Georgetown, TX 78626
(800) 436-8696 or (512) 930-3545
visitgeorgetown.com

Salado Chamber of Commerce
831 N. Main St.
Salado, TX 76571
(254) 947-5040 or (254) 947-8634 (for
visitor information)
salado.com

day trip 02

Belton Area Convention and Visitors
Bureau
PO Box 659
412 E. Central Ave.
Belton, TX 76513
(254) 939-3551
beltonchamber.com

Killeen Civic and Conference Center and
Visitors Bureau
3601 S. W.S. Young Dr.
Killeen, TX 76541
(254) 501-3888
killeenciviccenter.com

Temple Convention and Visitors Bureau
101 N. Main St.
Temple, TX 76501
(254) 298-5388
templechamber.com

day trip 03

Lorena City Hall
107-A S. Frontage Rd.
Lorena, TX 76655
(254) 857-4641
ci.lorena.tx.us

Waco Convention and Visitors Bureau
106 Texas Ranger Trail
Waco, TX 76706
(800) WACO-FUN or (254) 750-5810
wacoheartoftexas.com

northeast

day trip 01

Hutto Chamber of Commerce
122 East St.
PO Box 99
Hutto, TX 78634
(512) 759-4400
huttochamber.com

day trip 02

Greater Taylor Chamber of Commerce
PO Box 231
1519 N. Main St.
Taylor, TX 76574
(512) 352-6364
taylorchamber.org

day trip 03

Burleson County Chamber of Commerce
301 N. Main St.
Caldwell, TX 77836
(979) 567-0000
burlesoncountytx.com

Visit College Station
614 E. Holleman Dr., Suite 1100
College Station, TX 77840
(979) 260-9898
visit.cstx.gov

Destination Bryan
3891 S. Traditions Dr.
Bryan, TX 77807
(979) 721-9506
destinationbryan.com

east

day trip 01

Manor Chamber of Commerce
810 N. Caldwell St., Bldg. B, Ste. 200
Manor, TX 78653
(512) 272-5699
manorchamberofcommerce.com

Elgin Chamber of Commerce
114 Central Ave.
Elgin, TX 78621
(512) 285-4515
elgintxchamber.com

Giddings Area Chamber of Commerce
183 E. Hempstead
Giddings, TX 78942
(979) 542-3455
giddingstx.com

day trip 02

Burton Chamber of Commerce
507 N. Railroad St.
Burton, TX 77835
(979) 289-3402 (City Hall)
burtontexas.org

Brenham–Washington County Convention
and Visitors Bureau
115 W. Main St.
Brenham, TX 77833
(979) 337-7580
visitbrenhamtexas.com

southeast

day trip 01

Bastrop County Museum and
Visitors Center
904 Main St.
Bastrop, TX 78602
(512) 303-0904
bastropcountyhistoricalsociety.com

Smithville Area Chamber of Commerce
100 NW First St.
Smithville, TX 78957
(512) 237-2313
smithvilletx.org

La Grange Area Chamber of Commerce
220 W. Colorado St.
La Grange, TX 78945
(800) LAGRANGE or (979) 968-5756
lagrangetx.org

day trip 02

Round Top Area Chamber of Commerce
103 Henkel Circle
Round Top, TX 78954
(979) 505-1200
exploreroundtop.com

Fayetteville Chamber of Commerce
Visitor Center
123 N. Washington St.
PO Box 217
Fayetteville, TX 78940
(713) 598-6331
greaterfayettevillechamber.org

south

day trip 01

Lockhart Chamber of Commerce
702 S. Commerce St.
Lockhart, TX 78644
(512) 398-2818
lockhartchamber.com

Luling Area Chamber of Commerce
421 E. Davis St.
Luling, TX 78648
(830) 875-3214
lulingcc.org

day trip 02

Flatonia Chamber of Commerce
208 E. North Main St.
PO Box 610
Flatonia, TX 78941
(361) 865-3920
flatoniachamber.com

Schulenburg Chamber of Commerce
618 N. Main St.
PO Box 65
Schulenburg, TX 78956
(866) 504-5294 or (979) 743-4514
schulenburgchamber.org

day trip 03

Gonzales Chamber of Commerce
and Agriculture
414 St. Lawrence St.
Gonzales, TX 78629
(888) 672-1095 or (830) 672-6532
gonzalestexas.com

Shiner Chamber of Commerce
817 N. Avenue E
PO Box 221
Shiner, TX 77984
(361) 594-4180
shinertx.com

Yoakum Area Chamber of Commerce
105 Huck St.
Yoakum, TX 77995
(361) 293-2309
yoakumareachamber.com

day trip 04

San Marcos Convention and Visitors
Bureau
617 I-35 North
San Marcos, TX 78666
(888) 200-5620 or (512) 393-5930
visitsanmarcos.com

day trip 05

Seguin Convention and Visitors Bureau
116 N. Camp St.
Seguin, TX 78155
(800) 580-7322 or (830) 379-6382
seguinchamber.com

southwest

day trip 01

San Antonio Convention and Visitors
Bureau Visitors Center
317 Alamo Plaza
San Antonio, TX 78205
(210) 244-2000
visitsanantonio.com

day trip 02

Gruene Historic District
1281 Gruene Rd.
New Braunfels, TX 78130
(830) 629-5077
gruenetexas.com

New Braunfels Convention Center and
Visitors Bureau
390 S. Seguin Ave.
New Braunfels, TX 78130
(800) 572-2626
playinnewbraunfels.com

day trip 03

Wimberley Valley Chamber of Commerce
14100 Ranch Rd.
PO Box 12
Wimberley, TX 78676
(512) 847-2201
wimberley.org

Blanco Chamber of Commerce
300 Main St.
PO Box 626
Blanco, TX 78606
(830) 833-5101
blancochamber.com

day trip 04

Comfort Chamber of Commerce
630 TX 27
PO Box 777
Comfort, TX 78013
(830) 995-3131
comfortchamber.com

Greater Boerne Convention and Visitors
Bureau
282 N. Main St.
Boerne, TX 78006
(830) 249-7277
ci.boerne.tx.us

day trip 05

Bandera County Convention and
Visitors Bureau
126 TX 16 South
PO Box 171
Bandera, TX 78003
(830) 796-3045
banderacowboycapital.com

west

day trip 01

Lake Travis Chamber of Commerce
14425 Falcon Head Blvd.
Austin, TX 78738
(512) 387-3180
laketravischamber.com

day trip 02

Johnson City Chamber of Commerce and
Visitors Center
100 E. Main St.
Johnson City, TX 78636
(830) 868-7684
johnsoncitytexas.info

Stonewall Chamber of Commerce
250 Peach St.
Stonewall, TX 78671
(830) 644-2735
stonewalltexas.com

day trip 03

Fredericksburg Convention and
Visitors Bureau
302 E. Austin St.
Fredericksburg, TX 78624
(888) 997-3600 or (830) 997-6523
visitfredericksburgtx.com

day trip 04

Kerrville Convention and Visitors Bureau
2108 Sidney Baker St.
Kerrville, TX 78028
(800) 221-7958 or (830) 792-3535
kerrvilletexascvb.com

West Kerr County Chamber of Commerce
3186 Junction Hwy.
PO Box 1006
Ingram, TX 78025
(830) 367-4322
wkcc.com

northwest

day trip 01

Lake Travis Chamber of Commerce
14425 Falcon Head Blvd.
Austin, TX 78738
(512) 367-3180
laketravischamber.com

Lakeway City Hall
1102 Lohmans Crossing
Lakeway, TX 78734
(512) 314-7500
lakeway-tx.gov

day trip 02

Marble Falls/Lake LBJ Chamber of
Commerce & CVB
916 Second St.
Marble Falls, TX 78654
(830) 693-2815
marblefalls.org

Kingsland Chamber of Commerce
1309 FM 1431
PO Box 465
Kingsland, TX 78639
(325) 388-6211
kingslandchamber.org

day trip 03

Cedar Park Tourism Services
450 Cypress Creek Rd., Bldg. 3
Cedar Park, TX 78613
(512) 401-5070
cedarparkfun.com

Greater Leander Chamber of Commerce
100 N. Brushy St.
PO Box 556
Leander, TX 78641
(512) 259-1907
leandercc.org

Burnet Chamber of Commerce
101 N. Pierce St., Ste. 1
Burnet, TX 78611
(512) 756-4297
burnetchamber.org

Lake Buchanan/Inks Lake Chamber
of Commerce
19611 E. TX 29
PO Box 282
Buchanan Dam, TX 78609
(512) 793-2803
buchanan-inks.com

day trip 04

Llano Chamber of Commerce
The Railyard Depot
100 Train Station Dr.
Llano, TX 78643
(325) 247-5354 or (866) 539-5535
llanochamber.org

Mason County Chamber of Commerce
108 Fort McKavett St.
PO Box 156
Mason, TX 76856
(325) 347-5758
masontxcoc.com

day trip 05

Lampasas County Chamber of Commerce
205 US 281 South
Lampasas, TX 76550
(512) 556-5172
lampasaschamber.org

festivals and celebrations

Texas undoubtedly has more festivals than any other state. Regardless of the weekend, you'll find some town whooping it up with parades, music, and lots of food. There are festivals for every interest, whether yours is pioneer heritage, German food, or watermelon. For a searchable listing of festivals, go to traveltex.com.

january

Hill Country Gem & Mineral Show. Fredericksburg. (830) 456-5419. For more than five decades, this popular rock show has included gems, minerals, fossils, meteorites, and more with plenty of jewelry, gold panning, and exhibits. Held at the Pioneer Pavilion at Lady Bird Johnson Municipal Park.

february

San Antonio Stock Show and Rodeo. San Antonio. (210) 225-5851; sarodeo.com. Spanning 18 days in Feb, this Texas-size event is one of the top five PRCA rodeos in the country and attracts over one million visitors. Along with a rodeo, the event includes a horse show, livestock show, carnival, top country music performances, and more.

Williamson County "Gemboree." Georgetown. (800) 436-8696; wcgms.org/gemboree .html. Dealers from around the US showcase and sell the latest gems and minerals on the market. Demonstrations, exhibits, and lectures are given throughout the day.

Wine Lovers Trail. Fredericksburg. (866) 621-9463; texaswinetrail.com. More than 40 Hill Country wineries participate in this event. Sample the products of these vineyards and enjoy special events.

march

Best Little Cowboy Gathering in Texas. La Grange. (979) 966-7846. This weekend event celebrates cowboy culture with western dancing, country western musical shows, western art displays, and a barbecue cook-off. Held at the Fayette County Fairgrounds.

Sherwood Forest Faire. 1883 Old Highway 20, McDade; (512) 222-6680; sherwoodforest faire.com. Held on weekends in Mar and April, this annual celebration of medieval times draws thousands of visitors to eat, drink, and watch (or become) kings, queens, knights, jesters, and other medieval folk. Some visitors camp on the grounds, while others opt for hotels in Elgin or Giddings during their stay.

Rajun' Cajun Throwdown. Luling. (830) 875-3214; cityofluling.net/291/Rajun-Cajun -Throwdown. Food lovers gather in downtown Luling to celebrate mouthwatering Cajun specialties at this annual cooking competition. Visitors take in live zydeco music while sampling the spicy creations.

Texas Independence Day Celebration. Washington-on-the-Brazos. (936) 878-2214; tpwd.texas.gov/state-parks/washington-on-the-brazos. This two-day event at Washington-on-the-Brazos State Historic Site celebrates the birth of the Republic of Texas. Activities include live music, food, craft demonstrations, and historical reenactments at the spot where the Texas Declaration of Independence was signed in 1836.

april

Round Top Antiques Week. Round Top. (512) 237-4747; roundtoptexasantiques.com. Held the first weekend of Apr, this show features dealers from across the nation. It has been called the best antiques show in the state.

Balcones Songbird Festival. Lago Vista. (512) 965-2473; friendsofbalcones.org/festival. This late Apr event celebrates two local endangered bird species—the golden-cheeked warbler and the black-capped vireo—as well as other songbirds, butterflies, and wildflowers. Guided nature talks, family activities, photo hikes, and more. Held at the Balcones Canyonlands National Preserve.

Cotton Gin Festival. Burton. (979) 289-3378; texascottonginmuseum.org. Held at the historic Burton Cotton Gin, this family-friendly event includes a parade (complete with tractors), children's petting zoo, carnival rides, folk demonstrations, arts and crafts, live music, and more.

Highland Lakes Bluebonnet Trail. Burnet, Buchanan Dam, Llano, and other communities. lakesandhills.com. The fragrant bluebonnet is the state flower of Texas. For two weekends in early Apr, a self-guided driving tour will take you past the area's prettiest bluebonnet fields. Each town on the trail, from Burnet to Llano, celebrates with art shows and a festival atmosphere. Maps are available from the Marble Falls CVB (830-693-4449) or the Lake Buchanan Chamber of Commerce (512-793-2803).

Smithville Jamboree. Smithville. (512) 237-3282; jamboreesmithville.com. This longtime event includes parades; a livestock show; softball, volleyball, and horseshoe tournaments; nightly dances; an antique car show; a carnival; and canoe races.

Texas Ladies' State Chili Cookoff. Seguin. (830) 379-6382; seguinchamber.com or texasladiesstate.com. Women from around the state test their skills at this chili cook-off. Along with taste tests, visitors enjoy live entertainment.

may

Fredericksburg Crawfish Festival. Fredericksburg. fbgcrawfishfestival.com. Have a Cajun good time in Fredericksburg on Memorial Day weekend. The annual event at the Downtown Marketplatz features activities for the entire family, incluing live music, a fun carnival, delicious Cajun food, and shopping galore. The festival is sponsored by the local Jaycees as a fundraiser to support local organizations.

Hill Country Run Motorcycle Rally. Luckenbach. (830) 997-8515; hillcountryrun.com. Held from Friday through Sunday at the Luckenbach Dance Hall, event fans say it is "not just your plain ol' motorcycle rally." Featuring music, dancing, food, and drink, plus a bike show and auction, the rally is sponsored by the Optimist Club of Fredericksburg to help fund children's programs.

june

Boerne Berges Fest. Boerne. (830) 428-8778; bergesfest.com. This festival, scheduled for Father's Day weekend, includes arts and crafts, live music, and a celebration of summer.

Peach JAMboree. Stonewall. (830) 644-2735; stonewalltexas.com. The peach capital of Texas shows off its crop on the third Fri and Sat of June. The baking contest includes entries for peach cobbler, peach preserves, peach salsa, peach pie, and peach creative baking, which had a prize-winning entry one year of peaches and cream eggroll.

Taylor International BBQ Cook-Off. Taylor. www.facebook.com/TaylorBBQCookoff. Barbecue beef, chicken, and sausage reign supreme at most Texas barbecue joints. Over 100 teams compete in categories ranging from best BBQ sauce and best margarita to kids' grilled cheese.

Watermelon Thump. Luling. (830) 875-3214; newsite.watermelonthump.com. On the last Thurs, Fri, and Sat of June, you can enjoy seed-spitting and watermelon-eating contests and championship melon judging. There's also an arts and crafts show, carnival, live entertainment, and street dances. A Guinness World Record was set here in 1989 for spitting a watermelon seed almost 69 feet.

Western Days Festival. Elgin. (512) 285-4515; elgintxchamber.com. Held the fourth week of June, this event includes the Tiny Tots Parade; Tennis Court Dance; volleyball, softball, and horseshoe tournaments; a carnival; arts and crafts; and more.

july

4th of July PRCA Rodeo. Belton. (254) 939-3551; beltonchamber.com. Since 1924 this popular rodeo has pitted bulls against riders. Held at the Bell County Expo Center, the event features bronc riding, roping, steer wrestling, and barrel racing.

Fourth of July Celebration. Round Top. (979) 505-1200; exploreroundtop.com. One of the oldest Independence Day celebrations in the country winds through Round Top.

Freedom Festival. Seguin. (830) 379-3212; seguintexas.gov. Get ready for a red, white, and blue party known as the biggest small-town Fourth of July parade in Texas. The annual Freedom Fiesta has been drawing onlookers and participants since the early 1900s. Activities start with a patriotic parade, followed by food booths, arts and crafts, family entertainment, and kiddie rides, for an old-fashioned street fair atmosphere. That evening, a street dance will keep the mood festive, as will the grand fireworks display in Max Starcke Park.

Frontier Days. Round Rock. (512) 255-5805; roundrockchamber.org. Come to Round Rock for the Fourth of July. There's plenty of food, games, parade, and the atmosphere of a summer festival.

Half Moon Holidays. Shiner. (361) 594-4180; shinerhalfmoon.com. Shiner celebrates summer with a brisket cook-off, barbecue dinner, fireworks, carnival, horseshoe-pitching tournament, dance, and lots of live music.

Watermelon Festival at the McDade Fairgrounds. McDade. (512) 332-1270; mcdade texas.com. The festival includes prizes for the largest watermelon and best watermelon seed spitting, as well as bingo and horseshoe- and washer-pitching competitions. Other activities include a grand parade through downtown McDade, a car show, live music, and food vendors. Festivities conclude with a barbecue dinner and the crowning of the Watermelon Queen. Held the second Sat in July.

august

Gillespie County Fair. Fredericksburg. (830) 997-2359; gillespiefair.com. This event holds the record as the longest-running county fair in the state. The festivities include old-fashioned family fun from carnival rides to food booths with an emphasis on agriculture.

LBJ Birthday Celebration. Johnson City. (830) 868-7684; johnsoncitytexas.info. The legacy of this Hill Country president is remembered with a wreath laying at the president's grave and ranch tours. Held on the anniversary of LBJ's birth: August 27.

Salado Art Fair. Salado. (254) 947-5040; visitsaladotexas.com. More than 30 artists set up booths on the grounds of the Salado Civic Center, 601 N. Main St. This weekend festival in early Aug is one of the most popular art shows in the state. Features live music and Artists in Action, artists working on site demonstrating their talent and technique.

september

Comal County Fair. New Braunfels. (830) 625-1505; comalcountyfair.org. This long-running fair ranks as one of the largest (and one of the oldest) in the state. The event includes everything from a PRCA rodeo to carnival rides to children's play areas.

Oatmeal Festival. Bertram. oatmealfestival.org. This Labor Day weekend festival is named for the nearby community of Oatmeal, and all the events, from the street parade to the midway, continue the theme.

Texas Heritage Music Day. Kerrville. (830) 203-6280; texasheritagemusic.org. Held every Sept on the campus of Schreiner University, thousands attend to learn about the heritage, history, music, and culture of Texas. Includes a tribute to the father of country music, Jimmie Rodgers.

Round Top Antiques Week. Round Top. (512) 237-4747; roundtoptexasantiques.com. Called by some the best such show in the state, this extravaganza features antiques dealers from across the US. Held mid-Sept through early Oct, it attracts shoppers from around the country.

october

Czhilispiel. Flatonia. (361) 865-3920; flatoniachamber.com. When tiny Flatonia needed a doctor years ago, local citizens decided to send a hometown girl to medical school. To fund her education, they began this chili cook-off (now the second largest in Texas) and festival held in late Oct. There's lots of music, a quilt show, "the world's largest tented biergarten," and a barbecue cook-off as well.

Deutschen Pfest. Pflugerville. (512) 990-6350; deutschenpfest.com. This annual event celebrates Pflugerville's Old World heritage with a 5K "Pfun" run, a parade through the historic downtown, rides, live music, and food.

Fort Croghan Day. Burnet. (512) 525-4025; highlandlakesofburnetcounty.com. Step back to Burnet's frontier days at this special event on the second Sat in Oct. The day includes demonstrations of pioneer chores ranging from blacksmithing to bread making. Admission and parking at the event are free.

Fredericksburg Food and Wine Fest. Fredericksburg. (830) 997-8515; fbgfoodandwine fest.com. In late Oct the Fredericksburg Food and Wine Fest highlights Texas's top wineries. Along with award-winning vineyards, the event showcases an array of vendors who offer a taste of Texas through spices, salsas, cheeses, and more. Two stages offer musical entertainment, and the whole family finds plenty of just-for-fun activities such as grape-stomping and cork-tossing.

Folkfest. New Braunfels. (800) 572-2626; texashandmadefurniture.com. This event, held at Heritage Village and the Museum of Texas Handmade Furniture, showcases the work of New Braunfels craftspeople and furniture makers through demonstrations, food, and live entertainment. Guided tours of local historic buildings also available.

Heart o' Texas Fair and Rodeo. Waco. (254) 776-1660; hotfair.com. This 12-day fair draws over 200,000 visitors for a look at a championship rodeo, livestock shows, an art show, and nationally known entertainment.

Hogeye Festival. Elgin. (512) 229-3217; hogeyefestival.com. Called "a time for warm hearts and hot guts," this family-friendly event celebrates the sausage heritage of Elgin with events like the Hogalicious Dessert Contest, a hog-calling contest, cow patty bingo, and a pork barbecue contest.

Kerrville Folk Festival. Kerrville. (830) 257-3600; kerrvillefolkfestival.org. Founded in 1972 by Rod Kennedy, it is the longest continuously running music festival in North America and a mecca in the songwriting community. For 18 straight days and nights, the festival offers concerts and activities for all ages. Held at Quiet Valley Ranch, just 9 miles south of Kerrville.

Oktoberfest. Fredericksburg. (830) 997-4810; oktoberfestinfbg.com. On the first weekend in Oct, head to the "Old Country" by visiting this German Hill Country town. You'll find polka dancing and sausage galore, as well as arts and crafts, a street dance, and rides for the kids.

Texas Mesquite Arts Festival. Fredericksburg. (830) 997-8515; texasmesquiteartfestivals .com. Visitors have the opportunity to shop for one-of-a-kind woodwork at this annual show. A gathering of more than 50 artists who work primarily in mesquite showcases collectibles, cabinets, mantels, sculptures, musical instruments, and other artwork made from the often-maligned tree.

november

Gathering of the Scottish Clans. Salado. (512) 947-5232; saladomuseum.org. Put on your tartans and grab your bagpipes for the oldest Scottish gathering in the Southwest. If there are Gaels and Celts in your ancestry, you can learn more about your family genealogy. Even if you're not a lass or laddie, enjoy traditional folk dances, Highland games, lots of bagpipe music, and Scottish foods like meat pies and scones.

Nature in Lights. Killeen. (254) 287-4916; hood.armymwr.com. Held at the Belton Lake Outdoor Recreation Area, this drive-through event features 5.5 miles of holiday lighting displays as well as a Santa's Village. Begins in early Nov and continues through New Year's.

Walkway of Lights. Marble Falls. (830) 693-4449; marblefalls.org. This virtual tunnel of lights is made of more than two million lights that reflect off the waters of Lake Marble Falls, one of the most spectacular lighting experiences in the region. Stroll beneath the lights evenings from late Nov through early Jan.

Wurstfest. New Braunfels. (830) 625-9167; wurstfest.com. Early in Nov, pull on your lederhosen, take out your beer stein, and join the fun at this celebration of sausage making. One of the largest German festivals in the country, Wurstfest features oompah bands and great German food.

december

Christmas at Old Fort Croghan. Burnet. (512) 525-4025; fortcroghan.com. This festival is a re-creation of a pioneer Christmas. Fort Croghan is lit by glowing lanterns. Visitors on the candlelight tour are met by carolers and costumed volunteers.

Christmas on the Chisholm Trail. Belton. (254) 933-5860; beltontexas.gov. Held on the first Sat evening of Dec, this family event begins with the lighting of the tree in the historic downtown. Other events include madrigals in Victorian dress, cowboy Christmas tales from "The Singing Cowboy," arts and crafts vendors, and more.

Christmas Stroll. Georgetown. (512) 930-3545; mainstreetgeorgetown.org. The court-house square is lighted with thousands of miniature white lights followed by an evening of shopping, storytelling, and visiting a children's village. The town also hosts a holiday homes tour through several historic structures.

Hill Country Regional Christmas Lights Trail. Johnson City, Llano, Fredericksburg, Burnet, Boerne, Wimberley, and Marble Falls. tex-fest.com. The Hill Country joins together for this trail of Christmas lights and festivities. Blanco's historic courthouse square is lit with festive lights, and Marble Falls celebrates with a walkway of lights every evening. Fredericksburg puts on Weihnachten and candlelight tours of homes. Llano features a Santa Land. Johnson City, the boyhood home of LBJ, is aglow with more than a quarter-million lights.

Lights Spectacular. Johnson City. (830) 868-7684; lightsspectacular.com. One of the biggest displays in the state, this dazzling event features more than 600,000 lights illuminating homes, businesses, and churches, transforming this quiet Hill Country community into a glittering wonderland. The largest light display is on the Blanco County Courthouse, a historic building aglow with more than 100,000 tiny white lights. Maps are available at the courthouse for a self-guided drive of Johnson City's fantastic home light displays, erected by local citizens who play a big part in spreading the holiday spirit. The community also has "light art displays," illuminated panels with up to 1,200 lights. Also a large Christmas tree in Memorial Park on US 290 is illuminated with thousands of colored lights.

Main Street Bethlehem. Burnet. (512) 756-4481; fbcburnet.org. Held the first two weekends in Dec, this festival depicts a biblical-era village, complete with live animals and Mary, Joseph, and baby Jesus.

A Timeless Christmas in Johnson City. Johnson City. (830) 868-7128; nps.gov/lyjo/index.htm. Celebrate the season with lamplight visits to the LBJ boyhood home, thousands of holiday lights, and a chuckwagon camp at the Johnson Settlement.

Wassailfest. New Braunfels. (830) 221-4000; nbtexas.org. Merchants throughout the downtown area prepare the traditional English holiday drink of wassail and serve it to the evening guests who enjoy live music, horse-and-buggy rides, and a visit from Santa. Look for open houses, caroling, and bell choirs on this special evening of holiday fun.

appendix a

especially for winter texans

If you're among the many lucky travelers who've adopted the Lone Star State as their winter home, welcome to Texas. You've chosen a destination where you can enjoy the excitement of the West, the zest of Old Mexico, the tranquility of the Gulf, and the history of a rambunctious republic, all in one place. Some of the best seasons and reasons to see the state include the changing post oak leaves in fall, the glittering Christmas festivals, and the often sunny Texas winter days.

Texas has an excellent network of state parks, most of which provide campsites with hookups. Generally there is a 14-consecutive-days limit for camping at each park. The central reservation number for all Texas state parks is (512) 389-8900 on weekdays 9 a.m. to 6 p.m. or see tpwd.texas.gov/state-parks/park-reservation-information/reservations for online, email, and fax reservations.

Winter Texans will also be interested in state park passes. The **Texas Parklands Passport** (which is also called a Bluebonnet Pass) is for those who meet one of these eligibility requirements:

If you are age 65 and over and a Texas resident, you can receive 50 percent reduced entry. Residents and nonresidents who turned 65 before September 1, 1995, are entitled to waived entry fees at state parks.

Veterans of the US Armed Forces with a 60 percent or more service-connected disability will receive waived entry fees to state parks.

Travelers who have been medically determined to be permanently disabled as a result of a mental or physical impairment (including blindness) are entitled to a 50 percent discount.

To get this Texas Parklands Passport, apply at any state park or at the headquarters in Austin. If you don't qualify for the Parklands Passport, you can also purchase an annual pass called the **Texas State Parks Pass.** It's valid for 12 months and is presently priced at $70 for a one-car membership; a second pass for someone at the same address is an additional $25.

appendix b

texas state parks

Texas has an excellent system of state parks offering camping, angling, hiking, boating, and tours of historical sites. Facilities range from those with hiking trails, golf courses, and cabins to others that are largely undeveloped and exist as an example of how the region once looked.

Reservations are recommended for overnight facilities. Pets are permitted if they are confined or on a leash shorter than 6 feet. The central reservation number for all Texas state parks is (512) 389-8900, Mon through Fri 8 a.m. to 6 p.m., or see tpwd.texas.gov/state -parks/park-reservation-information/reservations for online, mail, and fax reservations. For TDD service, call (512) 389-8915 weekdays. To cancel a reservation, call (512) 389-8900.

For travelers 65 years or older (or those with at least a 60 percent VA disability), there is the free or discounted (depending on age) State Parklands Passport. This windshield sticker permits free entry into any park. For information on park passes and discounts, see Appendix A.

For more information on Texas state parks, call the Texas Parks and Wildlife Department at (800) 792-1112 Mon through Fri during working hours, or at (512) 389-4800 in the Austin area. Texas Parks and Wildlife Department also maintains an excellent website: tpwd .texas.gov.

appendix c

guide to tex-mex food

You'll find Tex-Mex food everywhere you go in Central and South Texas. It's a staple with all true Texans, who enjoy stuffing themselves at least once a week with baskets of tostadas, the Mexican plate (an enchilada, taco, and rice and beans), and cold *cerveza*. Unlike true Mexican food, which is not unusually spicy and often features seafood, Tex-Mex is heavy, ranges from hot to *muy caliente,* and can't be beat.

cabrito—young, tender goat, usually cooked over an open flame on a spit. In border towns, you'll see it hanging in many market windows.

cerveza—beer.

chalupa—a fried, flat corn tortilla spread with refried beans and topped with meat, lettuce, tomatoes, and cheese.

chile relleno—a stuffed poblano pepper, dipped in batter and deep-fried.

enchilada—a corn or flour tortilla wrapped around a filling and covered with a hot or mild sauce. The most common types are beef, chicken, and cheese, and sometimes even sour cream and shrimp.

fajitas—grilled skirt steak strips, usually served still sizzling on a metal platter, with condiments (pico de gallo, sour cream, cheese) and flour tortillas.

flauta—a corn tortilla wrapped around shredded beef, chicken, or pork and fried until crispy; may be an appetizer or an entree.

frijoles refrito—refried beans.

guacamole—avocado dip spiced with chopped onions, peppers, and herbs.

margarita—popular tequila drink, served in a salted glass; may be served over ice or frozen.

menudo—a soup made from tripe, most popular as a hangover remedy.

mole ("MOLE-ay")—an unusual sauce made of nuts, spices, and chocolate that's served over chicken enchiladas.

picante sauce—a Mexican staple found on most tables, this red sauce is made from peppers and onions and can be eaten as a dip for tortilla chips; ranges from mild to very hot.

pico de gallo—hot sauce made of chopped onions, peppers, and cilantro; used to spice up tacos, chalupas, and fajitas.

quesadilla—a tortilla covered with cheese and baked; served as a main dish.

sopapilla—a fried pastry dessert served with honey.

tamale—corn dough filled with chopped pork, rolled in a corn shuck, steamed, and then served with or without chile sauce; a very popular Christmas dish.

tortilla—a flat, cooked round of flour or cornmeal used to make many main dishes, and also eaten like bread along with the meal, with or without butter.

verde—green sauce used as a dip or on enchiladas.

appendix d

lcra parks

When it comes to parks, Austinites have only one problem: selecting from a long list of excellent facilities located near the capital city. Many of these parks are the products of the **Lower Colorado River Authority** (LCRA; 800-776-5272; lcra.org), a conservation and reclamation district that generates and transmits electricity produced by the powerful Colorado River. The LCRA also manages the waters of the river and assists riverside and lakeside communities with their economic development.

Among travelers, the LCRA is best known for its parks. These sites, which vary from unimproved sites along the riverbanks to full-fledged parks with boat ramps, fishing piers, and camping, are favorite summer destinations. Scattered from the shores of Lake Buchanan, down through the rest of the Highland Lakes, and along the riverbanks of the Colorado River all the way to Matagorda County on the Gulf Coast, these waters offer vacationers a great place to relax.

index